Balance and Bias in Journalism

Also by Guy Starkey

RADIO IN CONTEXT

Balance and Bias in Journalism

Representation, Regulation and Democracy

Guy Starkey

First published 2007 by
PALGRAVE MACMILLAN
Houndmills, Basingstoke, Hampshire RG21 6XS and
175 Fifth Avenue, New York, N.Y. 10010
Companies and representatives throughout the world

PALGRAVE MACMILLAN is the global academic imprint of the Palgrave Macmillan division of St. Martin's Press, LLC and of Palgrave Macmillan Ltd. Macmillan® is a registered trademark in the United States, United Kingdom and other countries. Palgrave is a registered trademark in the European Union and other countries.

ISBN-13: 978–1–4039–9248–2 hardback
ISBN-10:   1–4039–9248–7 hardback
ISBN-13: 978–1–4039–9249–9 paperback
ISBN-10:   1–4039–9249–5 paperback

This book is printed on paper suitable for recycling and made from fully managed and sustained forest sources.

A catalogue record for this book is available from the British Library.

Library of Congress Cataloging–in–Publication Data
Starkey, Guy.
   Balance and bias in journalism: representation, regulation and democracy / Guy Starkey.
    p. cm.
  ISBN–13: 978–1–4039–9248–2 (cloth)
  ISBN–10:   1–4039–9248–7 (cloth)
  ISBN–13: 978–1–4039–9249–9 (pbk.)
  ISBN–10:   1–4039–9249–5 (pbk.)
1. Journalism––Objectivity. 2. Journalism––Objectivity––Great Britain. I. Title.
PN4784.O24S73 2006
302.23––dc22

10   9   8   7   6   5   4   3   2   1
16 15 14 13 12 11 10 09 08 07

Printed and bound in China

To my parents, Eveline, Frederick and Jean.

Contents

Figures

Tables

Preface

This book began as an investigation into the nature of balance and bias in the *Today* programme on BBC Radio 4 during the general election campaign in the United Kingdom (UK) in 1997. From the original, relatively narrow focus of 39 programmes broadcast over seven weeks has developed a much wider brief, addressing the main broadcast media and the press worldwide. The subject of inquiry is itself widely debated by journalists, politicians and other interested parties, as well as by viewers, listeners and readers, and is often in the media. This is because representation and democracy are inextricably linked, with regulation offering only partial safeguards for balance and against bias.

Even as publication of the book coincides with radio's centenary,[1] with television well into its second half-century and the Internet firmly established as a major source of news and information, many of the key issues remain unresolved. In democracies and dictatorships alike, the ability to shape representations in the mass media bestows considerable power on those who have it. Used responsibly, it can be beneficial to a range of different stakeholders, and damaging to few. In the wrong hands, it can be at best misleading, and at the other extreme a force for evil. Many journalists understand and accept the responsibility this bestows upon them. Many others do not.

Accepting responsibility does not in itself resolve matters. Achieving balance is more problematic in practice than in principle, not least because we may not all agree on the nature of that 'balance'. This book seeks to discuss the associated phenomena of balance and bias in ways that will be acceptable to a wide readership. We all consume – or are at least affected by – the media, and many of us are practitioners. Even this text, though, will be subject to the same kind of scrutiny it prescribes for others, and indeed the author would expect it to be. It too can only be a partial account of 'realities' perceived and reinterpreted by a single proxy, a concept developed further in Chapter 1. As in the reporting it seeks to analyse, pragmatic decisions have had to be made over its scope, organization and focus, many of which may have been different if taken by somebody else. However, just as the book seeks neither to condemn nor to discourage responsible journalism in any of its forms, we hope it will be read in the same spirit with which it approaches those other texts: that is, sceptically rather than cynically.

There have been other studies of balance and bias in the media, and just as in their time they introduced new material into the public domain, this study has also generated some original material, which you will find in the case studies in the final chapter and elsewhere in the text. Rather than extensively reviewing earlier works, it is on this more recent data that the book concentrates. New data emerge every day, yet many of the analytical approaches to that data – and the conclusions drawn – will remain relevant as long as the media lack the transparency of personal experience and so make representations that can affect the democratic processes at the heart of society.

Acknowledgements

The author wishes to acknowledge, with thanks, the support of the Centre for Research in Media and Cultural Studies at the School of Arts, Design, Media and Culture of the University of Sunderland, England. Grateful thanks, too, to Robert Ferguson of the Institute of Education, University of London, for support and inspiration at the beginning of the project.

Abbreviations

ABA	Australian Broadcasting Authority
ABC	Australian Broadcasting Commission
ANN	Arabic News Network
BBC	British Broadcasting Corporation
CBC	Canadian Broadcasting Corporation
CRBC	Canadian Radio Broadcasting Commission
CRS	Compagnies Républicaines de Sécurité
CRTC	Canadian Radio-television and Telecommunications Commission
DAB	Digital Audio Broadcasting
DRM	Digital Radio Mondiale
DTH	direct-to-home transmission
FCC	Federal Communications Commission
FCO	Foreign and Commonwealth Office
IBA	Independent Broadcasting Authority
ILR	Independent Local Radio
IRA	Irish Republican Army
IRN	Independent Radio News
ITA	Independent Television Authority
ITV	Independent Television
MBC	Middle East Broadcasting Centre
MEP	Member of the European Parliament
MMR	measles, mumps and rubella vaccine
MRP	Mouvement Républicain Populaire
NGO	non-governmental organization
NPR	National Public Radio
NUJ	National Union of Journalists
Ofcom	Office of Communications
ONO	Organization of News Ombudsmen
PBS	Public Broadcasting Service
PCC	Press Complaints Commission
PCF	Parti Comuniste Français
PCI	Partito Communista Italiano
PR	proportional representation
PSB	public service broadcaster
RAJAR	Radio Joint Audience Research
RFE	Radio Free Europe
RNI	Radio Northsea International

RSS   Really Simple Syndication
SLD   Social and Liberal Democrats
SNP   Scottish Nationalist Party
UKIP   United Kingdom Independence Party
VOA   Voice of America
VT   videotape (inserts)

Introduction

Balance, bias, impartiality and objectivity: early definitions

Balance and bias are mutually exclusive terms that – despite their essential incompatibility – coexist in the discourse of representation, which is itself inherent in the study of journalism. Put simplistically, balance is the absence of bias, and bias is the absence of balance. Presenting a balanced account would normally require impartiality, or at least adopting an objective, rather than a subjective position and remaining true to it. In a phrase: 'telling it like it is'. That is the 'uncommitted way' in which Wilson, for example, contends issues must be presented in order for that account to be 'balanced' (1996: 45). Being objective means not placing undue emphasis on one part of a representation, in order to distort it, for whatever motive. Therefore objectivity implies detachment from an issue, or at least, representing it in as 'balanced' a way as could be achieved by someone without a vested interest in it. Likewise its antonym, subjectivity, implies common cause with persons or perspectives within an issue.

The concept of bias is itself complex. McQuail suggested four different kinds of bias: partisan, propaganda, unwitting and ideological (1992). The first is explicit support for a particular position and the second more implicit – apparent only to those who are sensitive to the value-laden nature of the comment, descriptions and attitudes in the reporting. Unwitting bias is forced on journalists by the physical constraints of their craft: there is only so much room in a newspaper or time in a bulletin, while McQuail's fourth category, ideological bias, may not even be apparent to those who produce it, because it is rooted in their own preconceptions and attitudes, values and beliefs, which they rarely, if ever, question spontaneously. Useful though those categories may be, they are not incontrovertible and McQuail himself redefines bias in later works (2005: 127).

Problematizing the problematic

Why, though, is impartiality so easily controvertible, and why does it follow that, depending on the context and the complexity of the representation, accusations of bias are so common (Street, 2001: 4)? Unfortunately, it is here that the usefulness of simplistic approaches diminishes, not least because *demonstrating* the presence or absence of balance and bias is essentially problematic. One person's 'balance' may be another person's 'bias', particularly if their perspectives differ widely, as we shall see. What may seem to one person to be objective may be considered highly subjective by the other.

Even the relationship between objectivity and impartiality is complex: the first assumes there is a single empirical truth about which it is possible to be objective. The second accommodates a relativist's view of the world, in which perspectives may be interchangeable, depending on the values of the person describing the world (Lewis, Inthorn and Wahl-Jorgensen, 2005: 10). This distinction may be purely academic, in the sense that it may be of no consequence, particularly as Hall argued convincingly that despite the importance of both terms in journalism, neither objectivity nor impartiality exist in practice, but are part of an 'operational fiction' (1974). Schlesinger's observational account of working practices in the British Broadcasting Corporation (BBC) (1987) had already led him to doubt that impartiality was achievable (see Chapter 1). So, what of the 'single empirical truth', or the validity of the different perspectives accommodated by the relativists?

The mass media routinely present images and descriptions that are necessarily partial, as opposed to complete. Often these are detailed and expressive, sometimes they are vivid and even moving, yet for all the investment in technology, the skill and dedication of practitioners, and the considerable appetite of audiences for their output, the media are quite unable to recreate any original experience of the world except in relatively limited detail. Their audiences witness even live events by proxy: they are not at the scene, although they may view what they are shown, read what they are told and hear what is played to them. They may not, however, independently look around, open a closed door, change perspective, ask their own questions or discover information they might themselves have chosen to access if they were truly there. Of course, someone else is there for them – that is, the proxy who has gone to the scene on their behalf – and that someone must choose how to present (or *re*present) the real-life experience of being there.

Representation being only a partial – again meaning incomplete – account of a place, an event or an issue, necessarily involves choices being made over what is included and what is not. A representation that is selective might still be widely considered 'fair' if competing perspectives have been 'balanced' in such a way that none of them gain any advantage from the act of mediation taking place. However, because bias lies in the absence of balance, it exists when one aspect of the place, one take on the event or one side of the argument has been given undue prominence that promotes it unfairly over others, either to its advantage or its disadvantage. Audiences are then further distanced from the realities they seek to experience through the media, because the representations they are being given are less accurate than they could be: in essence, distortions of what they might have found for themselves.

If as journalists we could achieve a perfect balance in our reporting, we could accurately claim to be impartial, as could other broadcasters in television and radio and writers in the press and other text-based media. Unfortunately, someone working in the media claiming to be impartial becomes problematic – and often acutely so – when others dispute that 'impartiality', instead perceiving bias where the originator claims none. In some contexts and over some issues (for example, party politics), being impartial is inherently more difficult, simply because different people may already have aligned themselves with a particular perspective, either through allegiance or because they share common values or beliefs.

There are, however, circumstances in which journalists would not wish to be impartial. Certain issues require partiality, or common cause with a single perspective, to the detriment of another. In what in the West may be termed 'enlightened' democracies, for example, racism is widely perceived to be not only morally wrong but obnoxious. In certain countries, legislation proscribes racist attitudes or such actions as the 'incitement to racial hatred', defined in Great Britain by the Public Order Act 1986 as using words which are threatening, abusive or insulting about a particular racial or ethnic group (Welsh and Greenwood, 2003: 353–4). Even if a sense of decency towards other human beings doesn't inhibit a journalist from 'balancing' the views of a proponent of equal opportunities with those of an outspoken racist, the possibility of a fine and up to two years' imprisonment probably would. Thus is established in law the principle that impartiality is not always acceptable, although such circumstances are of course exceptional, rather than the norm, because in democratic states there are few issues over which legislation is used specifically in order to constrain freedom of speech.

More controversial is the desirability of impartiality over issues where consensual notions of what may be deemed 'common sense' may be considered to be in conflict with a perspective that, although considered maverick by many, may still be shared by others. For example, should the merits of caring for the environment be equally balanced against those of harming it? Should advice about health and safety be carefully balanced with information on how to be reckless? Apparently uncomplicated dilemmas can become more problematic under different circumstances. What if harm to the environment would result from creating new jobs where unemployment is high? How should overwhelming medical evidence suggesting smoking is harmful be balanced against the freedom of individuals to decide their own fate, irrespective of any ambition on a journalist's part to educate and inform?

An academic study which randomly sampled 636 articles out of a total of 3543 about climate change published in the *Los Angeles Times*, *The New York Times*, *The Wall Street Journal* and *The Washington Post* between 1988 and 2002 found that more than half effectively 'balanced' what the researchers called 'generally agreed-upon scientific discourse' against the conflicting opinions of relatively small numbers of sceptics (Boykoff and Boykoff, 2004: 125–36). They considered 'norms of balanced reporting' to be distancing press coverage of global warming from a common scientific understanding of it as being attributable to humankind, and instead presenting as equally likely the minority view of it as a naturally-occurring and eventually self-correcting phenomenon.

Equally weighting competing yet unequally authoritatively-shared perspectives on an issue can have more immediate – and potentially disastrous – consequences for individuals within audiences. In the UK, a vast amount of scientific data about the combined measles, mumps and rubella vaccine (MMR) was already in the public domain, while from 1998 controversy raged in the media over whether it had caused autism in some children (Batty, 2004). Overwhelmingly, the majority of the medical community, including the Chief Medical Officer and the National Institute for Clinical Excellence, considered MMR safe (Boseley, 2002) and many of them repeatedly said so (Speers and Lewis, 2003: 913–18). Yet the presence of a small number of dissident voices, none of which has ever been able to prove a causal link between MMR and autism, was sufficient for journalists to regularly present what became a terrible choice facing young parents as a simple, although critical, 50–50 between one view and another: either the vaccine was safe or it wasn't, so take your pick, or perhaps even toss a coin (Sandall, 2003). Some estimates considered vaccination rates to have fallen the most dramatically amongst relatively well-educated middle-class, broadsheet-reading listeners to the BBC's 'intelligent speech' network, Radio 4 (Speers and Lewis, 2004: 171–82).

'Balancing' competing perspectives, however sound, may simply be done as a way of producing 'good' copy. Often, for broadcasters, a regulator may demand as much impartiality as is possible, while paradoxically, in the press, promoting a particular perspective over others might be a requirement of the job. That is, in certain territories broadcasting is subject to content regulation: such as in the UK, where Ofcom (Office of Communications) requires the commercial sector to maintain 'balance' in news and current affairs. The BBC is also expected to be 'impartial', because the charter under which it operates, and which is supposed to guarantee its independence from government, says it must (see Chapter 2). However, the British press face no such obstacles to both overt and covert support for individual political parties and perspectives, sometimes because of readership expectation – that is, what readers want to read – and often subject to the whim of the proprietor, who may have a political agenda in addition to the desire to sell newspapers (Allan, 2005: 7–13 and see Chapter 3). In both regulated and unregulated contexts, the implications for democracy are considerable.

Demonstrating impartiality depends on being able to evidence 'balance', that is, to prove the absence of bias. It may be easier for a protagonist, a regulator, or some other stakeholder in a representation to identify the *presence* of bias or the *absence* of balance, and therefore an absence of impartiality, but neither approach to the issue is unproblematic. Identifying bias could hardly be uncontroversial, but measuring and so quantifying it according to methodologies that might produce a consensus presents further difficulties. Gunter's review of methodological approaches to measuring bias on television acknowledged many of the pitfalls inherent in both quantitative and qualitative analyses, suggesting that even the concept of bias would be difficult to define (1997: 5). Yet, he went on to identify a large number of such studies carried out by academics, broadcasters and regulators alike, each of which has its own constituency of sponsors and audiences (see Chapter 2). Similarly, just as the Glasgow University Media Group pressed on in the face of opposition to their early *Bad News* studies (Street, 2001: 25–8), in studying any aspect of journalism neither should we be deterred by difficulty, even if by considering balance and bias in particular we are problematizing the already problematic.

Understanding balance and bias

This book examines balance and bias in journalism in a number of ways. In the first chapter we will consider the relationship between the reality of first-hand experience and representations of it in the media. Then Chapter 2 examines the implications of balance and bias for the proper working of democracy, and the ways in which broadcasting is often regulated in order to protect it. Chapter 3 considers the relatively unregulated environment of the press, in which constraints on journalistic representation may be few or ineffective, and questions the appropriateness of a tradition that bestows influence through the often dubious privilege of ownership. The following two chapters distinguish between bias in the complementary but quite distinct processes of production and reception: in creating and interpreting media representations or, in essence, encoding and decoding individual texts. Because international contexts sometimes require a reinterpretation of core principles and values, lest our very freedom to hold them should be lost, Chapter 6 attempts to reconcile a number of globalizing forces with often transitory national interest, and asks to what extent ideals should be compromised in times of danger. The final chapter presents a number of case studies from regulated contexts where obligations to aspire to balance have inevitably been met with only qualified success, and one that suggests that with greater freedom may come deceit.

CHAPTER 1

A Question of Balance: Reality and Representation

Representing 'reality'

Although journalists very rarely draw their audiences' attention to the incompleteness of their reporting, every such media representation is a construct, formed from elements chosen in whole or in part to offer those audiences an insight into a 'reality' in which they are supposedly interested. It follows, therefore, that the chances of these being wholly accurate representations are remote. Even if unintentional, representing 'reality' within the time and resource constraints upon all media can introduce distortions that obfuscate more than they illuminate.

For example, on 28 October 2004, as the then Palestinian President Yasser Arafat was being taken to France for medical treatment – in what subsequently turned out to be his last journey – BBC Radio 4's *The Six O'Clock News* was reporting that controversially Israel had guaranteed that he would be allowed to return to his compound, should he recover. Paradoxically, *Channel Four News* produced by Independent Television News (ITN) was saying there were 'no guarantees' from Israel he could return, a position that could easily have been understood to be harsh, given Arafat's critical condition. Audiences to either report may have unquestioningly believed the 'reality' it presented to be true, whereas only someone who heard both conflicting accounts would have been given reason to doubt the truth of one of them, while being quite unable to establish from the broadcasts alone which was correct.

That realities exist, and that they may be experienced by people first hand is not in question. What is problematic for others is *knowing* how well a reality has been represented. This became evident long before the development of the broadcast media, and while print was in its infancy. The development of different European movements in art and literature – the mass media of their time – reveals how common understandings of representation have changed in the past. The realist movement in the arts was a reaction to the idealistic portrayals of life by the Romantics of the late eighteenth and nineteenth centuries. While Romantic artists imagined historical, biblical and fictional scenes based on ancient texts, legends and popular fiction,[1] 'realists' sought to show life as they themselves experienced it (Winston, 1995: 26–9).

Often the detailed, almost photographic images of the early realists' own observations shocked the art world, because through painting they brought to the attention of the middle classes the great poverty and desperation in the lives of the working class people they rarely met themselves.[2] In literature, writers began to weave into their fiction long, detailed descriptions of people, places and practices based on observed fact, being far removed in their gritty detail from the escapism of the Romantics.[3] Then 'naturalists' wanting something new to sell to their public, meticulously researched detail but integrated it less digressively with their narratives.[4]

Though quite possibly sincere, the efforts of the realists and the naturalists were not universally perceived as the unmediated accounts of life they wanted them to be, because of the awkward inconsistency of 'the inherent disproportion which exists between the small flat surface of a book and the vast arch of life which it undertakes to mirror', as Edmund Gosse noted in his 1890 article, 'The limits of realism in fiction' (in Becker, 1963: 390). On considering the pioneers of the realist movement in retrospect, Grant saw realism as 'not only a technical, but also a philosophical impossibility' (1970: 64–5), but the point was not lost on their contemporaries: some of whom, in turn, reacted against them by producing works that would highlight the mediation taking place. Among them were impressionists, led by the artist Claude Monet (1840–1926), whose work recognized some of the limitations of realism and sought to add to their representations of life as they had experienced it their own impressions, feelings and moods.

Most provocative of all were the surrealists. By juxtaposing often absurd still images with either contradictory or simply unlikely titles, or in film deliberately disrupting the normal conventions of narrative structure, they vividly drew attention to the acts of mediation taking place in the presentation of 'reality' to audiences, challenging those audiences to resist given meanings and to construct their own.[5] The novelist Alain Robbe-Grillet (1922–) wrote a manifesto for a 'new' form of novel (1963), which offers readers subjective and often competing 'realities' seen from the perspectives of the characters, rather than the observations of the realists' omniscient narrators (Starkey, 2004a: 184). Some writers used dreams – even drug-induced hallucination – to inspire colourful but intentionally 'unreal' narratives, and the stream-of-consciousness style of *Ulysses* by James Joyce (1882–1941) defies most attempts to situate its depiction of a single day in Dublin within the realist paradigm.

Even without the deliberate confusion in surrealism, 'realism' is further complicated by the potential of individuals within audiences to each make 'readings' of the same media 'texts' in different ways (Hall, 1981: 67). The same television news report, for example, may provoke an emotional response in one viewer, but complete indifference in another. For historical or cultural reasons, one media outlet may be more trusted than another (see

Chapter 4). Most media texts are also subject to the double hermeneutic framework identified by Giddens (1984: 284): that is, the audience is interpreting the journalist's interpretation of events, each interpretation of which may in turn be flawed (see Chapter 4).

Some media forms are more likely to encourage alternative, or what producers may term 'rogue' readings, than others. For example, there are parallels between impressionism in painting and the radio feature, which often uses drama and music to depart from the more journalistic conventions of reportage found in the documentary genre (Kaye and Popperwell, 1995: 75). Any dramatization – however 'realistic' a 'reconstruction' or a drama-documentary may purport to be – implicates the producer in interpretation (McWhinnie, 1959: 35). Similarly, the parliamentary sketch in the British Press owes little to the verbatim record of proceedings published in *Hansard*, and both political cartoons and the tradition of television satire famously established by the BBC in *That Was The Week That Was* (1961–3) major on impressions rather than empirical data (Carpenter, 2000).

To what extent, then, can any representation be considered 'fair'? This is the gulf between ontology (which concerns the nature of existence), and epistemology (the nature of knowledge), described by Scott and Usher as routinely subject to compromise (1993: 63). Audiences interpret media output in ways that accommodate information in the text that is new to them within established frameworks of knowledge and understanding. They will reference new information to prior knowledge, attitudes and expectations they have already developed either first hand or through proxies – perhaps accepting some or all of it as credible, or rejecting some or all of it as incredible (see Chapter 4).

This does not, of course, inhibit the media in routinely claiming to depict 'reality'. Newspaper and magazine news and feature pages, and the various news and documentary genres in radio and television, all present their accounts as 'windows on the world' through which audiences may see for themselves aspects of real life they cannot personally experience. A range of technical and symbolic codes are consistently deployed in their output in order to signify at various times importance, seriousness, urgency, sincerity, rigour, and generalizability – but always authenticity of content. For example, a common convention of opening sequences of television news bulletins is showing the world, either as a turning globe or as individual countries or continents, often combined with brief shots of people and places, some recognizable from past reports and others not, all backed by dramatic music which simultaneously connotes both gravitas and movement. The clear implication is that the world is big and ever changing, but that the news organization is both perceptive and agile, and able to focus in on certain people and events of particular significance.

This is compounded by the recent fashion among television producers in the West to present both live and edited 'fly on the wall' footage of people engaged in both routine and unusual situations that audiences themselves are content to describe as 'reality TV'. The obviously false premise inherent in such output is that these are 'real' people (presumably as opposed to the more commonly shown 'unreal' ones) doing what they would be doing anyway. The premise is false because even when these often incongruous groups of people have not been assembled in a location constructed for the purpose, as in *Big Brother* (Endemol), or one otherwise far removed from their natural habitat, as in *I'm a Celebrity, Get Me Out of Here!* (Granada), they can hardly be unaware of the presence of the cameras or, in many cases, the radio microphones and transmitter units they are required to wear. At best this is human drama – some of it spontaneous and inevitably some of it planned – but none of it may incontrovertibly claim to faithfully constitute events that would have happened anyway, had the cameras not been present. As Bignell notes, the illusion of reality in the genre is little more than a recognition of its difference from the imaginary narratives presented in televised fiction (2005: 61).

Even the most apparently insignificant and seemingly innocuous items may be flawed in their own ways. For example, in discussing a study of socio-economic trends revealed by 1991 and 2001 National Census data suggesting an increasing disparity between the 'north' and the 'south' of the UK, BBC Radio 4's flagship breakfast-time daily news and current affairs programme, *Today*, chose to contrast the two sides of this 'divide' (08:10, 30 June 2004). In the 'north', defined by the researchers as a region of almost 30 million people, reporter Bob Walker was despatched to carry out interviews in the depressed former steel-manufacturing town of Corby. The chosen location for the piece was the 'greasy-spoon' café The Greedy Pig, where the interviewees were the owner and a builder who had come in for a 'fry-up'. One effect of this London-based programme – centred in the south and peopled largely by apparently 'southern' journalists and contributors, sending a reporter on an expedition to the 'north' – may have been to unnecessarily accentuate the divide by reinforcing stereotypical assumptions held elsewhere. This was particularly likely because of the choice of location: one where it would be unusual to find many of the stockbrokers, bankers, academics, business people, doctors and other types of professionals who are also among the region's population and who may have been able to bring interesting – and different – perspectives to the debate.

Such close textual analyses as this, however brief or relevant, do not appear prominently in the various outlets of the mass media. Their own processes – and so, limitations – although widely discussed in the relative backwater of academic media studies, are usually not on the agenda of the media themselves. When the Glasgow University Media Group (1976: 267–8) analysed television news broadcast over six months and then concluded that bias not only exists, but is born of 'inferential frameworks' which favour establishment positions and assumptions, the broadcasters roundly condemned the findings as flawed, and various 'right-wing' elements sought to explain the research as ideologically biased and untrustworthy

(McNair, 1994: 33). In the United States, *Now* (PBS) and *On the Media* (WNYC), in France *Le Canard Enchaîné* and in the UK *NewsWatch* (BBC News24) and the *Media Guardian*, as well as columns such as 'Street of Shame' and 'Hackwatch' in the satirical journal *Private Eye*, do provide regular insights into journalistic practice. There are also many and varied websites, such as Accuracy in Media, Fairness and Accuracy in Reporting, the Centre for Media Literacy and the Freedom Forum,[6] each offering its own critique of the mass media. With a few exceptions, including *Media Watch* (ABC) in Australia, such commentaries are, however, on the periphery, and it would also be unusual for any of them to subject their own analyses of other publications and broadcasts to equally rigorous scrutiny.

Knowing 'reality'

What, then, is the 'reality' the media might try to represent? Cultural relativism is a paradigm in post-war Western philosophy which rejects the possibility of absolute truth: there may simply be a number of *understandings* of the world, some of which will differ greatly from the others, some of which will have a lot in common (McNair, 1998: 72–3). Yet, philosophers have recognized knowledge as problematic *at least* since Socrates, an Athenian widely considered to have lived from around 469–399 BC. As Socrates is thought to have written nothing down (although we cannot be sure), even our knowledge of him is reliant on the writings of his pupil, Plato (c.428–c.348 BC), which may or may not represent him correctly. Today, 'good' journalistic practice involves cross-referencing information, sometimes called triangulation, in order to ensure one person's account of a phenomenon tallies with those of others, rather than relying on a single source, as historians may forever have to rely on Plato's depiction of Socrates (Sanders, 2003: 10).

Checking sources is not always possible. In the UK's biggest political controversy of 2003, definitively ascertaining what the government scientist Dr David Kelly had said to the then BBC journalist Andrew Gilligan before Kelly committed suicide proved as difficult then as it has been for centuries to more accurately assess Plato's account of Socrates. Because Gilligan's description of his briefing with Kelly was so controversial, and the BBC and the government became locked in a bitter dispute over what he may or may not have said about weapons intelligence concerning Iraq (Born, 2004: 452–65), even four official inquiries failed to produce a widely-shared consensus on his claims among those who had been opposed to military intervention to overthrow Saddam Hussein and those who had supported it (Ahmed, 2003).

Inevitably, certain facts are knowable, and others are not, but simply being outside someone's experience does not make something nonexistent. On a person's death, some knowledge may die too, and unless recorded in some form, their testimony may be lost. Just as one person may know something another one does not, there may be much about the world that none of us know, not least because many more scientific discoveries could yet be made by humankind. Dissemination of information has vastly increased since Socrates' time, largely through advances in communication technology, but many phenomena he could not have known about were just as real then as now. That is, collectively or as individuals, we may only know part of the 'reality' around us, but that does not invalidate what we don't know or make it any less real.

Like most sciences, philosophy has its own controversies: empiricists consider that we know things through experience – the evidence of the five senses – and rationalists say that we learn by deduction. Most people's experience suggests some virtue in both paradigms. Educated and preferably experienced journalists arriving in unfamiliar situations may experience some things and deduce others, synthesizing from this variety of data accounts they may then present as 'complete' to their audiences. Deduction though can be fallible and providing evidence behind it may subsequently be necessary to validate it. In that 2003 example, Gilligan's 'island' – his own isolation as the sole surviving witness to the conversation with Kelly, in a sea of either supportive or denying conjecture – was one of his own making, in that he did not make the recording or such sufficiently clear contemporaneous notes as could have later served to verify his claims (Hutton, 2004: paragraph 241). Following a judicial inquiry by Lord Hutton into the circumstances surrounding Dr Kelly's death, the BBC instigated a thorough review of its journalistic practices, and reiterated the importance to reporters of generating such evidence (Neil, 2004: 12).

Interestingly, in his report, and despite the expression of uncertainty in places, Hutton's own use of the phrase 'the reality was' (2004: paragraph 467 (2)) may betray a confidence in the epistemological validity of his findings, which others would dispute. The inquiry involved five months of hearings, deliberations and report writing, £1.68 million of public expenditure and the consideration of well over 1000 documents. Even the full extent of those documents cannot be adequately represented in this book, for there is no total word count of them here – nor does this description offer any indication of the provenance of each of those documents, which might allow readers of this book to draw conclusions over their validity. For more information, it would be necessary now to read more detailed, though also partial, reports of the process, or the Hutton report itself.

Unusually, it is possible to visit the official website where transcripts of the proceedings and most of the primary material have been made publicly available at www.the-hutton-inquiry.org.uk/. Few people will do so, and predictably, Hutton's conclusions were welcomed by those they exonerated and condemned by those they indicted, while legions of partisan commentators, both professional and amateur, adopted positions on either side of the debate, usually according to the preconceptions they had already brought to the issue from their own responses to the wider war in Iraq (Born, 2004: 462–3). The then Director-General of the BBC, Greg Dyke, whose resignation was precipitated by the report, still insists it was Lord Hutton, and not the BBC, whose interpretation of events was 'fundamentally wrong' (Dyke, 2004: 287, 258). Similarly, on publication of the 1996 Scott Report into arms sales to the Middle East, rival interpretations of that text were hotly contested by those indicted in it, by the various political parties and interest groups who had already adopted positions on the issue and even by the author (Scott, 1996).

If not as widely shared as he might have liked, Hutton's conclusions were Hutton's reality, like Scott's had been Scott's, and those who might carefully consider the same evidence in the same way with the same wider knowledge as was available at the time could construct their own versions of that 'reality'. Such new 'realities' may be similar to Hutton's or quite different, but they all share some epistemological instability with any that could now be conceived by someone who was not actually present when Gilligan met Kelly, or now even by Gilligan himself, who just four months after the controversial meeting told the inquiry he had forgotten certain details of the conversation (DCA, 2003: 198). Dyke's autobiography devotes many pages to his own version of events, including a whole chapter entitled 'Why Hutton was wrong' (2004: 287–317), but none of his own descriptions of Gilligan's meeting with Kelly are drawn from personal experience of the encounter. The passage of time may also alter even widely-shared 'realities' as new information emerges. As Kelly's briefing with Gilligan was about the preparedness of Saddam Hussein to use weapons of mass destruction and the validity of Western intelligence about it, subsequent lack of success in finding any in Iraq may itself destabilize Hutton's assessment of what Kelly may have said. That did not discourage Channel 4 from broadcasting a dramatization of the events leading up to Kelly's death, alleging that Gilligan's notes were changed more than a month after the meeting (21:00, 17 March 2005). However, we cannot even now know if the 'reality' perceived by Kelly himself as he spoke with Gilligan on 22 May 2003 might have been affected by the subsequent, empirically convincing findings of the Iraq Survey Group, had they come earlier, as they declared themselves unable to uncover actual weapons, but what they called 'goals' (Duelfer, 2004).

The conclusions of official inquiries normally command wide respect, because of the authority accorded to those who carry them out. Coroners, for example, investigate deaths considered to be unusual according to a range of different criteria in a number of different territories, including Australia, Canada, Ireland, UK, USA and New Zealand. In France the sudden, unexplained and violent death of Diana, Princess of Wales, in 1997 was investigated by examining magistrates who concluded that her chauffeur, Henri Paul, was driving under the influence of very high levels of alcohol, and so they blamed the accident on him. Although unpopular verdicts at inquests can provoke anger among families of the deceased – such as suicide, or death

by misadventure when they feel someone else is to blame – such determinations of 'reality' are rarely contested, and in English law there is no automatic
right of appeal (Welsh and Greenwood, 2003: 163–5).

The official verdict on Dr Kelly was suicide, and despite suggestions of
involvement by the security services, due to the weight of evidence described
by those first at the scene, this has been generally accepted. The explanation
produced by the French judicial system has not, however, been sufficiently
convincing to quash widespread conspiracy theories over Diana's death,
largely because the French authorities repeatedly refused to submit the chauffeur's blood sample to DNA testing that would establish whether or not it
was actually his, or blood taken accidentally or otherwise from another body
in the hospital on the same night. When, in January 2004, the Coroner for
the English county of Surrey, Michael Burgess, finally opened and then
adjourned an inquest until 2005 so that sufficient evidence might become
'available', he commented that 'speculation and speculative reports are not
themselves evidence, however frequently and authoritatively they may be
published, broadcast or repeated' (Burgess, 2004).

Widespread confidence over the ability of forensic investigation to conclu-
sively provide evidence where appropriate eyewitness accounts are
unavailable or unconvincing, bears comparison with the insistence of empiricists to be able to establish truth through their own senses. We cannot be at
the scene of the crash, at the time it happened, but we can examine hard
scientific 'fact' in case it establishes direct causal relationships that provide
clear links between the event and its aftermath. In Diana's case, obstructing
access to such evidence was bound to fuel speculation that the 'reality' being
presented as conclusive lacked epistemological rigour – or in other words,
that there was some sort of 'cover up'.

Other widely disputed 'realities' surround the assassination of President
John Fitzgerald Kennedy on 22 November 1963, in Dallas, Texas, the killing
of John Lennon on 8 December 1980 in New York, and the shooting dead of
Martin Luther King, Jnr on 4 April 1968 in Memphis, Tennessee. That each
of these men died on those dates in those places is rarely disputed, and in each
case a 'killer' was identified (MacGregor, 1997: 130–1). The existence of a
plethora of books and websites each dedicated to presenting different 'truths'
behind the shootings (Knight, 2003) suggests that theorizing the wider background to each of them – disputing 'realities' – is a popular activity. In 2005
DNA evidence finally caught up with a number of conspiracy theories
surrounding the 1984 death in Shropshire, England of a 78-year-old
campaigner against the Sizewell 'B' nuclear power plant. Claims that Hilda
Murrell had been killed to silence her articulately put case, or in a bungled
operation by the intelligence services to search her house for missing papers
from a nuclear submarine, now seem more fanciful following the conviction
of a local petty criminal who at the time was a 16-year-old resident of a
children's home, and whose DNA was found on the elderly lady's body
(Carter, 2005).

Other conspiracy theories dispute more conventional claims about a wide range of issues, from state espionage to suppressed inventions, from the declaration of war to encounters with extraterrestrials and so on. In fact, almost any falsifiable data could provide people ranging from the purely sceptical to the clinically delusional with the opportunity to dispute someone else's 'reality'. In religious belief, agnosticism benefits from the epistemological instability of competing faiths in that empirical proof of divine intervention in the tangibles around us is hard to establish. Atheism, though, is no more provable than belief. So in many respects the relationship between knowledge and the knowable will remain problematic. Consequently, at least in the way it is presented, responsible journalism seeks to separate fact from fiction, to distinguish between experience and conjecture, and to present a 'balanced' range of evidence used to verify its own versions of 'reality'. Where it doesn't act responsibly, journalism is in fact creating false 'realities' of its own.

Constructing 'reality'

The celebrated news anchor Walter Cronkite used to close the *CBS Evening News* in the United States with the words 'and that's the way it is'. His successor, Dan Rather, was more accurate with his own catchphrase 'and that's part of our world tonight', because to imagine that the content of a news bulletin or a newspaper accurately reflects all that is happening in the world, or even what may be all the most important events in the world to the target audience, is to grossly underestimate the role of journalists in constructing the discourse they articulate and then illustrate using other audio and visual material. Because of time and resource constraints routine events are normally excluded from news bulletins and the news pages, confined if merely interesting or intriguing to other programmes and the feature pages. The business section of a newspaper, for example, or such similarly specialized news channels as CNBC and Bloomberg, would apply its own particular 'news values' to the prioritization of stories within its field, rather than attempting to show the sum of commercial activity that could be described as the business world.

Irrespective of any specialism, most of human activity is simply not newsworthy, but any of it has the potential to suddenly become so, should routines become disrupted in some way which is either novel or has some greater or wider significance (Anania, 1995). The role of the editor is to determine which such disruptions are of sufficient interest to the audience to deserve coverage within the spatial limitations of the particular medium, and then to prioritize them (McNair, 1998: 77–80). Galtung and Ruge's model of selective gatekeeping attempted to rationalize the various levels of selection between the original event and its representation, if any, through the news media (1965), and Allan neatly summarizes the range of literature on news values which followed (2004: 57–8). Naturally, although often agreeing, different editors, even serving similar audiences, will at times make different decisions: one story may lead all the evening news bulletins broadcast on different channels and all the next day's front pages, or they might all disagree which story should be the lead. Despite this, Hall noted the innocence with which journalists rationalize their application of news values, as if 'events select themselves' (1981: 234).

Proprietorial influence aside, though, journalism does not exist in an institutional vacuum: the need to build and maintain audiences and circulation figures leads editors to prioritize stories within popular themes, which may be racier than others and unusual in some way (McNair, 2000: 7). For example, on 28 February 2005 ITN's *Evening News* on ITV1 (18:30) led on the beginning of the Michael Jackson trial, ahead of a guilty plea in court by a would-be aeroplane shoebomber, political controversy in parliament over new powers of house arrest for terrorism suspects, and the largest number of civilian deaths yet, in a suicide bombing in Iraq. The same organization's *Channel Four News* (19:00), aimed at a more 'upmarket' audience, relegated Jackson to third place, after the first commercial break, and it is easy to situate the apparent 'dumbing down' of news values in the ITV1 bulletin within the 'critical paradigm' described by McNair as elitist (2002: 192). 'Market-driven journalism', as defined variously by Koch (1990: 23), Underwood (1993: 163) and others, may promote consumer-orientated and human interest items over more 'worthy' ones, simply because they provoke emotional responses (McManus, 1994: 89), but journalism is also driven by other factors, such as newsroom culture, sensitivities towards advertisers or even not 'putting audiences off their dinners' (Sheridan Burns, 2002: 7–10). Lewis, Inthorn and Wahl-Jorgensen explained how the citizens who make up audiences usually have the least influence on news values (2005: 9–11).

Certainly, although merely by convention rather than by diktat, the often compelling nature of 'bad' news does tend to prioritize it over 'good' news. The BBC television newsreader Martyn Lewis publicly criticized this practice, to the obvious annoyance of many of his colleagues (MacGregor, 1997: 81), but his indictment of institutional negativity is routinely justified in practice. A 30-year record in employment levels in the UK announced on 15 December 2004 was barely mentioned in the broadcast media, even before the resignation of the Home Secretary David Blunkett later that day, because they were consumed by allegations he had 'fast-tracked' the immigration application of his then lover's nanny. That a single job – two including Blunkett's – could transcend in direct importance to most individuals the country's need for a stable and prosperous economy stretches belief, but had the trend in employment figures been negative, rather than positive, it is likely they would have received much greater attention (McNair, 1998: 81).

Sometimes an event may be deemed so significant – or 'newsworthy' – that bulletins will be extended, extra pages will be added and extraordinary coverage will only be replaced by normal output when its compelling nature begins to subside. For example, while it was expected broadcasters in the UK would follow appropriate obituary procedures in the event of the deaths of certain members of the royal family, it was the tragic and unexpected death of Diana, Princess of Wales, which provoked unprecedented departures from normal radio and television programming (McNair, 1998: 48–9). In April 2002, though, the relatively muted response to the not entirely unexpected passing away of the 101-year-old Queen Mother drew sharp criticism that even rebuked the BBC television newsreader, Peter Sissons, for not wearing a black tie to make the announcement (Pierce, 2002). The shock value of the September 2001 ('9/11') terrorist attacks on New York's World Trade Center was probably anticipated by those who planned them, and worldwide editorial reactions were typified by the BBC's mixed news and sport network, Radio Five Live, abandoning live sports coverage for five days (Starkey, 2004b: 35).

Because the application of news values necessitates the prioritization of some stories over others, it follows that even far less dramatic events than 9/11 will dominate news coverage to the demotion or even exclusion of lesser ones which, had chance dictated differently, might otherwise have admirably led bulletins and made front pages. Prince Charles was reported to have considered ITN's coverage of his grandmother's death to be more respectful than the BBC's (Pierce, 2002), yet even the same organization may produce different news for different audiences, reflecting perceived variations in audience interests in their selection from and presentation of the same material. Young people were typically affected much more by Diana's death than that of the Prince's grandmother. An event not receiving coverage, though, in particular outlets or even at all, does not render it any less real a phenomenon – it is just less known about than it could have been.

News values determine the extent of coverage, as well as what is included. Some aspects of a story, by their very nature, will receive more coverage than others, thus making them more apparent. For example, journalism interviews victims, so reporters will usually show more Palestinians than Israelis, perhaps, as some studies suggest, by a ratio of 4:1, because of the nature of the conflict in the region. The dissenting hero is also considered more newsworthy than someone conforming to the mainstream, so the Israeli who disagrees with Israel's policy towards the Palestinians and makes a stand against it will receive more coverage than the other Israelis who agree. It simply is not news if an Israeli defends Israel, but it may be news if an Israeli attacks his own country.

The determination of an outlet's news values, and their routine application, can rarely be value free. Choices cannot be made arbitrarily, and because journalism does not exist in a vacuum, resource and institutional pressures will inevitably impact upon them (see Chapters 2 and 3). Schlesinger's study of the processes taking place in the BBC's radio and television newsrooms provided an important insight into what is, in effect, a relatively tiny elite of editors who research, sift, editorialize and finally disseminate information about the world in which we live, and their attempts

as broadcasters to achieve the balance required of their reporting. He identified a tendency among BBC journalists to believe in a 'myth of value-
freedom', created for public consumption in order to maintain the trust of
their audiences, and a consequent tendency to consider their own objectivity
and powers of perception to be beyond reproach (1987: 203–4).

Journalists and those who theorize journalism often rationalize the
dichotomy in this wielding of power and privilege, while treating powerful
others including governments with scepticism (and yet expecting audiences to
trust *them*), within linguistic frameworks of 'professionalism'. Citing notions
of 'ethics' as well as formal professional codes of practice, the training literature is largely unequivocal: journalists are able to act 'responsibly',
regulating themselves and their own conduct within the institutional and
wider regulatory frameworks that under normal circumstances cannot scru-
tinize their work as effectively as their own consciences (Sheridan Burns,
2002: 11–12). Another study of the culture in the BBC, by Burns, identified
benchmarking of this self-regulation against journalists' peers, to the extent
that as long as their work received the approval of colleagues in the newsroom, criticism of it from 'lay' observers could be dismissed as amateur and
hence unqualified (1977: 137).

Another example of this might be the then incoming Chairman of the
BBC, 'self-made millionaire and businessman' Sir Christopher Bland,
explaining his own political affiliation to the Conservative Party and those
of other BBC governors as inevitable because only a 'political eunuch'
could fail to bring political baggage to the job. He told the listings magazine *Radio Times* that he was, however, very able to recognize this and act
impartially, being his 'own man, an independent spirit' (30 March 1996).
In just the same way as Burns had observed among BBC producers, Bland
then claimed high profile members and supporters of the then opposition
Labour Party, Melvyn Bragg, Greg Dyke and Margaret Jay would confirm
his impartiality. Because the media are themselves so often controversial,
with frequent allegations of bias in even closely regulated broadcast media
(see Chapter 2), claiming impartiality – even if authenticated by peers – is
often insufficient to silence critics. The inevitability of this is explained by
Patterson's view that the interpretive element in journalism positions the
journalist in the foreground, while the social actors in the story, like the
'facts', assume a secondary, merely illustrative role (1996: 101–2).

Notwithstanding Giddens' double hermeneutic framework (1984: 284)
though, Fink recognized this fallibility in every one of us: that we are all
'shaped' by our origins and experiences – our perceptions and our actions
being inevitably, even if sometimes imperceptibly, influenced by values and
beliefs we bring to bear on our readings of texts and situations. Fink also
suggested that 'ethical' journalists might be able to partially overcome this by
aspiring to objectivity while simultaneously recognizing the impossibility of
achieving it (1988: 18). As *everyone* has a background and a set of personal
values and beliefs, the only realistic solution is to adopt such an informed

standpoint from which to consider, to measure and to analyse data subsequently produced. Otherwise, because of this 'reflexivity' no journalism would ever be attempted, and nor would any research ever be undertaken. Various scholars, though, have considered whether value-freedom may be achieved in any kind of research into the world around us. Among them, Scott and Usher explained the unlikelihood of 'decontaminating devices' ever eliminating the various forms of 'value-laden' intervention inherent in selectivity (1993: 59).

Only subsequently to the ethnographic observations of Schlesinger and Burns inside the BBC have technological and institutional advances allowed certain audiences to develop their own limited editorial autonomy. Huge growth in the number of radio stations and television channels has enabled individuals to select for themselves from a range of different perspectives and approaches, and the introduction of interactive services via digital broadcasts and the Internet allows them to set editorial filters according to their choices from different parameters or to actively seek out the items and the sources they want. Despite, for example, the development of Really Simple Syndication (RSS) software in 1999 and a growing interest in audio podcasting from 2004 (see Chapter 3), audience customization of the journalism they consume is still a relatively minor phenomenon as more traditional, streamed rather than interactive, versions of the print and broadcast media are likely to predominate for the foreseeable future. Today, most news is received, in bulletins that form part of a wider diet of programming, or in newspapers that command loyalty among regular readerships.

Making 'reality'

If journalism can never be a wholly benign, blamelessly passive activity, devoid of reflexivity in the sense that even honest journalists might simply report what is happening without bringing any influence to bear on those events, there are different degrees of reflexivity. Misreporting of 'reality' does not need to be malicious, or at all intentional. As with cameras and microphones in so-called 'reality TV', the mere presence of a reporter can actually cause events to happen. A journalist accompanying a graffiti artist to research or record the act itself may be the catalyst that caused the resultant graffiti to exist. While it is arguable that the graffiti depicted in the subsequent report may just be typical of others that have been and will be created by the artist, it may not itself have been created had it not been for the presence of the reporter: the artist might otherwise have decided to stay home that night or performed somewhere else where, perhaps, lighting conditions may not have been so good.

Similarly, it is debatable whether the fuel protests in the UK in September 2000 would have begun as they did – or even if they would have begun at all – if a leading activist, David Handley, wasn't already the subject of a documentary for Channel 4 Television about the pressure group Farmers for Action (Brown et al., 2003: 40–8). It can hardly have escaped the attention of those involved that if they were being followed around by a camera crew for a year, that they must be of considerable interest to at least a part of the media. It is impossible to know to what extent the farmers' protest may have been buoyed up by the attention they were receiving and their confidence boosted by the immediate reactions they were provoking, but the subsequent footage, played and replayed in contemporaneous bulletins and retrospective analysis, was always portrayed as showing what happened, rather than what may have resulted from the presence of the cameras.

On 16 September 2004, for example, 502 days after US President Bush declared major combat operations over in Iraq, the BBC was still allowing the conflict to skew its representation of events, when compared with the news values of other media serving similar domestic audiences in the UK. This was despite, just a month previously, an opinion poll suggesting 'ordinary voters' ranked Iraq tenth in a list given them of possible 'election issues' (Travis, 2004). On the previous day, protesters against the passing of legislation in the British Parliament, outlawing hunting with hounds, had spectacularly burst into the Chamber of the House of Commons, interrupting the debate, while outside the building violent clashes were taking place between police and large numbers of demonstrators apparently intent on storming the legislature. This was the first invasion of the actual floor of the Chamber in living memory; it was that morning's lead in all the country's broadsheet news-papers, and it had dominated radio and television news bulletins the afternoon and evening before. However, in Radio 4's 08:00 news bulletin the first three items concerned Iraq, and the issue of security at Westminster was relegated to fourth place.

The lead item was a report that 'three British men' had been kidnapped at gunpoint in a residential district of Baghdad. Second was the United Nations Secretary-General Kofi Annan newly stating an opinion that the war in Iraq had been illegal, and that force should not have been used in 2003 until after a further resolution from the Security Council specifically authorizing it. Third was the former British army commander Colonel Tim Collins, criticiz-ing the lack of preparation by the coalition forces for the aftermath of the overthrow of Saddam Hussein. Although the lead was clearly an important breaking story that had happened only hours earlier, the presence in the bulletin of the second two Iraq stories was neither incidental nor due to 'events' in the world. Both assertions, on the legality of the war and the nature of contingency planning by the coalition, were, of course, of undoubted news value. They were, though, both entirely initiated by the BBC, being taken from interviews carried out by Owen Bennett-Jones in New York and John Humphrys in London. Both extended interviews were broad-cast that morning during *Today*, and during the course of his, Collins confirmed he still supported going to war, but it was his criticisms that made it into the headlines.

By contrast, the version of 'events' from Independent Radio News (IRN) at 08:00 was quite different: they led on security at Westminster, relegating the 'three Britons' kidnap story to second place and prefixed by 'in other news'. Their three-minute bulletin placed Kofi Annan third, then fourth was the killer Hurricane Ivan arriving at the US coast. Other stories that morning being covered by both the BBC and IRN, but with less prominence, were an initiative on asylum seekers by Prime Minister Tony Blair, and the British and Dutch company Corus unusually making a profit from steel manufacturing in the UK. By 09:00 on IRN the kidnapped 'three Britons' had become one Briton and two Americans, and by 10:00 IRN had dropped Kofi Annan altogether. Other news organizations around the world did carry the Annan story, and by their 50-minute 19:00 programme, *Channel Four News* had television footage of him repeating his opinion to camera. However, they ran it second, for a single minute, after leading for 20 minutes on the Commons invasion – the first 'since the seventeenth century' – followed by three minutes on the kidnappings and then a further item wondering whether Iraq was drifting into civil war.

That the BBC felt the legality of the decision in 2003 to attack Iraq was still the most important issue that day is demonstrated by its domination of the prime slots in the morning's *Today* programme. The Annan interview ran for nearly six minutes at 07:09 immediately after the 07:00 bulletin, and the Collins interview was the centrepiece in a sequence running for 20 minutes from 08:10, between the ten-minute bulletin described above and the headlines at 08:31. This was wrapped with a brief discussion with Christopher Greenwood, Professor of International Law at the London School of Economics who had advised the British government on the legality issue and still considered the war to be legal, and the Liberal Democrat MP Sir Menzies Campbell, who had always considered it wasn't. It is interesting to consider whether the news values in the bulletin were driven by programme content in *Today* that had been planned before the Commons protest story broke, or by an obsession with Iraq (see the discussion of institutional polemic in Chapter 5). The following morning, with *The Sun* newspaper claiming one of its own reporters had now systematically breached Commons security, *Today* realigned itself with the rest of the country's news media, with interviews about the protests at 07:09 and 08:10: some 42 hours after the actual storming of the Commons.

Although no less acute an issue for the protesters from one day to the next, both the hunting issue and that of Commons security were soon eclipsed by the kidnappings. The holding of Briton Ken Bigley, the kidnappers' threats to behead him unless Iraqi women 'prisoners' were released and, perhaps because they demonstrated Mr Bigley's precarious situation, the summary beheading of the two American hostages taken at the same time, dominated the domestic news media in the UK for the next week. It became clear over the period that the media were themselves being manipulated, at first by the kidnappers – who may not have perceived any value in holding Bigley and posting staged addresses to camera on the Internet if it were not for the attention they would have received – and then in turn by the hostage's family, who made successive appeals for his release. By 25 September, the story's grip on the media was even beginning to be questioned by, among others, the former editor of the *Guardian* newspaper, Peter Preston (08:14, *Today*, Radio 4). That same day, the BBC was reporting that 500,000 Muslims in the country were being sent leaflets advising them of their rights if arrested under anti-terrorism legislation. By contrast, IRN was simultaneously reporting that the leaflet was urging Muslims to report suspicions of terrorist activity in their community. These twin but quite different stories, with the widely differing implications of each take on the leaflets, were by no means mutually exclusive, but once again the 'reality' being described to two different audiences was in each case different from the other.

The next Briton to be kidnapped in Iraq, aid worker Margaret Hassan, received only a fraction of the coverage in the UK media that was accorded to Bigley. This could be variously attributed to her dual British and Iraqi nationality, being born in Ireland, having lived in Iraq for 30 years, the insistence of the British media (later denied by her family) that she had become a Muslim, having married an Iraqi or simply her gender – depending on what one wants to believe. Certainly, journalism favours novelty, and a second kidnapping may never be considered as 'newsworthy' as the first. However, a consensus did appear to develop among politicians and the media, that excessive coverage of such stories was playing into the hands of the kidnappers. On the discussion programme *Any Questions* (20:05, 22 October 2004, Radio 4), although the first questioner asked the panel what the government's response should be to the kidnappers' demands, in turn each of the four guest contributors briefly – and for the programme, uncharacteristically – dismissed the question as one best not discussed, lest it harm Mrs Hassan or encourage further such kidnappings.

Sadly by then, and like the two Americans kidnapped with him, Ken Bigley had been shown brutally murdered on the Internet. It is worth considering to what extent such actions by extremists in whatever cause are carried out in order to themselves make the news. In July 1985, Prime Minister Margaret Thatcher, proclaimed it to be in the interest of democratic nations to 'starve the terrorist and the hijacker of the oxygen of publicity' they need. Even lawful protest, or the relatively benign yet often more effective phenomenon of civil disobedience, like the hunting protests, is usually inspired by the publicity it can attract, with the intention of influencing public opinion and that of decision makers.

Arguably, if the mass media did not exist, then neither would many of the phenomena they describe. Paradoxically, one very positive role of 'free' media can of course be to expose wrongdoing, which can exist anywhere in society, but which governments in particular may be well placed to hide. Campaigning journalism may be not simply revelatory, but a mobilizing force in inciting public or official action. The ability of both press and broadcasters to drive events forward in the manner described by Pujas (2002: 151), particularly in the context of a political scandal, bestows on editors significant, but not unlimited, power over the world they 'report' (see Chapter 3).

Competing realities

When Sarah Montague told the *Today* audience on the day after the death of the celebrated BBC presenter John Peel (1939–2004) that he had begun his career as a disc jockey on Radio 1 (08:24, 27 October 2004, Radio 4), it was untrue. In fact, Peel had first broadcast on KLIF in Dallas, Texas, before working on two more American stations, KOMA in Oklahoma City, then KMEN in San Bernardino before returning to his native England in 1967 and joining the offshore pirate station Radio London, months before the BBC launched its own popular music station. Those *Today* listeners who knew this, or at least some of the detail of his early career, would have recognized Montague's statement as an error, probably assuming it to be casually made. To anyone else listening, this was a 'reality' they could readily accept, probably remember, and perhaps repeat to others. So, distorted in this way by inaccurate reporting, quite distinct from the reality audiences cannot perceive first hand, are false realities created through misrepresentation, which themselves gain currency by being further transacted within the human consciousness. Mistaken journalism is bad enough, though sometimes unavoidable, but the false realities created through malicious journalism are worse, because at their heart lies a malign intent to deceive and often to cause damage. It takes many forms, but includes the deliberate slur of a politician, the invention of false witnesses to discredit other accurate testimony, and even the book review that deliberately misquotes an author in order to make a fallacious, even facetious point.

The representation of reality may be at its most damaging when it distorts differences between people, or attributes false differences to large numbers of them. The media routinely make representations through individuals, because it is impossible to meaningfully depict all members of one demographic group and describing populations through examples is not only more practical but it allows audiences to feel 'human interest' in identifiable others. The central problem in using individuals in this way, either in fiction or in journalism, is one of representativeness. It is reasonable to ask to what extent specific examples of a population may be sufficiently representative to display only traits that are generalizable to others within that population (Starkey, 2004c: 3–25). People may be grouped according to gender, ethnicity (including colour, race, religion, country or region of origin), age, sexual orientation, disability and even class, so the potential for stereotyping is enormous. This matters because audiences may not always be discriminating enough to distinguish between generalizable and uncharacteristic behaviour.

Human fallibility aside, there are often significant perceptual differences that can intervene to disturb the processes of mediation. It is hard to imagine a more telling clash of perspectives than Victoria Derbyshire's regular interviewee on BBC Radio Five Live, a cancer sufferer called Michelle, taking Derbyshire gently to task over being labelled as 'dying from cancer', rather than the more positive 'living with cancer' that she preferred, despite the increasingly intrusive therapeutic and palliative care she was receiving at the time (10:20, 27 October 2004). These interviews were brief but moving insights into the progress of Michelle's disease, and Derbyshire acknowledged the vast difference between the two perspectives on her condition, readily conceding to Michelle in adopting hers, 'however accurate' her own had been.

Human emotion may also intervene, as in the case of BBC reporter Barbara Plett, telling listeners to Radio 4's *From Our Own Correspondent* (11:30, 30 October 2004) that as Yasser Arafat's helicopter left his compound in Ramallah she started to cry (Plett, 2004). Distributed worldwide via the Internet and the BBC World Service, and so heard extensively in the Middle East, this admission was not lost on the then deputy Prime Minister of Israel, Yosef Lapid, who was able to use it to exemplify his claim of institutional sympathy in the BBC with the views of the Palestinian Liberation Organization Arafat had led (*Today*, 07:13, 11 November 2004).[7] The force of Lapid's argument may be seen in the reluctance of the normally combative interviewer, John Humphrys, to dispute his assertion: 'impartial' journalists don't normally confess to emotional involvement with the subjects they report on, and Humphrys simply moved on, neither acknowledging the claim nor denying its pertinence to listeners' perceptions of the BBC's ability to be impartial over the continuing conflict between Israel and the Palestinians.

Normally, though, such assertions as Lapid's are summarily dismissed as being themselves based on partial readings of a text (see Chapter 4). Sometimes a lack of impartiality may be coincidental, and at others it may be deliberate. A major factor in the routine distortion of 'reality' is the existence of rhetoric: the art of persuading an audience to certain actions or beliefs through the deliberate use of language. Rhetoric may intervene at any stage in the production and the consumption of media output. If he had felt such a response were justified, Humphrys could have attempted to dismiss Lapid's opinion as mere rhetoric, just as his colleague Jonathan Dimbleby told the *Today* audience in a programme trail for *Any Questions* that he routinely distrusted what politicians told him (07:31, 26 November 2004).

Even when attempting to 'balance' an account of 'reality', a journalist's own research may have been influenced by rhetoric introduced into a situation by someone else: the evidence of a source may not be as robust as the source actually claims. The role of rhetoric in the art of media manipulation may be as old as party politics itself because what is today called 'spin' can be traced back to the late seventeenth century and the emergence of party politics in the government of England. Fierce rivalry between Whigs and Tories, the development of a 'free' press and elections often so frequent as every two and a half years created a climate in which such politicians as the Tory Robert Harley (1661–1724) first realized the impact of political communication on an albeit relatively limited electorate (Knights, 2004: 210–14).

Rhetoric appears to us, however, to have first been described in the literature of Ancient Greece, in the persuasive oratory of Odysseus in Homer's *Odyssey*, for example (2004 edition). In Sicily in the fifth century BC, when a series of land confiscations was followed by a number of legal attempts to reclaim the land, paid rhetoricians helped the plaintiffs to prepare and deliver persuasive oratory before the court in an attempt to convince it of their case. Rhetoric became well established in the democratic system in Athens where skill at speaking in deliberative and forensic contexts became essential to successful politicking (Hobbs, 1996). Plato considered rhetoric to be a dangerous vice, as inherently untruthful and often gratuitously playing to the prejudice of partisan audiences who didn't want to hear less partial accounts of matters on which they had already formed their opinions. He criticized the itinerant teachers of rhetoric, the Sophists, for distorting truth in order to win arguments (2004 edition) and their legacy is the term 'sophistry', now used by some to condemn as plausible but fallacious, arguments with which they disagree. Plato's pupil, Aristotle (384–322 BC), took a more sympathetic view, considering rhetoric to be a necessary part of the adversarial nature of politics, through which competing positions may be tested against each other (2004 edition). Later, in Ancient Rome, Cicero (106–43 BC) and Quintilian (c.35–95 AD) perceived rhetoric as essential to good government, because it could create empathy among the people: in today's language, keeping them 'on-side'. Rhetoric may also be an essential of opposition, and the putting of counter-arguments that is often called 'devil's advocacy' (see Chapter 5).

The difference between rhetoric and lies can be contentious, and many condemned the case for war in Iraq made in 2003 by President Bush and Prime Minister Blair as the latter. However, in an ironic twist of logic, such assertions by their critics may themselves contribute nothing more tangible to that particular controversy than a new layer of rhetoric, based on the critics' perceptions and preconceptions, often choosing to discount the unanimity of the United Nations Security Council over what they thought was Saddam Hussein's breech of previous UN resolutions. One rhetorical position may satisfy one community of thought – as evidenced by the record box office takings of Michael Moore's partial 'documentary' *Fahrenheit 9/11* (2004) – while another may be just as satisfying to another group of people who share their own common understandings and perspectives on the same issue.

Debate may be healthy, but when disagreement results in violence, the consequences may be tragic for some. To imagine that the world is a more contentious place post-9/11 is to underestimate the huge political, ideological and religious divisions between sections of humanity throughout history. Conflict between nations, ethnic groups, religious adherents and tribes is not a recent phenomenon, and such issues as the relationship between Israel and Palestine, the Cold War, the Third World and religious fundamentalism of several kinds have long been controversial. However, as the communications theorist Marshall McLuhan (1911–80) predicted in 1964, one effect of the mass media drawing disparate communities together in a 'global village'

(2001: 334) is that we now know more about each other than ever before. On a global scale, as individuals and governments feel ever more entitled to comment on and even take action in distant lands, there may be a new crisis in objectivity: a Western perspective on democracy and freedom becoming increasingly at odds with beliefs and understandings elsewhere (Hendy, 2000: 139–40, and see Chapter 6). The mass street protests of 2006, some of them resulting in violence and death, over the publication in Denmark of political cartoons considered insulting by many Muslims, are a good example of how one set of values – for example freedom of speech – may easily compromise another.

Due to the partisan nature of most participants in party politics, rhetoric can be particularly difficult to separate from 'reality' in political journalism, but rhetoric can usually be found wherever there is controversy. In fact, many politicians might take issue with Dimbleby's assertion about their honesty, if they believe themselves to have always been candid with him – and of course, rhetoric may be just as easily inserted into a representation by a journalist as by a politician or any other contributor. Dimbleby presented a two-part television series entitled *The New World War* (23:10, 31 October 2004 and 23:00, 1 November 2004, ITV1), 'inextricably linking' terrorism, climate change and world poverty (Dimbleby, 2004), which to some viewers may have appeared partial in its selection of evidence and the conclusions he drew from it. The combative style of some mainstream current affairs broadcasting, such as the major US television network programmes, *Meet the Press* (NBC), *Face the Nation* (CBS) and *Larry King* (CNN) often requires even openly right-wing journalists to adopt rhetorical arguments in order to draw more interesting responses out of their interviewees (Fallows, 1997: 16–20), and it is often just as difficult to separate objective reporting from politically-motivated rhetoric in the partisan press (see Chapter 3) as it would be from political propaganda produced by the parties themselves.

Confronted by so many uncertainties, we may be able to agree, with luck, that in determining the exact nature of reality, individuals who are discerning enough to care, face significant challenges in separating reality from rhetoric, knowledge from faith, opinion from fact and suspicion from ignorance. The difficulties inherent in balancing competing evidence, upon whatever it is based, render representation as problematic for the realities the media seek to describe as for the audiences who consume their output. If we respect our audiences, problematizing balance – and therefore bias – should concern us all as journalists, writers, producers, presenters and academics. Certainly, politicians – and among them legislators – have deemed this too important an issue to be left to professionals alone. So let us consider now the role of regulation and its prospects for the promotion of democracy.

CHAPTER 2

Balance in Broadcasting: Representation and Regulation

Democracy and 'impartiality'

In dictatorships, power over the people and the institutions that both control and support them is held by those who have taken it by force. Except where insurgency, perhaps in the form of counter-revolution, results in protracted conflict that might even escalate into civil war, political control changes hands as a result of internal struggles that involve relatively few of the country's citizens. By contrast, most democracies are complex power structures, usually contextualized within such arrangements as a constitution, the rule of law and a judiciary that is independent of the executive. These are structures in which political control of the nation-state has to be won in elections. Instead of armed struggle, competing groups or individuals vie for power through democratic processes, which test through the ballot box the appeal of different underpinning ideologies, practical policies and – inevitably – public personalities.

It should be a *sine qua non* of democracy that the operation of elections and the disparate influences on the electorate taking part in them are governed by the highest democratic principles. Of course, in most democracies they are not. Newspapers and other parts of the media are controlled by those who would seek to influence electoral outcomes, large and small parties have different levels of funding with which to pay for advertising, leafleting, operating call centres and other kinds of promotional activities. Without such infrastructure, individuals working alone normally find it hard to campaign effectively against established parties. For example, in the UK it is rare for an 'independent' to be elected to the House of Commons (as was the former BBC war correspondent Martin Bell in unusual circumstances in 1997 – see Chapter 4) just as in the 2004 presidential elections in the United States the third candidate Ralph Nader polled only 0.3 per cent of the vote, lacking the financial backing of either the Republican or Democratic parties, who were each estimated to have spent in excess of US$ 300 million on their campaigns.

Notwithstanding the ability of the press to try to influence elections (see Chapter 3), it is common in democracies to find widely-shared expectations that public service broadcasting, at least, will be 'fair' to those who have or want political power. That is, to aspire to 'fairness' *and* to achieve it. In the UK for example, many people depend on the BBC for the information upon which they then make decisions – including how they each cast their vote. Generally, the BBC is a trusted source, widely held in high esteem, and despite ITN's nearly 50-year history of sometimes breaking news, and sometimes setting trends in news presentation, the BBC remains the service viewers turn to in the largest numbers for coverage of important events (Cozens, 2005). Individuals uncritically consuming the BBC's output, be it radio, television or on-line, may unwittingly be influenced by that output, simply because of their expectations of it (see Chapter 4).

Politicians, too, expect at least 'fairness', where advantage cannot be bought. Because of its privileged status and guaranteed licence fee income – effectively a tax on watching television – a BBC which didn't represent all the people would be undemocratic, in the way that campaigners for democracy since the nineteenth century Chartists and those who won the American War of Independence (1775–83) before them legitimately demand 'no taxation without representation'. This has been recognized recently in other ways, such as the then Director-General, Greg Dyke, telling listeners to Radio Scotland he considered the Corporation to be 'hideously white' in its attitudes and staffing, in that it underrepresented as an institution the ethnic minorities amongst its audience (21:00, 7 January 2001). Furthermore, many expect the BBC to set standards to which others can aspire, construing it as a principled foil to the corruption and partiality of the press.

Certainly, the BBC is highly regarded internationally, and the radio World Service has traditionally been perceived overseas as fiercely independent of British governments, despite the different funding arrangements for overseas broadcasting (see Chapter 6). Channel 4 is also a state-owned public service broadcaster (PSB), which is governed by a body of non-executive directors appointed by the regulator, Ofcom, yet neither it nor public service television and radio in the United States have achieved such significance either nationally or internationally as the BBC. Fallows' analysis (1997), for example, although subtitled *How the Media Undermine American Democracy*, barely mentions National Public Radio (NPR) or the Public Broadcasting Service (PBS), so marginalized is non-commercial radio and television in the US.

The significance of the BBC today – and the reason it is singled out for greater scrutiny in this book than Channel 4 or the commercial sector – derives largely from its long-held monopoly of British broadcasting, and the way it became very firmly established in the UK, before facing serious commercial competition. Its incorporation as a public body responsible for all broadcasting from 1 January 1927 was following a recommendation of the parliamentary Crawford Committee on broadcasting, which saw such an arrangement as a prerequisite to 'scrupulous fairness' in matters of public controversy (Crawford, 1926: 14–15). Regulation would be by a single Board of Governors, bound to ensure the Corporation operated within the terms of the Royal Charter, renewable every ten years, under which it was to operate. The committee considered this essential in a public service which was then intended to enjoy a monopoly of British broadcasting, confined as it was in the 1920s to the new phenomenon of 'wireless' (Briggs, 1961: 21).

Then, the use of the radio frequency spectrum was much less efficient than such subsequent technological advances as FM, Digital Audio Broadcasting (DAB) and Digital Radio Mondiale (DRM) afford today. So, in the UK the liberal tradition of a free press, with a variety of titles and a diversity of ownership, was deemed inappropriate for a new medium benefiting from only a very limited number of possible channels. There was no television, either analogue or digital, and no Internet, be it dial-up or broadband. While anyone who disagreed with the existing range of views in the press could – with deep enough pockets – launch a new newspaper or magazine, the radio spectrum was a finite, and in practice, very limited resource. Considering that podcasting developed as recently as 2004, in the 1920s it was inconceivable that there could ever be sufficient channels available to sound broadcasting to even begin to satisfy possibly infinite demand (Crisell, 1994: 18). This contrasts strikingly with the more recent development of the Internet, where theoretically infinite capacity and minimal operating costs mean it is much easier even to launch a new website, than to challenge the existing press with a new newspaper, journal or magazine. Consequently even the most modestly resourced individuals, associations and pressure groups are quick to create a web presence if they want to promote a particular perspective (see Chapter 3).

The Crawford solution to the problem of scarcity of radio frequencies was not, however, the only one possible. The USA favoured privately-owned commercial stations regulated by a number of bodies whose duties were later assumed in 1934 by a merged Federal Communications Commission (FCC). In Canada, the first private stations were licensed in 1922, but because of fears of Americanization a 1932 parliamentary committee recommended the creation of the Canadian Radio Broadcasting Commission (CRBC) to operate in competition with the growing number of private stations, and in 1936 this became a crown corporation: the Canadian Broadcasting Corporation (CBC) of today. In the Netherlands a timeshare arrangement allocated frequencies on a rolling basis across the week to different religious and political groups. In France, private radio stations were tolerated, in competition with the early state-owned stations (Kuhn, 1995: 84), while in Italy with the formation of the Unione Radiofonica Italiana in 1924, the government of the time reserved two hours per day for itself, as well as the right to interrupt other programming with 'important' announcements (Monteleone, 2003: 23).

Several Western democracies were decisive enough to choose the public service monopoly model, though, like the UK. Examples include Danmarks Radio in Denmark (1925) and belatedly, NRK in Norway (1934). This approach necessitated a new interpretation of the liberal tradition, because creating a monopoly of broadcasting was a concentration of ownership and 'share of voice' (in today's terms), which democratic principles suggested should recognize the power of the new medium of radio. In the absence of open access to this emerging market, as had always been the case in print, the BBC as a monopoly PSB, owned and operated by state institutions, adopted a policy of 'benign paternalism'. It characterized itself as 'scrupulously neutral' towards political parties and organized interest groups, and it was able to do so largely because it was insulated from the government in power by its ability to rely on receiving licence income from its public (Thompson, 1990: 258). This is authoritarianism 'with a conscience' (Williams, 1976).

Such arrangements were considered essential for such a privileged and monolithic organization to claim to be acting in the public interest, and this rationale has preserved the BBC's relative independence from government into the twenty-first century. Because the independence of the BBC is predicated on its performance not disrupting the post-Crawford consensus within the main political parties, the internal self-perceptions of 'impartiality' in British broadcasting discussed in Chapter 1 can be traced back to the BBC's first Director-General, John (later Lord) Reith (1889–1971). However, when the former privately-owned British Broadcasting *Company* was granted its Royal Charter and became a *Corporation*, Reith had already compromised his own 'operative ideal' of neutrality, having abandoned it in practice during the General Strike of May 1926 (Thompson, 1990: 258). During the nine-day national emergency, the British Broadcasting Company had been 'broadly pro-government' in its editorial policy towards the strike (Crisell, 1994: 20). Reith's submissiveness then is characterized by some as more pragmatic than motivated by party politics: he had chosen to support the government against the strikers in order to resist calls for the BBC to be 'commandeered' for the duration of the strike, saying that:

> ... since the BBC was a national institution, and since the Government in this crisis were acting for the people ... the BBC was for the Government in the crisis too; ... we had to assist in maintaining the essential services of the country, the preservation of law and order, and of the life and liberty of the individual and of the community.
>
> (Briggs, 1961: 365)

Whether pragmatic or not, adopting such a position may have set a damaging precedent. It certainly raises important questions. What, after all, constitutes a crisis so important as to abandon 'neutrality'? Perhaps crises might come in degrees, each smaller one demanding partial abandonment. Who are 'the people' if they do not include large sections of the working population who, in 1926, chose to strike? (Reith probably meant the 'establishment' – a more than notional ruling class – rather than the whole population.) In what way was the then government 'for' the people, if, in a democracy, the role of the opposition is to represent those people who voted against the government?

Uncomfortable an accommodation as it may seem, the inescapable conclusion of many was that in 1926 Reith chose – albeit perhaps out of necessity – to temporarily align the BBC with the government, even banning leaders of the Labour Party and trade unions from putting their case 'on air' (Briggs, 1961: 374–7). Adopting such a blatantly partial stance in a matter of great public controversy, he justified it in terms of the national interest. Defining in a crisis what constitutes the national interest is itself essentially problematic (see Chapter 6) because different people and parties will inevitably have different perspectives, so public service broadcasting carries the hidden risk that intended 'neutrality' will in practice be compromised by systematic favouring of establishment perspectives (Thompson, 1990: 259).

Influence and control

'Benign paternalism' has not always been systematically achieved. Although arguably Western journalism has in many cases become much more cynical than in the 1920s, deference having become relatively unfashionable (Goodwin and Smith, 1994: 191–4), sympathy for establishment perspectives was evident in the discourse of Radio 4 *Today* presenter Jack de Manio, as late as July 1968. His on-air *faux pas*, most memorably his inability to give correct time checks, were legendary, but he began one programme in July 1968 by suggesting 'raising our hats' to the London policemen whose weekends had again been 'mucked up' by 'a lot of silly hooligans' (Donovan, 1997: 29). De Manio's 'hooligans' had been in Grosvenor Square, demonstrating against the war in Vietnam, and a range of contemporaneous evidence from the protest suggests they included large numbers of thoughtful and sincere people who simply disagreed with US foreign policy in the Far East.

Considering de Manio's comment charitably, this act of political positioning on air was probably not part of a deliberate editorial policy of the BBC regarding Vietnam, demonstrations, dissent or freedom of expression, as Reith's positioning of the BBC had been in 1926. This was a case of a presenter reflecting a reactionary, 'establishment' perspective on a controversy, and lending that view a legitimacy not intentionally accorded to any counterbalancing opinion. Just as de Manio was in a position of influence, he may himself have been influenced by attitudes around him, although the discussion on pages 44–5 of synergies between the liberal tradition and the BBC would suggest his views may have been more maverick than endemic to the organization. The divide between stated policy and the effect of presenter discourse is discussed more fully in Chapter 5.

Nor has 'benign paternalism' always been effectively applied as a model throughout Europe. In France, despite strikingly *laissez-faire* attitudes to radio in the 1920s, 'impartiality' had become an issue by the end of the 1932 election campaign, during which the medium was first used in defiance of the press for political coverage (Kuhn, 1995: 85). An original consensus among the political elite that radio news should be 'neutral' (Miquel, 1984: 75) began to break down, and during the 1930s radio became increasingly politicized. This was compounded by radio's wartime role during the German occupation of the north, when it was used by Hitler's forces to broadcast German propaganda. It was also used by the collaborationist Vichy government in the south of the country to try to foster public support for its rule, and by, among others, the exiled Brigadier (later General) Charles de Gaulle (1890–1970), who broadcast from London to France via the BBC, rallying popular resistance against the Germans (Kuhn, 1995: 86–9).

To the irritation of British governments and the BBC alike, in the 1930s private stations had broadcast popular entertainment programming to the UK from the European continent, often winning larger audiences than the BBC (Crisell, 1994: 22), but this was nothing compared to the disquiet felt in London when the Germans commandeered the powerful transmitters of Radio Luxembourg and used them to transmit propaganda in English designed to spread disinformation and unease among the population. Broadcasting from Hamburg, the pro-fascist Irish-American William Joyce (1906–46) was the better known of two announcers who were nicknamed Lord Haw Haw by the *Daily Express*, and whose opening drawl of 'Germany calling, Germany calling' heralded what was widely perceived to be less a statement of 'reality', than a product of the German propaganda Ministry of Joseph Goebbels (see Chapter 6).

Even if Joyce's carefully constructed monologues had little effect on British morale, the potential of radio to inform selectively and even to persuade listeners in large numbers became widely accepted. The role of the media in wartime places additional strains on notions of 'balance'. Neither during the Vietnam War nor the Gulf Wars of the more recent past were the USA or the UK in any real danger of attack. Yet, during the Second World War the threat of invasion by Hitler's forces was a very real one for the UK. The temptation for any government in such circumstances to commandeer broadcasting organizations and use them exclusively for the purposes of morale boosting and propaganda at home must be very strong.

The BBC was not commandeered, as Reith had feared would happen 13 years earlier, and abroad it was widely considered 'an island of truthfulness amid a sea of rumour and propaganda' (Crisell, 1994: 23). In Australia, though, vulnerability to attack from Japan brought strict censorship to the Australian Broadcasting Commission (ABC), which had been formed in 1932. In addition to a brief period during which the evening news bulletin was actually produced by the Ministry of Information, many programmes had to be submitted for approval three weeks before transmission. Even drama had to play its part in the war effort, although this concerted propaganda campaign was not received uncritically, and the programme *The Jap As He Really Is* received special mention in the Commission's 1942–3 report, warning of loss of effectiveness in the event of any undermining of public confidence in the network's 'impartiality and integrity' (ABC, 2005).

After the war, although it was business as usual for the ABC and the BBC, in other democracies the war's legacy was the potential it had demonstrated for exercising influence. During the de Gaulle presidency (1958–69), the French state directly controlled and censored television news, using it to circumvent the political institutions and processes that could have moderated and contested its message, and address the people directly. Buoyed by the success of his wartime use of radio, de Gaulle used the new medium of television unashamedly, through the appointment to key positions of sympathizers who actively promoted his policies not just at elections, but routinely at other times too, reinforcing Gaullist ideology on a range of issues (Kuhn, 1995: 113). There, as in other countries which had failed to insulate their national broadcasting organizations from direct political control, senior broadcasters themselves became part of the kind of media–political elites identified by Roncarolo as broadly distinguished by the nature of the democracies themselves (2002: 74–9). Those which produce majority governments are more likely to have robust broadcast media with central if interchangeable control whereas those which produce inherently unstable coalition governments need to be more accommodating of political difference in order to maintain the political consensus around which the media–political elite is gathered.

An Italian solution to the problem of political editorial control was to openly dedicate each of the country's national public television networks to a different political party: an arrangement called *lottizzazione* (Monteleone, 2003: 387, 399–401). Each channel's director-general was a political appointee, who would dictate its editorial policy: so from 1975 RAI-1 became a Roman Catholic network, controlled by the Christian Democratic Party and RAI-2 became a voice of the Socialist Party. In 1979 a new, third channel called RAI-3 represented the Communist Party (Roncarolo, 2002: 72, 86–7). While minority parties were excluded from this arrangement between the coalition partners in the then government, and the communists could also claim to be disadvantaged until the launch of RAI-3, Italian citizens at least benefited from the relative transparency of knowing from which political perspective any issue was being represented (Menduni, 2002: 53–6, 122–4). Just as in choosing which newspaper to buy, and as Plato had observed about the rhetoricians' audiences 2400 years previously, now on Italian state television individuals could choose which coverage suited their own perspective, and watch only that.

State monopolies of broadcasting in a number of European countries began to collapse with the growth of 'free' radio and television transmitted either across national borders or in defiance of national law. In Italy, RAI's monopoly had long been purely notional because Radio Monte Carlo had begun regular broadcasting in Italian from the neighbouring principality of Monaco in 1966. Tele Monte Carlo followed in 1974. The further development of cable television, ruled by the Italian Constitutional Court in 1974 as outside state regulation (Anania, 1995), also disrupted the simplistic appeal of *lottizzazione*, because it was the catalyst for a rapid proliferation of hundreds of private radio and television stations across the country.

Among those at the forefront of the Italian broadcasting revolution was the ambitious young house builder Silvio Berlusconi, who launched TeleMilano on cable in 1974, developing it into a national service in 1978. These were Berlusconi's first steps towards his own reinvention as a centre-right politician and his eventual election as Prime Minister for seven months in 1995. He returned to power for a second, for Italy uncharacteristically enduring, period in office from 2001–05, and a third from 2005–06. As RAI had ceased to be Italy's only domestic television broadcaster nearly 20 years before, in 1993 *lottizzazione* was replaced by a new system of effectively a 'regulated' domestic duopoly of RAI and Mediaset. As the latter is owned by Berlusconi's company Fininvest, the duopoly divided Italian television into two politically polarized camps. In the 1990s Mediaset's popular programming provided him with an important political platform from which to secure the tight political control later wielded across Italy by his party, Forza Italia (Roncarolo, 2002: 82–4), albeit unable as it was to secure a decisive victory in the 2006 general election.

In France the initial *laissez-faire* attitude to privately-owned radio had been replaced by a thinly-disguised monopoly contrived through state control of Radio France and the apparently independent *périférique* (or peripheral) stations: Radio Monte Carlo, Radio Sud (Andorra), Radio Luxembourg and Europe 1 (Sarre). Although they all broadcast from outside France, shareholdings by the state companies Sofirad and Havas enabled President Valéry Giscard d'Estaing to appoint his own supporters to key posts in each of them during his presidency (1974–81) (Kuhn, 1995: 94–5). Inspired by the Italian example, it was the growth of pirate stations that brought about a *de facto* end to the monopoly in all but legislation. The first, Radio Verte, in 1977, was set up by members of the growing ecological movement, but others were inspired by industrial unrest and run illegally by trades unions – as in the case of Lorraine Coeur d'Acier and Radio SOS Emploi – or even by political parties themselves. Radio Riposte was the biggest opposition party, the Parti Socialiste's high-profile Parisian station, but others followed, such as Radio K in Marseille which began broadcasting just months before the 1981 presidential elections.

Even though the often violent riot police (the Compagnies Républicaines de Sécurité (CRS)) were involved in clashes with supporters of Lorraine Coeur d'Acier and the state organized regular jamming of their transmissions (Charasse, 1981), a group of President Giscard d'Estaing's own followers even set up their own station, Radio Fil Bleu, so great was the desire to acquire a 'voice' in the burgeoning 'free' radio market (Kuhn, 1995: 95–9). As the socialist leader and one of many summonsed to appear in court for illegal broadcasting, François Mitterrand (1916–96) made the ending of the monopoly an election promise (1981), and it is quite possible that his subsequent victory was due at least in part to the popular wave of support for the new stations. Following legalization, the then mayor of Paris, Jacques Chirac, among many hundreds to exploit the new liberalization of the airwaves, launched his own Gaullist station, Radio Tour Eiffel.

Despite the intense activity elsewhere in Europe, effective challenges to the BBC's monopoly were slow to produce legal concessions to those who, for political or commercial considerations, wanted to control a part of British broadcasting. Just as the war silenced the 1930s continental radio stations, leaving a fitter, more populist BBC in its wake and only the nighttime broadcasts of a similarly rejuvenated Radio Luxembourg to compete with it, the offshore music pirates, led in 1964 by Radio Caroline, were all but seen off by legislation in 1967. While the Conservatives had introduced privately-owned, commercial Independent Television (ITV) in defiance of objections on quality grounds in 1955, the Labour government of Harold Wilson (1916–95) was ideologically hostile to the idea of belatedly introducing commercial radio. In enacting the Marine Broadcasting (Offences) Act, which closed all but Radio Caroline, it required the BBC to begin all-day broadcasting of pop music on a new network it named Radio 1, and to develop local radio to counter the London-centricity of the national services (Crisell, 1994: 31–3).

Although the pirates had broadcast mainly music and advertisements, there had been a limited amount of news coverage, constrained of course by the stations' being based on board ships or disused military forts just outside the country's territorial waters. In most cases this consisted of rewriting and reading out versions of the BBC's news, monitored off air. Inevitably, the pirates were broadly opposed to Wilson's government because he was about to put them out of business, but as the 1967 Act was being debated and its enactment approached, on air campaigning against it was surprisingly muted. After Radio Caroline fell silent, hit by financial and business problems associated with the more clandestine logistics of operating without the benefits of legal status in the UK, it was a new pirate, Radio Northsea International (RNI), which campaigned most effectively against Wilson's government.

Using an approach typified by the re-recording of a mock wartime hit previously released in 1969 by Bud Flanagan, as *Who Do You Think You Are Kidding, Mr Wilson*, RNI broadcast an aggressive propaganda campaign aimed at swinging votes to the Conservative Party in a number of marginal constituencies in London and the south-east of England, in the general election of June 1970. The station's transmissions were extensively jammed by the British authorities in an attempt to stem this loss of political control of broadcasting (see Chapter 6), but this was the first time 18-year-olds had voted in a British election, and many commentators agreed that it was the youth vote that secured the Tories their small Parliamentary majority (Street, 2002: 112). Like Mitterrand would 11 years later, the incoming Prime Minister Edward Heath (1916–2005) had promised to introduce commercial radio, and as had been the case with television in 1955, when the first Independent Local Radio (ILR) station began broadcasting in October 1973 the Crawford legacy to the BBC of a monopoly of licensed, land-based domestic radio was finally ended.

Regulation and broadcasting

The lessons of the twentieth century for the western democracies, about controlling and influencing broadcasting, are that neither is dependent on physical ownership. That is, for a state to control the content of radio and television, for better or worse, it does not need to own the means of either production or transmission. When, under the Television Act 1954, ITV was set up as a federal system of private companies sharing regionally-produced programmes they distributed to a national audience, mixed with a small amount of complementary regional programming, even the 'pro-business' Conservative government of the day ensured the transmission facilities were firmly under state control. The country's first statutory regulator of commercial broadcasting, the Independent Television Authority (ITA), planned coverage, allocated franchises to the various companies and built and operated the transmitter network. Transformed by the Sound Broadcasting Act 1972 into the Independent Broadcasting Authority (IBA), it also ran ILR's radio transmission network on the same basis (Crisell, 1994: 34).

Despite their many ideological and policy differences, the UK's biggest political parties were nonetheless complicit in the so-called 'post-war consensus' which kept extreme change out of British politics until the polarization of the Thatcher years (1979–90) (Born, 2004: 48). Margaret Thatcher's legacy to radio and television, The Broadcasting Act 1990, dismantled the IBA and transmission became the responsibility of the individual programme companies, as the existing technical infrastructure and real estate were privatized. Neither in 1955 nor in 1990, however, did the state relinquish ultimate control of broadcasting: not only because it retained the right, indirectly through the regulator, to issue the licence to broadcast, but also because it reaffirmed the broadcasters' subordinacy to the regulator on a range of content issues *including* 'due impartiality' on matters of controversy (HM Government, 1990: section 6; subsection 4). In times of what they may deem dire 'national emergency', most governments retain the power to take control of broadcasting if they wish.

So, with the passing of the Communications Act 2003, and the creation of Ofcom as a super-regulator of commercial broadcasting and other privately-owned forms of telecommunication, the UK found itself, at least in part, in a similar position to that of several other countries which have controls in place to, among other issues, limit bias. Section 320 of *The Ofcom Broadcasting Code* proscribes the expression by licensees of their own views on 'matters of political or industrial controversy ... and ... current public policy'. It also requires 'the preservation ... of due impartiality' and 'the prevention ... of undue prominence' of some perspectives over others (Ofcom

2005: 62–3). However, while Ofcom regulates the commercial sector in the UK, the BBC regulates itself in complying with the 'due impartiality' rule: the paradox underlying the Gilligan affair of 2003, as we shall see later. Few other countries that attempt to regulate against bias leave the state broadcaster to regulate itself. The Australian Broadcasting Authority (ABA), for example, regulates all radio, television and Internet provision, and 'political matter' is subject to limited controls under the Broadcasting Services Act 1992. The Australian Auditor-General also carries out a regular audit of the ABC, including matters of independence, accuracy and impartiality (Caine, Bartlett and Crossley, 2004).

Regulation of television and radio in Italy is by the Communication Authority, which enforces the '*par condicio*' law of 2000, guaranteeing all parties equal access and airtime (Roncarolo, 2002: 73). In France, the Conseil Supérieur de L'Audiovisuel is bound to issue broadcasting licences that will ensure political pluralism, either to services which will allow a wide range of views access to the airwaves, or to those representing alternative perspectives. For example, anarchists, socialists and the extreme right have their own 'opinionated' radio stations, which are expected to 'balance' each other's output. 'Internal pluralism' within non-opinionated television channels and radio stations is measured quantitatively and qualitatively, with access given to government, the opposition and groups unrepresented in parliament being subject to airtime quotas (CSA, 2000). In Sweden, the Radio- och TV Verket requires 'impartiality' in the commercial sector, while a second body, the Granskningsnämnden för Radio och Television, handles large numbers of complaints alleging political bias across the two industries.

In many other countries such forms of content regulation are not practised, even if they once were. In the United States the FCC had introduced the so-called Mayflower Doctrine in 1940, forbidding editorializing by radio stations. It was replaced by an expanded 'fairness doctrine' in 1949, requiring 'balancing' opinions to be included in all matters of political controversy. Some commentators considered that rather than encouraging freedom of expression, editors began to avoid certain issues because of the effort required to find 'balancing' material. Others considered the fairness doctrine incompatible with the First Amendment rights to freedom of speech enshrined in the American constitution (Rowan, 1984), and during the 1981–9 presidency of the free market deregulationist Ronald Reagan (1911–2004) it came into disrepute, and was abandoned in 1987. That allowed the rise of the right-wing political 'shock jocks', whose rhetoric today rages undiminished on some of the country's highest-rated talk stations (see Chapter 5). One caveat: even in the USA today, election advertising is regulated, in that legally recognized candidates must be given equal access to *purchase* airtime.

The Canadian Radio-television and Telecommunications Commission (CRTC) requires that where airtime for paid-for advertising or even free time is afforded to a party or a candidate, opponents must be given equal access. In Canada, broadcasters must also ensure their audiences are 'informed of the main issues and positions of all candidates and registered parties', but editorial judgement is the responsibility of the broadcaster.

In New Zealand, the Broadcasting Standards Authority has regulated political advertising during elections since it was set up in 1989. It also requires programmes to be 'fair and accurate' and that broadcasters maintain procedures for correcting factual errors and redressing unfairness. There, though, as elsewhere, the recent trend has been towards deregulation – or at least, the relaxation of controls on broadcasters (Wall, 2005: 2). Foreign ownership has become an issue in New Zealand in particular, where two non-Kiwi groups rapidly came to dominate the national radio market (Shanahan and Neill, 2005).

So, even where regulators concern themselves with issues of 'impartiality', approaches vary widely. Where external regulators require advance viewing of a television programme or hearing of a radio broadcast, as both the ITA and the IBA would do over matters of political controversy, regulation is at its strongest. Otherwise, action can only be taken against individual broadcasting organizations *after* the item has been transmitted. The former IBA even banned the 1971 *World in Action* documentary, *South of the Border* (Granada), which included interviews with the then Irish Republican Army (IRA) Chief of Staff and the Sinn Féin President, without even seeing it (BFI, 2001). Despite *World in Action*'s long history of challenging British government policy towards Northern Ireland and so Granada Television's fractious relationship with the regulators, the city of Manchester in which it is based was bombed in 1996.

Regulators may act against broadcasters outside their national boundaries, where they control the means of distribution, but international cooperation is necessary for such controls to be effective where broadcasts cross frontiers. On 13 December 2004 France banned the French-based satellite broadcaster Eutelsat from rebroadcasting the Lebanese television channel, Al Manar. Run by the militant Palestinian group Hezbollah, its broadcasts were considered to be anti-Semitic and inciting violence against Jews. On 17 March 2005, following intense lobbying from France, the rest of Europe followed suit, under the European Union Rules and Principles on Hate Broadcasts (Council of Europe, 1989: Article 22a). The other pan-European satellite broadcaster, Luxembourg-based SES, then had to remove the channel from its Astra satellite system. On a more routine basis, such regulators as Ofcom may control channels that broadcast internationally from within their territories, such as Iran NTV, broadcast from the UK.

An alternative to state regulation is, of course, self-regulation, as practised by the BBC. There are other parallels in broadcasting with the self-regulation over matters of privacy operated in the UK, for example, by the press (see Chapter 3). Broadcasters not wishing to be penalized later may take unilateral action now to avoid contravening the regulations and facing the regulator's sanctions later. In September 1988, for example, Channel 4 cancelled an edition of the round-table discussion programme *After Dark*, which was to feature the new Sinn Féin President Gerry Adams, following advance complaints from an individual who may have been on the political right (Moloney, 1991). Within weeks, the then government passed legislation banning the voices of that party's spokespeople from all broadcasting, because it wanted to deny them the 'oxygen of publicity' because of alleged links with the IRA (McNair, 1998: 96). Self-regulation as a form of self-imposed discipline includes adherence to any professional codes of conduct (see Chapter 1). Typical is clause three of the National Union of Journalists (NUJ) (of Britain and Ireland) code of practice, which states they should 'strive' for fairness and accuracy, avoid confusing 'comment and conjecture as established fact' and not allow 'distortion, selection or misrepresentation' in their reporting (NUJ, 2004). Also inherent in expectations of professional conduct may be a moral sense some broadcasters have that in a democracy they should be 'fair' to all.

However, Tiffen's detailed account of Australia's 'cash for comment' scandal (2002: 131–48) is an excellent example of how morality cannot be relied upon in every case to ensure that 'fairness' prevails. Two popular radio phone-in presenters on 2UE in Sydney were accepting secret payments from private companies for favourable coverage. In the frenzied media scandal which ensued, they hit back, citing the way travel writers compliment destinations which look after them generously, and other journalists who receive goods and services, tickets to events and expensive lunches without disclosing them to their audiences. A memo also emerged that had instructed presenters not to be critical of McDonald's on air because they were important advertisers on the station.

Although there was no obvious party political element to the 'cash for comment' scandal in Australia, two significant issues are raised by it. Firstly, despite the scale of the deception, involving Aus$4 million, and the existence of legislation and regulation intended to prevent it, it remained undiscovered for so long: the subsequent ABA investigation concluded that the programme code had been breached 95 times. Secondly, it is worth remembering that political journalists are regularly dined out by politicians as part of the briefing processes underpinning their craft and, for example, although there is no suggestion here of professional wrongdoing, BBC2 *Newsnight* presenter Kirsty Wark was publicly criticized for allowing impressions to be created of a conflict of interest through her friendship with the Scottish first minister, Jack McConnell. Because, in what became known as Villagate, their families had holidayed together at her second home in Majorca, the Conservative Party alleged that Wark had compromised her ability to report impartially on Scottish affairs, given that she obviously had a longstanding friendship with a Labour politician (MacLeod and Foster, 2005).

That we know about 'cash for comment' in Australia and Villagate in the UK – as well as a myriad of other 'realities' that would otherwise have remained hidden from us – is due in part to appropriate investigative journalism. On a much bigger scale, the criminal activity behind the Watergate scandal was only exposed in 1972 because of Robert Upshur Woodward and Carl Bernstein, two reporters on *The Washington Post*, whose disclosures in effect precipitated the resignation of President Richard M. Nixon (1913–94) two years later (Olson, 2003 and see Chapter 3). Had they chosen not to pursue their story, for whatever reason, the course of US political history would probably have run very differently. Although frequently complaining at being 'spun' by politicians (Brants and van Kempen, 2002: 169–72), patently journalists also have the power to 'spin' stories themselves (see pages 152–6). The regulation of journalistic practice and the issues raised in this book are appropriate responses to the perennial question *Quis custodiet ipsos custodes?* Or, in this context, who watches over the watchdogs?

'Balance' in practice

Such extreme reactions as those of the IBA over *World in Action* and the ABA over 'cash for comment', precipitated as they were by unusual contexts, are however atypical of content regulation. The vast majority of broadcast output does not come under such scrutiny, and yet it is the generality of broadcasting that can have the greatest effect on democratic processes. As with Villagate, sometimes the media raise issues about 'impartiality', as sometimes do politicians themselves, usually where they see some potential electoral value for themselves. Equally, as the Conservatives did over Villagate, they might see it necessary to prevent their interests being damaged. To imagine that 'balance' is unimportant, because voters are not influenced by what they see and hear, is to underestimate the importance placed on the media by the politicians themselves.

Where political advertising is allowed in the broadcast media, such as in the USA, parties would not spend the large amounts they do if they didn't think controlling at least a part of the content and presentation of political discourse in the mass media would help increase their share of the vote. Even four months before the 2004 presidential election, incumbent President George W. Bush and challenger Senator John Kerry had already spent $188 million between them on television advertising (Timms, 2004). Different groups of supporters also purchase airtime to promote their preferred candidates. A 1990 opinion poll in Australia suggested television can be the most effective medium for political advertising, with 64 per cent of respondents claiming they had 'often' or 'sometimes' watched campaign advertisements on television, with 36 per cent citing newspapers and 33 per cent radio (McAllister et al., 1990). Advertising, where strictly controlled, is at least transparent: in the United States candidates are required to submit accounts to the Federal Election Commission showing how much has been spent. Television and radio stations are required to sell them airtime at comparable rates, without discounting for a preferred candidate or scheduling spots punitively for one they do not support.

Where free airtime is allocated for spot advertising or, as in the UK, Party Political and Party Election Broadcasts, the apportionment of time may be according to a formula agreed between the 'main' parties and the broadcasters. This does favour incumbency, because it is largely based on representation in parliament: so the two biggest parties will by definition receive the most exposure, while minority or new parties will receive less or none at all. The third party, the Liberal Democrats, have long campaigned for proportional representation (PR) to be the basis of election to parliament. Under PR their representation in the House of Commons – and so, their allocation of time – would be greater for subsequent general elections. There remains, though, that element of transparency found in political advertising where the originators of the material must declare themselves, which simply cannot be found in the editorial decision making behind routine coverage of news and current affairs.

The contexts for this are not confined to news bulletins, magazine programmes, phone-ins or documentaries either. The BBC and regulators of commercial radio in the UK have routinely banned the playing of songs that they felt might have a disproportionate effect on political 'balance' in a station's output. Examples include the 1997 Labour Party campaign song *Things Can Only Get Better* by D:Ream. During the 1996 US presidential campaign, the Republican challenger to Bill Clinton, Senator Robert Dole, was parodied mercilessly on such entertainment-based late night chat shows as *The Late Show with Jay Leno* (NBC) and *Late Night with Conan O'Brien* (NBC), while no balancing ridicule was meted out to Clinton. We may justifiably hypothesize that getting positive coverage on those and other apparently innocuous shows, such as the *Late Show with David Letterman* (CBS) and in the UK *Richard and Judy* (Channel Four) and *Steve Wright* (BBC Radio 2) may well swing sufficient votes in marginal constituencies to affect outcomes, as did RNI in 1970, but the difficulty inherent in this hypothesis lies in proving it. Often these 'soft' environments present political interviewees with less challenging questioning than they would receive on the political circuit of news and current affairs programmes (McNair, 2002: 197). Politicians may perceive them as providing more direct access to audiences than they get through broadcast dialogue with political journalists, because they are allowed more latitude in expressing themselves (see Chapter 5).

'Background' coverage of issues can be as damaging to individuals and parties involved in political processes as direct reporting. For example, polls by NOP and MORI suggested falling public support for the impending ban on hunting with dogs in England and Wales between its enactment in November 2004 and its coming into force in February 2005, which if correct could demonstrate large numbers of people changing their minds on the issue (MORI, 2005). As relatively small numbers of the population were directly involved in the sport, it would be reasonable to suspect that the media played a significant part in any widespread shift of opinion. Crucial to this may be the tendency of many reports to focus on South Shropshire Hunt master and

House of Commons invader Otis Ferry, and always position him as the son of million-selling 1970s and 1980s pop star Bryan Ferry (for example 18:30, 16 February 2005, ITV1). Similarly, on the eve of the ban, the reporting of one last legal hunt as 'emotional' was explained as a response to the ban being a threat to lifestyles, livelihoods and interests (08:02, 7 February 2005, Radio 4). Such a spin is deliberately sympathetic to just one side of the controversy. Without any 'balancing' material that would be equally emotive to an average listener – if one exists – such an approach is in itself biased.

There are similarities between the physical positioning of programme production among the infrastructure and paraphernalia of the hunting community and the observations of the Glasgow University Media Group (1976: 267–8) that cameras covering industrial strife were normally behind police lines, thus capturing most graphically aggression from the strikers facing them, rather than from the police who had their backs to the cameras. On the first weekend after the hunting ban, *Today* (19 February 2005) and *Countryfile* (BBC1, 20 February 2005) were both presented as outside broadcasts from 'just outside the kennels of the Beaufort Hunt' (*Today*, 07:09) in Badminton, South Gloucestershire. Typically, *Today* presenter Edward Stourton described being 'in the stable with a magnificent beast' and 'the picturesque scene of a hunt meet' (08:10) while in the studio co-presenter Sarah Montague remarked on the baying of the hounds as a 'fantastic sound effect' (08:59). Following an incident the previous day, when a Labour MP who had supported the ban was widely reported to have been attacked by a mob of hunt supporters, the contributions of two of Stourton's interviewees, Parmjit Dhanda, MP for Gloucester (another ban supporter) and Penny Little of Protect Our Wild Animals came remotely from another studio.

It is true that the practicalities of broadcasting according to today's 24-hour news agenda – to tight deadlines in sometimes poorly resourced environments that might make it difficult to meet audiences' expectations of high aesthetic production values – can make achieving 'balance' even more difficult. Getting appropriate contributors to central or remote studios, for example, rather than resorting to telephone or – often worse – mobile phone links for audio presents broadcasters with logistical difficulties, which should not be underplayed. Challenged on *NewsWatch* (BBC News24) to respond to a viewer's timings of interviews in the BBC's television news coverage of 19 February and his opinion that extensive interviewing of hunters by reporters effectively 'embedded' with them had been 'benign', Home News Editor Jon Williams admitted the BBC 'might have been more challenging' of both sides, but defended any concentration on hunt supporters on the grounds that the story had 'moved away' from the three-year-long debate of the rights and wrongs of hunting to coverage of a day of challenge to the new law (25 February 2005, 20:45).

The viewer's other criticism of the coverage was that the 'countryside' depicted bore little resemblance to that he knew as a country dweller in an area without a hunt, and where few people supported the principle of hunting. The viewer and Williams each contested the other's version of reality, neither being willing to concede that the other's was complete. The essential problem here lies in the unwillingness of most reporting to make clear its incompleteness, and the inability of audiences to discern this for themselves (see Chapter 1). Williams considered that the 'nature of balance' – or the demands it placed on his reporters – had changed as the enactment of the ban had associated one side of the debate with the government and similarly repositioned hunters as its challengers.

Holding governments to account is a legitimate journalistic activity, and a responsibility taken seriously by most political journalists. Inevitably, though, the tendency to oppose government raises legitimate concerns about broadcasters' 'impartiality', however honourable might be their motives. Following the second consecutive Labour landslide, in 2001, in his *Sunday Times* column, *Today* presenter John Humphrys assured readers that in the absence of a strong parliamentary opposition to hold the government to account, it would be the broadcasters who would save the country from 'elective dictatorship' and 'illuminate' that which 'politicians might want to keep in the dark' (McNair, 2002: 197). This manifests itself in an often combative and inquisitorial style that polling evidence suggests audiences readily perceive to be cynicism about politics and politicians generally, but it is usually the party in power that bears the brunt of such attacks. In turn, the broadcasters blame the politicians for causing them to forcibly extract the truth (Fallows, 1997: 62–3).

Despite the instinctive zeal of such combative political interviewers as John Humphrys and Jeremy Paxman in the UK and John McLaughlin and Tim Russert in the USA, not every issue involving government is a Watergate, though, or even a Villagate. Nor is every politician or official either naturally predisposed to dishonesty or inclined to lie or deceive when necessary, despite considerable evidence that some of them may have lied sometimes (Bradlee, 1997: 126–31). Yet the 'spiral' of routine journalistic cynicism about government, if admittedly less extreme than most conspiracy theories, can however be not only counterproductive, but unbalancing (Brants and van Kempen, 2002: 169–72). The 1997 Labour landslide was partly attributable to cynicism over the Conservative record of the previous 18 years, yet after a so-called 'honeymoon period' Labour in government was subject to the same sort of critical analysis that had so badly damaged the Conservatives before them. That the latter were so slow to recover electorally may also be attributable to the damage done to them in office by a media concentration on 'sleaze' in individuals, which came to unfairly and durably characterize them as a whole political party (McNair, 1998: 106).

This is not a recent phenomenon (Franklin, 1994, 1997; Capella and Jamieson, 1997) despite attempts in the UK to portray spin as an invention of 'New' Labour, as that party rebranded itself in the mid-1990s in order to distance itself from its own previous record in government. An analysis by the Times Mirror Center of the People and the Press used polling evidence to examine both public perceptions of journalism, and perceptions among journalists of their own work (1995). While the public were overwhelmingly cynical about the political class, the journalists surveyed were far less cynical about them than their reporting suggested, with 53 per cent even expressing confidence in public officials as both more honest and more honourable than the general public (Fallows, 1997: 202–3). Content-regulated broadcast media should not systematically misrepresent governments negatively, but neither should they do the opposite: by being unduly influenced by them into transmitting propaganda at the other extreme, by merely acquiescing over controversy or failing to raise challenging questions.

Achieving 'balance'

So, 'balance' in news and current affairs broadcasting is especially problem-atic, for those who would achieve it as much as for those who would 'measure' it. Well-meaning journalism routinely attempts to achieve 'balance' by juxtaposing binary opposites: government and opposition, groups for and against hunting, those who perceive a phenomenon one way, and those whose perception of it is a mirror image. Experience may tell us, though, that in life few issues are neatly organized into simple self-balancing opposites, presenting potentially equally attractive but mutually exclusive alternatives to the as yet undecided wider perspectives (Frost, 2000: 41–2). Elementary physics tells us that balance is achieved when two or more elements are each positioned with a fulcrum between them, in such a way that their relative mass and displacement from that fulcrum permits none of them to weigh more heavily than another.

Balance, though, does not exist merely in two dimensions. Despite the scope it offers for easily distinguishing between different perspectives, conceptualizing politics as a simple arrangement of positions along a simple axis spanning the divide between the extreme left and the extreme right is over simplistic. Political positioning, of people, policies and ideologies may occur instead at any point somewhere within a poly-dimensional space, more reflective of the complexities of the polity. Just as a toy spinning top struggles to keep its balance despite different gravitational and centrifugal forces pulling in different directions, so politics is much more than a simple dichotomy of the right versus the left. Degrees of allegiance to particular posi-tions vary and different issues might engender differential positioning within parties – for example, in the UK 'euroscepticism' (or 'eurorealism') often having been said to divide both the Conservative and Labour parties.

Nor are journalists necessarily uncommitted to every cause or perspective they encounter. Channel 4 news anchor Jon Snow chronicles in his autobiog-raphy a 'personal journey' beginning with a childhood ambition to be a Conservative MP, through his 'radicalization' as a volunteer in Uganda and then protesting against apartheid in South Africa, to the distinguished career as a reporter and presenter that followed (2004). Inevitably, we are – each of us – actively or passively positioned somewhere on a vast plane of opinion on just about every matter of public controversy we have ever encountered. In producing such crowd-pleasing partial narratives as *Fahrenheit 9/11* (2004), Michael Moore set his rhetoric within a journalistic framework, but excluded dissenting views. Some of us, though – journalists and academics alike – have professional responsibilities to try and prevent our own positioning from influencing what we say and do in certain contexts: or as John Humphrys once said, to leave any political views 'outside the studio door' (*Medium Wave*, BBC Radio 4, 28 January 1996). However, 'reading' and so determining the impact of our own work, and whether or not it is 'balanced', may be as problematic for us as reading broadcast and printed texts is for audiences (see Chapter 4).

Not everything about balance, though, is subjective. Just as in print journalism, there are measurable elements in broadcast speech and the use of images to reinforce spoken narratives on television that can be counted, timed and compared with like events (Gunter, 1997: 26–7). When some of these elements outnumber others that may reasonably be expected to counter them, this alone may demonstrate the presence of bias. In effect, on one side of the fulcrum one or more elements may be weighing more heavily than others. Determining the mass – or the impact – of a particular element is itself problematic: as Fallows (1997: 62–3) relates, in 1984 CBS reporter Lesley Stahl was astonished to be praised by a White House official for a damning report on the Reagan administration's 'hypocritical' attitude and policies towards mental health care. When Stahl challenged the official's reading of the report, she was told that the positive footage she had showed of the president speaking at a Special Olympics event for children with mental difficulties and opening a nursing home 'drowned out' the savage voiceover she had added to it (see Chapters 4 and 5).

Notwithstanding Reith's compromise over the General Strike, the claimed correlation between impartiality and broadcasters' professionalism (Burns, 1977: 137) renders it rather unusual that in 2003, at the height of the David Kelly controversy, the then BBC Chairman Gavyn Davies should have protested that the BBC had legitimately 'taken a different view' over Iraq from that of the government (Ahmed, 2003). In doing so, Davies raised an issue that is not only fundamental to the independence of the BBC, as he perceived it to be, but also one that is central to that key obligation of many broadcasters in different territories to remain impartial in matters of public controversy. In the privileged case of the BBC, being subject only to self-regulation, taking a different view from the government or, in different circumstances, the opposition should be as difficult to justify as if it were to associate itself with one interest group in a controversy – such as pro-hunters or those who oppose Britain's membership of the European Union – and then oppose those who disagree with their point of view.

Between the two instances, in which the Corporation apparently declared itself firstly *for* 'the establishment' and secondly *against* it, the BBC has almost unfailingly defended its self-perception of 'neutrality'. That might at times be a fair representation of the BBC's position, but such claims have not always been uncontroversial. Critics of its reporting of such episodes as the 1982 conflict with Argentina over British sovereignty of the Falkland Islands (or from the Argentinian perspective 'las Malvinas'), the American bombing of Libya in 1986 and the first Gulf War in 1991 alleged that the Corporation took its role as an impartial commentator too literally and sometimes lent credibility to the claims of Britain's enemies in the different conflicts. Critics alleged that in 1982 they revealed vital personnel and weaponry movements in the South Atlantic that the military would have preferred to be kept secret. Given the controversial nature of the 2003 war on Iraq, maintaining an 'impartial' stance on the conflict would have been more consistent with that recent tradition.

The 'different view' described by Davies in July 2003 was, of course, the BBC's apparently entrenched position on the report on *Today* by Andrew Gilligan about the 'sexed up' government dossier on Iraq (Ahmed, 2003) (see Chapter 1). Davies, the BBC governors, the *Today* team and others in the Corporation considered the report correct in its main allegation that the 'sexing up' was done by 10 Downing Street, even though during the Hutton Enquiry it emerged that doubts were expressed internally about 'loose language' in the report and home working by Gilligan, who was relatively unsupervised when not operating out of the newsroom (Wells, 2003a). The manner in which the BBC Board of Governors appeared to use its regulatory powers over a formal complaint from the then Chief Press Secretary to Tony Blair, Alastair Campbell, about the Gilligan report does suggest that the issue was allowed to grow out of all proportion from the original allegation because of the way it was handled. The governors gathered for an extraordinary meeting on 6 July 2003, but they accepted assurances from Davies and Dyke, as well as a number of other senior executives who joined the meeting, that Gilligan's report was correct. Some governors expressed concerns about procedural issues, and it was suggested that they await a more considered analysis of the BBC's output, but the minutes of the meeting show that they agreed the BBC's coverage of the war and the controversy around it had been 'entirely impartial' (BBC, 2003).

However, like Hutton, the parliamentary all-party Intelligence and Security Select Committee later concluded that Gilligan's single-sourced report was wrong (ISC, 2003). Hutton's conclusions were catastrophic for the BBC, with the same governors accepting resignations from both the chairman and the director-general within 24 hours of his report being published. Effectively, over Iraq the institution had abandoned the at least feigned equivocation in the event of disagreement over an issue, that it had been able to regularly lend to issues from the Falklands, Libya and the 1991 Gulf War, to more recent controversies over, for example, the ordination of gay bishops, the genuineness of asylum seekers or the MMR vaccination. In the aftermath of Hutton, with a lot of fence mending and face saving to do, the changes made to the BBC's editorial processes and practices following the Neil Report (2004) were a belated recognition by the Corporation that something had to be done.

In a parliamentary democracy such as the UK, inevitably it will be the actions of the government that journalists wish to challenge – although, at least in an election campaign, it is likely that other parties' manifestos and their previous records in government if they have them are at issue. Successive editions of the BBC's own *Producers' Guidelines* (2004a), now replaced by the *Editorial Guidelines* (2005a), maintained that the most important periods in the democratic cycle – elections – are, unlike times of crisis or civil unrest, moments in broadcasting which require particular care over the 'fair' representation of issues and participants in the political process. However, the BBC's record of 'fairness' in election periods is also inconsistent: for example, in 1995 only court action initiated by opposition parties prevented the broadcasting in Scotland of an extended interview with the then Prime Minister John Major on *Panorama* (BBC1), just three days before local elections were to be held there. The BBC had insisted that to transmit the programme was part of a normal balance of reporting over a period of time – the essence of the statutory definition of 'due' impartiality – while the Labour, Liberal Democrat and Scottish Nationalist parties successfully argued in court that their leaders should receive equal exposure at such a crucial juncture.

If the controversy over Gilligan's report was, as some commentators have characterized it, a 'war' between the Labour Government and the BBC, when the Conservatives were last in power, they too accused the Corporation of bias against them, being able to cite examples of 'worse' treatment than was being given to Labour politicians. Famously, in 1987 the Conservative Party Chairman Norman (later Lord) Tebbit telephoned the *Today* programme to complain it was being biased against his party in its coverage of the air raids on Libya launched from Britain. Being perceived in the 1980s as anti-Conservative and then two decades later by Alastair Campbell as anti-Labour over Iraq is not the sort of 'balance' over a reasonable period of time that is articulated by the *Guidelines*. If balance is not maintained over the short term, journalism will be mistaken for partisanship. After enjoying years of irreverent coverage in the USA, for example, of the 1989–93 presidency of Republican George Bush, Democrats considered certain journalists to be liberally-inclined political allies who would be more supportive of the subsequent administration of Democrat Bill Clinton (1993–2001). When the same kind of challenging, sceptical coverage was levelled at Clinton, many of them felt betrayed (Fallows, 1997: 63–5). Always doubting or being overwhelmingly cynical about government policies and statements – whichever party is in power – may be damaging to democracy itself, because of the wider cynicism and lack of interest in political processes that it may cause among audiences, in the manner discovered in the USA by the Times Mirror Center of the People and the Press (1995). Unless really deserved, it is also unrealistic and misleading for every administration to be depicted as flawed, malign or incompetent. Except in the most extreme of cases, democratically elected governments must by definition be preferable to life under a dictatorship, especially for those who would work in the mass media.

This is far removed from attempting to 'balance' elements around a putative fulcrum or 'journalism-in-the-round' which, though perhaps 'fairer' to all sides results in broadcasting that may be perceived as boring and less likely to improve audience ratings. The journalist John Lloyd identified this as, in its best forms, an 'attempt to come to grips with the complexity, nuances and constant shifts of public life' (2003). He also considered it to be part of the BBC's public service role, just as another former Director-General, John Birt (in office 1992–2000) was guided by a 'mission to explain' (MacGregor, 1997: 137–8). According to Lloyd, its antithesis is 'laser journalism', which relentlessly pursues and pinpoints minutiae of detail, often portrayed as the 'killer fact' that 'so clearly and fatally exposes the wickedness or mendacity at the heart of the state machine that heads must roll' (2003). While 'laser journalism' may be essential to exposing real corruption, as in Watergate (Olson, 2003) and Australia's 'cash for comment' scandal (Tiffen, 2002: 131–48), it can have undesirable – if also unintended – consequences. Dr David Kelly might not have contemplated suicide, if not for the certainty that sooner or later his identity as Andrew Gilligan's single source would have been teased out into the public domain by the media. Other examples include the Labour 'spin doctor' Jo Moore, hounded out of her job because of ill-considered language in a single e-mail sent on 9/11 before the enormity of the tragedy had become clear, and even pursued by the media into her new career as a schoolteacher, long after her mistake had been exposed and paid for.

'Impartiality' in broadcasting

That broadcasting can benefit the proper functioning of democracy is not in doubt – it can inform, educate and enlighten, even promoting participation in political processes (Coleman, 2000: 9–11). However, with the exception of such legally-constrained circumstances as racism or child abuse, the notion that impartiality is possible over any issue, be it party political or not – and a quality to be striven for – is one of the orthodoxies of modern broadcast journalism. It is considered by many to be not only routine, but as discussed in Chapter 1, a measure of professionalism (Sheridan Burns, 2002: 11–12). In successive editions of the BBC's *Producers' Guidelines* 'due' impartiality has been described as a 'core value' from which 'no area of programming is exempt' (BBC, 2004a: 36). Problematic though 'impartiality' may be, where broadcasting organizations are subject to outside regulation, or left to regulate themselves as in the case of the BBC, the public and those among them who are more closely involved in the political processes which inevitably underpin any democracy, are entitled to expect 'fairness'.

There are simple measurements which can be made, as much by producers as by listeners or academic researchers, and which can provide at least a partial assessment of how close to balancing elements around nominal fulcra a programme or a series has got. Those measurements can be made in advance, and they can inform the planning and production processes. Examples considered later in this book include frequency of appearance, duration of appearance, approaches to questioning, the inclusion of actuality and so on. In short: care can be taken by broadcasters in the planning stages of production over how long and how effectively access to their microphones is shared out, and over how they depict the issues, events and participants involved.

Many broadcasters make this a part of their routine already, and in the UK, until a relaxation of the rules through the passing of the Political Parties, Elections and Referendums Act 2000 they were obliged to by law, because the previous legislation, the Representation of the People Act 1983, provided some equality of treatment for all *candidates* in a ward or a constituency. The legal loophole that allowed broadcasters to avoid having to include many minority parties and maverick individuals in their programmes at all, lay in a liberal interpretation of the definition of the word 'candidate'. While many politicians were invited on television and radio, they were not interviewed in their capacity as candidate, but instead as spokespeople for their party, avoiding discussion of issues of direct relevance only to the constituencies in which they were standing for election or re-election.

Journalists who feel unbound by such mechanistic measures, may yet recognize an absence of 'fairness' in other contexts as newsworthy: the BBC quite unashamedly reported that in the 2004 presidential elections in Afghanistan, the interim President Hamid Karzai had enjoyed 'over 75 per cent' of all coverage by the state broadcast media during the campaign. The data had come from an international monitoring body which 'did not want' to be identified. It included coverage of what would otherwise have been routine events for the president (such as road openings), as positive coverage afforded him, but not 'balanced' with equal treatment for other candidates (North, 2004). There were no caveats to the report about journalists' difficulties when working in a dangerous country, the impracticalities of getting audio from other candidates based in remote locations or suchlike. Relatively, in both electoral and regulatory terms, Afghanistan was and remains, of course, bandit country, but the 'fairness' principle is a simple one, easily transferable across territories and regimes, and a concept that can be easily understood by Western journalists.

Whether in the absence of specific 'fairness' legislation or not, when broadcasters routinely abuse – either maliciously or through negligence – the trust placed in them it is appropriate to ask whether the regulatory regime under which they currently operate is sufficiently rigorous. Is market domination of broadcast news production by a single organization – producing news in different formats for different outlets from common source material

– compatible with notions of plurality in modern democracies? For example, in 2005 the BBC's share of all radio listening in the UK was around 54 per cent (RAJAR, 2005), whereas its share of television viewing was around 30 per cent (BARB, 2005). Certainly, in radio this was a domination of news provision that needed to be re-examined in the process of the Charter renewal that took place from 2004–06. Given the initial impotence of the BBC governors over Gilligan, the outcome of an earlier debate during the passing of the Communications Act 2003 over whether Ofcom should have a greater role in regulating the BBC, was not universally deemed to have been appropriate (Baldwin, 2003).

Damaged, but claiming not to be influenced by the Gilligan affair, the Blair government (1997–) commissioned a report into the funding and governance of the BBC, which proposed replacing the Board of Governors with a new independent body. With the suggested title of the Public Service Broadcasting Commission, it would be able to redistribute some income from the licence fee to other PSBs, such as Channel 4. However, the subsequent Green Paper (DCMS, 2005) proposed a new two-tier structure of internal self-regulation, establishing the BBC Trust as the body charged with holding the corporation to account, as opposed to also managing it (Gibson, 2005).

Such an arrangement may not be a wholly adequate solution to the problem of regulating a large, monolithic broadcaster, commanding a substantial 'share of voice' in the media marketplace, either in the UK or elsewhere. While readers may choose the newspapers they buy according to their political positioning (although, of course, many do not) in the absence of Italian-style *lottizzazione* (Monteleone, 2003: 387, 399–401), listeners and viewers cannot make such informed choices when seeking news and information from the broadcast media. Just as independent producers account for percentages of BBC programming that are set by quota, there may yet be a case for some of the BBC's news output being commissioned from outside providers. One or more of the Corporation's national radio networks, for example, could 'publish' news produced by another organization which would also be bound by tight external regulation.

It is worth considering the effect of the public service model of broadcasting on the sector's output. It may be that the way the BBC and other PSBs are financed makes them inherently more liberal in outlook than an organization that is both subject to and committed to the market place. The BBC's funding through, effectively, a tax on television viewing is state intervention in broadcasting, so it must by definition believe in state-interventionism. This is felt more strongly within the Corporation because the licence fee is so contentious outside it. In the USA, NPR is demonized by many right-wing commentators as 'liberal' because it represents a challenge to the notion that the market can provide whatever the public want, and some authoritative research suggests the voting record of journalists across the public and commercial sectors demonstrates predominantly left-wing allegiance, firmly concluding that they are liberal (Sutter, 2001: 439–41).

As well as their private voting habits, a predominance of arts graduates within its staff might give an organization a left-liberal 'mind': the collective beliefs and assumptions widely shared within the organization, and seldom if ever challenged among peers. There will be assumptions underlying many editorial decisions, which fit this paradigm: an ideological basis for the positioning of 'balancing' fulcra, which is itself, flawed. A tendency to read left-wing newspapers may translate into a greater likelihood of interviewing journalists from them 'on air'. 'Taking a position' on a government dossier or a whole war might be more inevitable. Certain issues that may be problematic for society will seem uncontroversial to producers. We can, however, only guess at the strength of such a hypothesis, unless the workforce is polled, and genuine responses confirm or refute it. Alternatively, we can consider evidence of such positioning within an organization's output.

For example, in the UK capital punishment is rarely raised as even potentially acceptable, even though it is practised today in several American states and its reintroduction is unswervingly supported in opinion polls by two-thirds of the British public. This is despite numerous revelations of miscarriages of justice that would have meant people, such as the Guildford Four, being executed and then eventually proven innocent (Summerskill, 2003). Like parliament, the BBC *and* commercial broadcasters routinely defy public opinion on the issue, rarely if ever pursuing politicians about this contradiction inherent in their role as the electorate's representatives. Both the BBC and parliament collectively believe they are right to do so. Put simply, left-liberal minds do not countenance capital punishment, while right-wing perspectives do.

As we move now from regulated environments in broadcasting to unregulated ones in the press, it is worth noting that there are data in Chapter 7 which suggest that regulation can be less than effective in ensuring 'balance'. Broadcasters may routinely favour one party or ideology over another, without such an imbalance being noticed or complained about very often by their audiences. If, despite regulation, such an ability to bias output exists, it should not be accepted as proper or professional. Of course, producing news and current affairs is a demanding business, and much live broadcasting is spontaneous and only achieved in spite of considerable technical and practical obstacles. However, if broadcasters are to demonstrate due professionalism in their work – in the terms of their audiences, their regulators and their peers – insofar as is possible they should still aspire to 'fairness'. That attempted 'fairness' should be according to the measurable parameters discussed in Chapter 5, as well as the immeasurable, because the existence of the immeasurable does not excuse their ignoring the measurable. Although complete impartiality is almost always an impossibility, in contexts that are regulated in order to promote democracy, and where it is appropriate, journalists should still *attempt* to be impartial in whatever ways they can. If not, we are entitled to suspect their motives, rather than assume their innocence.

CHAPTER 3

Power and Responsibility: The Press, the People and Self-regulation

Democracy and the press

If many broadcasters are constrained by legal and regulatory requirements to attempt 'impartiality' in their coverage of political controversy, the same concerns rarely trouble their colleagues in the print and online sectors. In theorizing cyberculture, academics note the considerable ease with which new websites may be conceived and set up within very short timescales at very little cost (McQuail, 2005: 137–42). The web has quickly become the ultimate democratic mass medium, in that in relatively 'free' societies the issues of access and gatekeeping associated with the ownership and regulation of broadcasting simply do not apply (Atton, 2004). The concessions made by Google in 2005 to the Chinese government, in agreeing to restrict its search engine's findings to 'approved' sites unlikely to voice dissent against the regime, are atypical, and Internet users in most parts of the developed world benefit from easy access to a wide range of uncensored sources. Online there is a virtual cacophony of different opinions, perspectives and 'realities', all vying for attention in the highly competitive environment of the World Wide Web. While governments, political parties and large corporations inevitably maintain elaborate Internet operations which allow them total control of the presentation of their own message through this burgeoning medium, humble gingerbread groups, pressure groups, clubs and societies can also establish and maintain an effective web presence with minimal expense, basic resources and fairly rudimentary information technology (IT) skills.

Even terror groups – of course, freedom fighters in their own terms – being hunted by the most powerful of Western nations can post text, still images, video and audio in order to communicate from the shadows in which they operate to the wider world without detection. Lone enthusiasts operating from their own bedrooms can create automated 'radio stations' or stream output from their webcams around the clock in the hope of finding interested

audiences 'out there'. This 'constant buzz of digital activity' has even galva-
nized mass protest on the scale of the 2003 anti-war demonstrations (Hassan,
2004: 134–6). While it is unlikely that soon every citizen will become an
editorially autonomous blogger, podcaster or webmaster – poverty remains
an issue for many, and others simply will not bother – the Internet has at least
the *potential* to be an ever greater influence for participatory democracy. In
practical terms, given the huge amount of material produced for dissemination online and the essentially onanistic nature of much web production, a lot
of it will rarely be read, seen or heard. The self-styled bedroom webcasters
actually reach very small audiences: most individuals who discover them,
after an initial dalliance, being unlikely to ever return for more.

The print industry is, however, very different. When Johann Gutenberg
(c. 1398–1468) invented the printing press around 1450, the first multiple
print runs ever – of the Bible – were immediately sold out. Development of
the new technology was inevitably slow, and it was the early 1500s before the
first postal services were developed, providing the rudimentary distribution
networks that would become essential to the circulation of early, often
sporadically published news-sheets. The *Oxford Gazette*, launched in 1665
at the behest of King Charles II, became the first daily English-language
newspaper. In the USA, the *Boston News-Letter* became the first regular
American weekly newspaper on 24 April 1704. Today, to launch a national
newspaper even in such a densely-populated territory as the UK would
require a large investment in capital and sufficient financial backing to
support it until the day it eventually breaks even.

That is why, despite the introduction of modern printing technology in the
1980s and the implications for production of onscreen editing and electronic
data transfer, as well as a number of high-profile – and very costly – launches
since then, there were only 11 national daily newspapers operating in the UK
in 2005. With the exception of the *Morning Star* (which describes itself as
'socialist' although it was launched in 1930 as the official newspaper of the
Communist Party of Great Britain), their audited average daily circulation is
shown in Table 3.1, as is their ownership.

When in 1986, during an often violent industrial dispute, News International moved production to new, fortified presses in Wapping in London's
Docklands, Rupert Murdoch effectively ended a number of restrictive print
union working practices that stood in the way of technological progress. In so
doing he unlocked large reductions in the cost of producing a national daily
(Littleton, 1992). The economic impact of these savings on the viability of
national newspaper production resulted in the 1986 launch in a blaze of colour
of a new title, *Today*, by regional newspaper proprietor Eddy Shah. Sensation-
ally, Shah's presses put rather blurred colour photographs on his front pages,
but despite the initial interest this attracted, and being bought by News International in 1987, the economic climate proved too tough and a large enough
readership too elusive for a progressive middle-market tabloid to compete with
the *Daily Mail* and *Daily Express*, so it folded in 1995 (McArthur, 1988).

Table 3.1 United Kingdom average daily newspaper sales and ownership,
30 January to 26 February 2006

The Sun (News International Newspapers Ltd)	2,999,642
Daily Mail (Associated Newspapers Ltd)	2,292,862
Daily Mirror (Trinity Mirror plc)	1,544,176
Daily Telegraph (Telegraph Group Limited)	852,109
Daily Express (Express Newspapers Limited)	788,322
Daily Star (Express Newspapers Limited)	683,550
The Times (News International Newspapers Ltd)	642,061
Guardian (Guardian Newspapers Ltd)	340,068
Independent (Independent Newspapers (UK) Ltd)	229,162
Financial Times (Financial Times Ltd)	133,816
Total	**10,505,768**

Source: Audit Bureau of Circulation.

Unlike the launch of *Today*, which was essentially a business decision, two subsequent launches were politically motivated. A combination of trade unions and local authorities provided the £10 million capital swallowed up by the tabloid *News on Sunday* (April–November 1987) and it was followed by the broadsheet *Sunday Correspondent* (September–November 1989). Both were left-wing in outlook, both were supporters of the then opposition Labour Party, and being published only weekly meant they needed only a fraction of the financial commitment of a daily, so their failure to build sufficient circulation and to attract enough advertising to survive even a few months, shows how difficult it is for alternative voices to be heard in the newspaper industry. A similar fate was suffered by Robert Maxwell's idealist weekly the *European* (1990–8) for which the largely eurosceptic UK was simply unprepared. Paradoxically, the *Independent* launched successfully in 1986, and a very slow build allowed the *Daily Sport* to become the only other enduring national daily launch in the UK since the *Daily Star* in 1978. It began as the *Sunday Sport* (1986–), becoming twice weekly by adding a Wednesday edition called the *Sport* in 1988 and then daily in 1991. The success of the *Sport* titles was built almost entirely on topless and almost-nude photography as well as such thinly disguised hoaxes as 'World War II bomber found on moon'.

Ownership and allegiance

The implications for democracy are clear if there are only a restricted number of newspaper titles, owned by an even smaller number of proprietors who can use their acres of daily column inches to promote their own views and political beliefs. Franklin identified the two brothers, Lords Northcliffe (1865–1922) and Rothermere (1868–1940), as well as Lord Beaverbrook (1879–1964), as 'perfect examples' of interventionist proprietors (1997: 99–100). Northcliffe in particular exploited the populist touch (Harrison, 2006: 56) that won large audiences to his titles, to try and dictate government policy over Germany, following its defeat in 1918. Beaverbrook told the first Royal Commission on the Press (1947–9) that he ran the *Daily Express* 'merely for the purpose of making propaganda', it was Stanley Baldwin (1867–1947), thrice British Prime Minister in the 1920s and 1930s, who called newspaper proprietorship 'power without responsibility', and Robert Maxwell suggested the *Daily Mirror* was by right his own personal megaphone (Curran and Seaton, 1997: 42, 48, 76).

In the absence of any 'impartiality' requirement, however much the press – and so, expression – may be characterized as 'free' by those who would resist any form of broadcasting-style content regulation, in practice there is little guarantee of internal 'fairness' or external pluralism. Newspapers are not expected either to be 'balanced' in their own output, or to 'balance' each other – not by most of the democratic states in which they operate – hence the almost total absence of content regulation. Partiality appears to be tolerated by their various audiences too: because newspaper purchase is voluntary (rather than obligatory as in the case of a broadcast receiving licence), those who disagree with a newspaper's editorial policy can simply move on to another.

Seymour-Ure's model for analysing 'press-party parallelism' proposes three useful criteria, each one representing a different type of relationship, becoming progressively more distant as a result. The first is actual involvement of a political party in ownership or management of the title or its parent company. Second is a non-controlling connection between press and party that might be an explicit relationship or merely a positively sympathetic editorial policy. Third order parallels are looser but would probably be detectable in the party affiliation of its readers, in that whether intentional or not, a predominance of one party's supporters may indicate that editorially the newspaper shares that party's values to a significant degree (1974: 157–9).

In the UK, while there is, with the obvious exception of the *Morning Star*, little evidence of party ownership of newspapers, second criterion relationships between the press and a party were most acute and most problematic for democracy in the Thatcher years, when all but the *Daily Mirror* and the *Guardian* were lined up in support of the Conservatives. For all its impassioned championing of left-wing values, even the *Guardian* could not bring itself to support Labour on polling day in the 1992 general election. The *Sun* headlines, 'If Kinnock wins today will the last person to leave Britain please turn out the lights' (9 April 1992), alongside the balding head of then Labour leader Neil Kinnock superimposed on a lightbulb, and 'Nightmare on Kinnock Street' (1 April 1992), were widely perceived as devastating, if skilfully populist examples of misrepresentation by exaggeration.

After 18 years of Conservative rule, it may well have been subsequent changes in press allegiance that acted as the catalyst for Labour's landslide victory in 1997. (Margaret Thatcher had been succeeded by John Major as party leader and so Prime Minister in November 1990, an office in which he was confirmed by a very narrow victory of his own in 1992.) One newspaper had already observed in a May 1992 headline, 'It's The Sun wot won it!' for Major (Street, 2001: 86), and it echoed that sentiment five years later with the variant 'It's The Sun wot swung it' (2 May 1997). McNair's analysis of the 'press deficit' in campaign coverage reconciles press bias among the major parties with votes cast, and notes that by the 2001 campaign the Conservatives were supported by only one national daily, the *Daily Telegraph*, representing just 7.6 per cent of national daily circulation (2002: 189–90). By contrast, Labour was endorsed by titles representing around 56 per cent.

It is arguable – if not provable – that the press were just following, as opposed to leading, a swing away to the left among the electorate, suggested by successive opinion polls, and encouraged by the weakness and indecision which characterized the Major years. Labour's rebranding and the initial charisma lent to its campaigning by Tony Blair undoubtedly contributed to this seismic shift in political allegiance, as well as voter apathy which led to a historically low turnout of only 71.2 per cent – then the lowest for 62 years (Butler and Kavanagh, 1997: 115). The most striking feature, though, of this democratic dichotomy – unlike broadcasters, the press have the freedom to champion one party, politician or political perspective – is that such decisions are normally taken by a single person: the proprietor. The magnification of one newspaper owner's influence on the outcome of an election, simply by virtue of wealth, is essentially undemocratic where the underlying principle behind any transfer of political power is based on one person, one vote. Some of the most powerful press 'barons' in the UK are not even UK citizens, and as such, they are not even members of the electorate.

In 2006, as well as *The Times* and the *Sun*, the Australian-born Rupert Murdoch's News Corporation also controlled the two biggest-selling Sunday broadsheet and red-top tabloid newspapers, the *Sunday Times* and the *News of the World*, which, for all its salacious interest in the more sordid antics of celebrities and royals alike, uses its pages unashamedly to promote Murdoch's political agenda. The Canadian-born Conrad Black's long-standing control through Hollinger of the *Daily Telegraph* and the *Sunday Telegraph* slipped into the hands of the Channel Island-based billionaires, Sirs David and Frederick Barclay in 2005, while in 1998 the Irish Independent News and Media Group, owners of the biggest-selling title in the Republic of Ireland, acquired the *Independent*.

The importance of the proprietors, whatever their national origins, is not lost on the politicians themselves, and as well as the routine briefings they may undertake with sympathetic correspondents, regular 'courtship' of Rupert Murdoch and others, even at party leader level, is well documented.

In a bid to win back the support of the Murdoch titles for the Conservatives, Michael Howard accepted flights and hospitality from News International in order to address the company conference in Cancun, Mexico, in March 2004 (United Kingdom Parliament, 2004). It was a similar *rapprochement*, by Tony Blair, which preceded the *Sun*'s switch to Labour in 1997.

Nor is the power of the press unrecognized by those who wield it. Sometimes, behind the scenes manipulation of politicians percolates through to the editorials, as when the *Sun* explicitly warned Labour that its support was entirely conditional on the party not holding a referendum to replace the pound sterling with the euro (28 May 2001), and that it would wage 'all out war' on Labour if it did so (McNair, 2002: 190). While both Labour and the Conservatives are at a disadvantage when out of favour, when in power neither has proven willing to introduce any kind of regulatory control that might force content regulation, broadcasting-style, on the press. Instead, both parties are guilty of collusion with friendly elements within the press in order to enjoy the electoral benefits this may produce.

This has the effect of reinforcing the two-party system that has dominated British politics since the eighteenth century. The third largest party, the Liberal Democrats has no natural allies among the press, with the possible, highly-qualified exceptions of the two ideologically 'liberal' titles, the *Independent* and the *Guardian*, who between them sell fewer copies than *The Times*, and both of which share values that often correspond to Liberal Democrat policies, but also perceive their non-aligned status as both a badge of honour and a marketing tool. Among the popular tabloids they find only rare support for their policies and politicians, until 2006 most attention focusing on popular characterizations of the then party leader, Charles Kennedy, as 'chat-show Charlie', deliberately depriving him of the gravitas and hence, credibility, that were the distribution of parliamentary seats different, he would have needed to be a serious contender for the role of Prime Minister. When he resigned under pressure from his parliamentary colleagues, readers suddenly became aware of an alcohol problem for which those characterizations had been the euphemisms of an unusually tolerant, if not exactly coy, press.

Given the modest but significant share of the vote the Liberal Democrats achieved in 1997, 2001 and 2005 (16.8, 18.3 and 23 per cent respectively), the notion that the press faithfully reflected popular opinion in shifting its support from right to left at the turn of the century significantly underestimates the potential of third party politics which the Liberal Democrats sought to exploit. Parties which have threatened to destabilize the political status quo by benefiting from temporary popular concerns unsatisfied by the three 'main' parties, such as the Greens in 1987, the Referendum Party in 1997 and the United Kingdom Independence Party (UKIP) in 2005 benefited from little, if any actual support in the press – another democratic deficit contributing in turn to shares in those elections for those parties of 0.3, 2.9 and 2.3 per cent respectively.

The criticisms above will not be unfamiliar to observers in other democracies around the world. News International's parent company is News Corporation, through which Rupert Murdoch's Australian interests extend to the country's only national broadsheet, *The Australian*, and via dozens of other titles, control of 68 per cent of the capital city and national newspaper market, 77 per cent of the Sunday newspaper market and 62 per cent of the suburban newspaper market (Jackson, 2003). In the US, where in 1985 his adoption of citizenship for commercial considerations resulted from tighter regulation of media ownership than in the UK, News Corporation's newspaper holdings are much more modest: the *New York Post*. However, Murdoch's worldwide media ownership extends to book publishing, magazines and various terrestrial and satellite broadcasting companies, such as Fox in the United States and Australia, Star in Asia and Sky in Europe.

The US market is much more diverse. The great nineteenth century media moguls, Joseph Pulitzer (1847–1911) and William Randolph Hearst (1863–1951) were eclipsed after the First World War, to the extent that by 1990 a total of 135 different groups owned 1228 daily newspapers. The largest chain, Gannett, with over a hundred daily titles including the best-selling *USA Today*, also owns 21 television stations covering 17.9 per cent of the country and had a turnover of $7.4 billion in 2004. Despite claims that sections of the US media are liberally inclined (see Chapter 2), the press generally favour the Republican Party, although not uniformly. At first, Hearst newspapers were used unashamedly to promote socialism and then, as the proprietor's outlook swung to the right, they espoused the ultra-conservatism that is of obvious wide appeal to wealthy proprietors, if not necessarily their audiences.

Despite the relatively wide newspaper ownership in the States, some extreme anti-Semitic commentators perceive an 'imbalance' between Jews and non-Jews owning or controlling American newspapers that is as high as 9:1, which may well seem sinister to those who feel threatened by the ethnic origin of others and use the Internet to propagate their concerns. In more party political terms, and discounting bigotry for the moment (see Chapter 4), it is certainly significant that since 1948, newspaper presidential endorsements have favoured Republicans by 78 per cent (Bagdikian, 1997: 74). This could have been anticipated when the First Amendment to the American constitution was introduced in 1791, had the future potential of the mass media also been foreseeable, because it effectively outlawed restrictions on the freedom of the press. Yet, although by the 1830s and 1840s both the *New York Herald* and the *New York Tribune* were trying to be less partisan than later was the case during the Civil War (1861–5), it was the Democratic Party Presidents Harry S. Truman (in office 1945–53) and Bill Clinton (in office 1993–2001) who may have been the most harshly treated by the American press (Fallows, 1997: 48–52).

In Canada, by 1999, the combination of Conrad Black's Hollinger International and a company in which it had a controlling stake, Southam, between them controlled 59 daily titles, representing nearly half of the daily newspaper market (48.2 per cent). Because of the uneven distribution of market share across the country, in some states it was much higher – the highest being 98.5 per cent in Saskatchewan. In 2000 a $3.2 billion deal handed CanWest Global Communications, already a major player in the private television market, control of over two hundred Hollinger titles. In Vancouver CanWest's domination of the media became the most pervasive, where their two TV stations BCTV and Global would complement two of the biggest selling dailies, the *Vancouver Sun* and the *Vancouver Province*. The CRTC, whose remit excludes the press, was powerless to prevent the merger, although paradoxically, some commentators predicted a less politically partisan approach from the newspapers than had been the case under Hollinger, as Black's influence waned.

Press partisanship is an accepted part of political life in Italy, and while 'fairness' is still widely expected of television with its origins as a publicly owned medium, in print a lack of 'impartiality' is rarely, if ever, contested (Roncarolo, 2002: 73). Newspapers have always been perceived, by publishers and their audiences alike, as both political 'tools' and fora for political conflict, as extensively documented by Murialdi (1996). Several newspapers meet or have met Seymour-Ure's first and second criteria of 'press-party parallelism' (1974), most notably *L'Unità* which, unlike the *Morning Star* and the British Communist Party in the UK, have certainly not been confined to the periphery of Italian politics. Founded by the activist and writer Antonio Gramsci (1891–1937) of the Partito Communista Italiano (PCI) in 1924, the fascists under Benito Mussolini (1883–1945) forced it into sporadic, underground publication between 1926 and 1944, when it re-established itself as a popular daily organ of the party until being sold due to financial difficulties in the 1990s and 'temporarily' confining itself to a web presence. Without its direct affiliation to the PCI, *L'Unità* remains sympathetic to the left. Another communist title, *Il Manifesto* is also struggling financially. By contrast, *Il Tempo* was founded in 1944 as a conservative newspaper of the far right, and despite a more recent drift towards the centre, it is still widely perceived as reactionary. Discounting the sport title *La Gazzetta dello Sport*, the best-selling *La Repubblica* targets left-wing liberals with an intelligent tabloid style: a compact in today's terms.

Cross-media ownership regulation has ensured that the Italian newspaper market has remained very diverse, with many regional titles being relatively widely read within their own editorial areas. Several are owned by family dynasties, such as *La Stampa*, third-best selling, published in Turin and owned by the Agnelli family, who also control the Fiat car company based there. Its closest rival *Corriere della Sera*, second-best selling and also owned by the Agnellis, bears a 'declaration of independence' from political control. However, despite the Italian tradition of establishing 'independent' newspapers, most have found themselves becoming aligned with particular parties and campaigning for them (Roncarolo, 2002: 73). Recent moves to deregulate cross-media ownership in Italy would allow Berlusconi's Forza Italia to benefit disproportionately from any relaxation of the rules. In 2005 his company Fininvest already controlled *Il Giornale*, and with the prime minister's control of both private and state television (see Chapter 2), any major newspaper purchases could have seriously reduced plurality in the Italian media, in a country where newspaper readership is already comparatively low. Certainly, the left-wing press, just as the political opposition, were powerless to prevent either Berlusconi's election to office or his consolidation of media influence once there.

In France, dramatic post-war changes in the press and the constitution have altered their relationship considerably. After the German occupation, during which several existing titles either suspended publication or published clandestinely, came the liberation. Despite the new freedoms of the new republic, establishing a newspaper then required authorization, and initially that was only given to political parties and the organized resistance movement. In 1946 the Parti Communiste published 51 daily newspapers, the Parti Socialiste 34 and the Christian democrat Mouvement Républicain Populaire (MRP) 27. All three parties were partners in de Gaulle's coalition government, and although the coalition soon collapsed, several titles lasted with their party affiliations intact until the 1970s. Further launches, such as the conservative *J'informe* and the socialist *Le Matin de Paris*, both in 1977, were independent of but supportive of particular parties, but declining partisanship among the French people over the second half of the last century and a greater tendency to change political allegiance deprived many titles of the committed constituencies needed to sustain them in a competitive market. *J'informe* closed after three months, costing 30 million francs, while *Le Matin* lasted until 1988 (Kuhn, 1995: 69–71).

Cross-media ownership is far less problematic in France than in many other territories due to a diversity of titles and proprietors. This is in striking contrast to the way the state has meddled in broadcasting (see Chapter 2). Only *L'Humanité*, the newspaper of the Parti Communiste Français (PCF), meets Seymour-Ure's first criterion of strong, controlling links with a party, which owns 40 per cent of it. As the largest shareholder the party makes appointments to the editorial board. Founded in 1904, its circulation – now fewer than 50,000 – has been in rapid decline along with the party's membership. *Libération* founded in 1973 in the wake of left-wing civil unrest, has three times the circulation and is broadly supportive of, but not controlled by, the more mainstream Parti Socialiste. By contrast, *Le Monde*'s supposed independence and non-partisan approach as France's best-selling national daily – the 'newspaper of record' – is guaranteed by diversified share ownership, particularly among its journalists. It was begun in 1944 at de Gaulle's request, and in accepting the role of editor he held until 1969, Hubert Beuve-Méry insisted on complete independence.

'Independence', though, does not exclude the possibility of an editorial policy meeting Seymour-Ure's second criterion. Under Beuve-Méry's editorship,

Le Monde was committed to 'socially progressive' centre-left goals he described as 'social liberalism or liberal socialism' (Kuhn, 1995: 73). This has been pursued by subsequent editors, lending broad support to Mitterrand's socialist presidency, and being critical of the rise of the Front National under Jean-Marie Le Pen. The second best-selling national daily, *Le Figaro*, 80 per cent of which is owned by the aeronautics group, Dassault, was founded in 1826 and is at least editorially aligned with the Gaullist right. This was most acute under the previous ownership of the publisher and once Gaullist deputy in the French *parlement*, Robert Hersant. Paradoxically, the country's biggest-selling daily newspaper by two to one is the regional *Ouest-France*, based in Rennes and owned by the Association pour le soutien des principes de la democratie humaniste (to paraphrase, a movement for democracy).

Three weekly news magazines often outsell the daily newspapers – Dassault controlling 80 per cent of *L'Express*, *Le Point* occupying the political centre ground, and *Le Nouvel Observateur* being generally socialist in outlook. However, despite the diversity of ownership, and the range of approaches, some analyses still detect a democratic deficit in France. Neither the communists' regular poll successes of around 20 per cent in the 1960s and 1970s, nor Le Pen's 14.38 per cent result in the first round of the 1988 presidential ballot were reflected in positive coverage in the press (Kuhn, 1995: 76), and Mitterrand complained of unfair treatment for the socialists in the 1970s (1981).

Bias in practice

Impartiality in the press is not a new subject, and some relatively early literature on ethics in journalism recognized its importance as long ago as the 1920s. Nelson Crawford's *The Ethics of Journalism* considered objectivity over three chapters (1924). A growing sense of objectivity as desirable both professionally and for the simple commercial motive of not deterring large numbers of readers from buying a title, gained considerable momentum in the late nineteenth and early twentieth centuries (Frost, 2000: 158). Equally, though, playing to the political prejudices of a particular target audience could be as profitable as attempting to be all things to all audiences. Then, as now, whether toeing a party line or broadly supporting a party's values, routinely promoting one political perspective at the expense of others is a lack of impartiality: in short, bias.

In some instances bias may be healthy, because the ability to express opinion is exercising freedom of speech, at least, for those who have it. Chapter 4 considers the relationship between rhetoric and reception, and the effects of positive and negative coverage for political perspectives in more detail, but partisan journalists must perceive some advantage in biasing their output or they would not do it, and the profit motive is a secondary consideration for some newspapers, such as *L'Humanité*, given their *potential* to precipitate events. Politicians themselves invest large amounts of time and effort into trying to secure positive coverage, and they often complain that they are being electorally disadvantaged through negative editorial policies.

Bias also exists in omission. A valid criticism of the French press is that it failed to uncover at the time the aspects of the Mitterrand presidency which a whole decade after his death became the country's biggest post-war corruption scandals, leading to criminal trials for arms trafficking, misuse of the state oil company's revenues and payments to two political parties while in government (Henley, 2003). The timing of the Watergate revelations was such that Woodward and Bernstein (see Chapter 2) caused the American Republican Party maximum political damage while in office, to the extent that Richard M. Nixon's resignation on 9 August 1974 was the first in the history of the USA. Although his Vice-President, Gerald Ford, succeeded him for the remainder of the presidency, the Republicans were defeated at the next election and the Democrat Jimmy Carter was returned to the White House in a decisive victory in 1976. The *Washington Post*'s story benefited the newspaper in a number of ways, not least in terms of its reputation for strong investigative journalism and any increase in circulation that brought (Olson, 2003). Notwithstanding any anti-Republicanism among its journalists, though, the American press was slow to pick up the Watergate story and similarly reluctant to criticize a range of policy failures over issues from McCarthyism to Vietnam (Bagdikian, 1997: 73).

Whatever their political views, or those of the newspapers they read, it is unlikely that individuals within audiences consume newspapers in a totally uncritical way, even if they do choose to buy them out of preference over the alternatives on the news-stands. The average daily circulation of the *Daily Mirror*, for example, dropped by 6.9 per cent over the year to March 2005, a fall attributed by its parent company Trinity Mirror to a drop in sales in May 2004, following the revelation that 'exclusive' photographs it published of British soldiers abusing Iraqi prisoners were fake (Trinity Mirror, 2005). Far from the dramatic and historic Watergate-style exposé that the pictures seemed to offer the then editor, Piers Morgan, the subsequent revelation that they had been staged in a 'calculated and malicious hoax' precipitated his resignation. Trinity Mirror's own data suggest some, but actually not many, readers reacted by turning away from the newspaper.

It is likely that the *Mirror* was so easily deceived because its long-established editorial policy had been to oppose the war in Iraq. The photographs on offer seemed to be further evidence to support its case. The difference between the illegal wrongdoing of the Watergate break-in and a government doing wrong in the opinion of a newspaper is certainly problematic: other British soldiers were found guilty at court martial of abusing Iraqis, as Morgan pointed out in his defence, and however dramatic the political scandal of the Watergate break-in and subsequent cover up, there was no loss of life in Washington on the scale of the war in Iraq. In one case the editor resigned, in the other the politician. That so few *Mirror* readers were sufficiently troubled by having also been deceived by the pictures might suggest that they too were prepared to readily buy into the idea of them as representative of a wider phenomenon that they opposed.

Another UK national daily that consistently opposed the war in Iraq was the *Independent*. Comment on the ethics of the war was extensively mixed up with the reporting of fact – often on the front page – and their Middle East correspondent Robert Fisk presented his own feelings about the war in long essays written from the war zone that concentrated on the negative effects of the conflict on the civilian population. These were prominently signed by Fisk, so readily identifiable as subjective, and they were undoubtedly well-suited to the perspective of the majority of the readership: it was an appropriate view of the war for the context, but not one that would have been welcome on the front pages of those newspapers which supported the military action. Their reporting focused more on military successes, hardware and the 'bravery' of the allied combatants, while featuring less of the human tragedy.

Both approaches amount to selective reporting: the one concentrates on immediate suffering while rarely, if at all, contextualizing it within the years of brutal repression of the Iraqi people by a corrupt dictator, and the other considers ends to justify means, by removing what was perceived to be a threat to stability in the region and elsewhere and arguing that a better future for Iraq will outweigh immediate loss and suffering. Many will consider neither position to be wholly correct, but if a number of newspapers consistently distance themselves from the fulcrum on a particular controversy, the essence of democratic plurality is that potential readers may be able to satisfactorily choose between them accordingly. Only those whose views are not represented by any newspaper may feel disenfranchised.

Over the most emotive issues, just as the war in Iraq polarized opinion in the UK more than any other issue since the Thatcher era, readers may perceive their choice of newspaper – often made ostentatiously – to be a mark of allegiance to a cause. It is clearly not in the interests of a newspaper's circulation figures for it to veer editorially about, appealing to the left on some issues and the right on the others, because it may alienate more readers than it attracts. So it is only rarely that a newspaper of the left will enthusiastically espouse right-wing attitudes and vice versa. This leads to readers forming expectations of their preferred newspaper, which journalists will be acutely aware of. Inevitably, in some instances the positions they take on issues – in framing stories and in both overt and covert editorializing – will be demand-led (and assumptions about demand may or may not be correct). In others, supply-side bias occurs where readers are perceived as divided or uncommitted, or perhaps where either editors or proprietors wish to influence democratic processes or debate.

While this may have the potential to offer sufficient diversity to meet the most democratic of principles, certain stories, perspectives and ideologies get ignored. For example, the distinguished British investigative journalist John

Pilger described such groups as the children of Iraq and those in debt-laden Third World countries as 'unpeople', in desperate situations that are largely unreported (1998: 3). Some of the most dangerous issues to face humankind have also been ignored: Pilger noted that between 1965 and 1980 the UK Parliament avoided all debate of the nuclear arms race (1998: 512). As well as producing programmes for ITV, the principal outlets for Pilger's work are the *Guardian*, the *Daily Mirror* and the left-wing weekly *New Statesman*, formed by a group of socialists in 1913. The extent to which he is a part of the subcultures both producing and consuming those titles can be judged by his dismissal of a press briefing at the Ministry of Defence as 'low grade' propaganda 'of the kind' found in editorials in the right-wing *Daily Telegraph* (1998: 512).

Adding bias – or, more kindly, a perspective – to news coverage can be done in many ways, from overt criticism to subtle nuance. The often-problematic boundaries between events and opinion can be blurred. Only certain sources need be quoted, and dissenting voices can be ignored or other material may be used to discredit them. This can be done in a routine, totally hidden manner by anyone involved in a story, from the reporter to the editor: covert practices intended to distort reality in order to support a particular position on a controversy. Normally such practices never emerge into the public domain, and audiences remain ignorant over the true nature of the 'reality' being presented to them.

Occasionally a controversy arises which reveals at least in part the unethical practice behind a story. For example, when Carmen Proetta became an eyewitness to controversial British Army shootings of IRA operatives in Gibraltar in 1988, five British newspapers pilloried her as being involved in such offences as drug dealing, prostitution and assault, with one labelling her 'The Tart of Gibraltar'. They may, as some have claimed, been deceived by mischievous, anonymous sources in the intelligence services they could not name, but because ethical journalism takes responsibility for its actions, it is more likely their motive in concentrating on those allegations was to support the then British Government's defence against national and international pressure to admit to a shoot-to-kill policy in respect of the IRA. Proetta's testimony was that the IRA suspects were shot without the warnings to surrender that could have spared their lives. Sowing doubt over her character would damage the credibility of that testimony, and it was because of the potential damage to her reputation that she began libel proceedings that are reputed to have been settled at £350,000 (Lamont, 2003).

Whether for or against a policy, proving a point through selective reporting is advocacy journalism, described by Fink among other commentators on the ethics of journalism, as ethical if done openly and honestly, making clear to all that this is part of a crusade. Fink condemns it as 'unethical and irresponsible' if the distinction is blurred between it and objective reporting. Advocates in the newsroom, just as in the courtroom, should declare their allegiances to parties, pressure groups, policies or ideologies so their audiences may appreciate their perspectives, and their prejudices. According to Fink, journalists masquerading as 'objective reporters', yet taking their lack of objectivity into the newsroom are in essence deceitful (1988: 18). It certainly conflicts strikingly with professional codes of practice that use the language of 'responsibility', 'ethics' and 'fairness' – all commonly found on the readily accessible Databank for European Codes of Journalism Ethics, and compiled by the University of Tampere in Finland (EthicNet, 2002). In the UK, for example, the NUJ Code of Conduct is most explicit in its condemnation of 'falsification' through 'distortion, selection or misrepresentation', and the 'expression of comment and conjecture' as fact (2004).

Yet, there are nonetheless many honourable examples of advocacy journalism at its best, and where 'fairness' is appropriate, competing accounts by opposing advocates on an issue can be given equal exposure within a newspaper. In some cases, it may be reasonable to consider the advocacy to be a just cause, perhaps underpinning a campaign either by the newspaper itself or by others: as, perhaps, to correct some injustice. Another British investigative reporter Paul Foot (1938–2004) worked tirelessly if often expensively to pursue stories which others may have shied away from, either because of the intricacy of detail needed to piece together all the relevant facts, or because of personal and institutional obstacles standing between them and the 'truth'. He exposed wrongful convictions in such notorious British cases as the Birmingham Six, the Guildford Four, the Cardiff Three and the Swansea Two, and sought to unveil institutional obfuscation over such controversial deaths as those of British nurse Helen Smith in Saudi Arabia (1979) and the newspaper boy Carl Bridgewater (1978), as well as the Thalidomide scandal of prescription drug-induced birth deformities in the 1960s, and more.

Foot's work, although important, is not unique, and the history of campaigning advocacy journalism is a long one. George Orwell (1903–50) reported on poverty and misery among the destitute, as well as the fighting in the 1936–9 Spanish Civil War, and long before him Daniel Defoe (1660–1731) wrote campaigning pieces attacking Tory governments of the early eighteenth century. Often advocacy journalism is politically inspired: Defoe came from a non-conformist background that made conflict with the early Tories and their policies towards religious dissent almost inevitable, if as some sociologists argue we are shaped by our environments (Bourdieu, 1986). Orwell, far from an impartial war correspondent, actually took up arms to fight alongside the Spanish Republicans, as did many socialists from around Europe. Foot, too, immersed himself in the politics of the far left, being a member of the Socialist Workers Party and standing in several parliamentary, European and London mayoral elections and by-elections, most recently for the anti-war Respect coalition in 2004. Whatever Fisk's position on the war in Iraq, there is no suggestion he actually fought against the invading forces.

Where advocacy journalism exposes injustice, it may attract broad support and, by extension, in such circumstances 'balance' may be inappropriate (as suggested about racism in Chapter 1). Where campaigning journalism departs from the correcting of injustice, we enter a more problematic arena in which bias may exist solely to promote one perspective. In the power broking that takes place within democracies, particularly but not exclusively at election time, misusing the various techniques of the craft of journalism can actually be harmful to democracy itself. In theorizing bias in the press, Edward Hernan and Noam Chomsky identify similarities between the routine daily output of private sector companies operating in free markets within pluralistic democracies and the propaganda of dictatorships from Germany under Hitler and Goebbels to the communist bloc of the cold war (see Chapter 6).

They argue that because inequality of wealth is inherent in capitalism, mass communication is a necessary controlling agent in regulating social and economic change in order to preserve stability. Their 'propaganda model' is one which protects elements of the *status quo* through filtering news, marginalizing dissent and encouraging conditions in which both governments and commercial interests may communicate and so reinforce preferred information and attitudes to the public (Hernan and Chomsky, 1994: 297). To do this, the 'presuppositions' of the state are accepted without question (Chomsky, 1989: 5), meaning, for example, such fundamental issues as the virtue of capitalism, the validity of parliamentary democracy in decision making, the right of the state to tax its citizens and then spend the proceeds in a way it determines in order to meet some of those citizens' needs, and – in some territories – the constitutional role of a monarchy are rarely if ever questioned.

Part of this phenomenon, like Pilger's publicity-starved 'unpeople' (1998: 3) may be due to issue fatigue, just as people are sometimes described as suffering from compassion fatigue in the wake of high-profile disaster appeals which damage regular charitable giving. Given the demand-led nature of much political bias, this may be because audiences, despite their differences, congregate around the political centre ground on a range of issues. According to occasional opinion polls, despite frequent scandals surrounding the Royal Family and their activities there is little public appetite in the UK for republicanism (although the position of the monarch is much less secure in some Commonwealth countries, such as Australia, where both distance and historical difference affect public perspectives, and the media are much less inclined to defer to royalty).

Similarly, supply-side bias towards the political margins simply fails to find mass audiences: the swing from Conservative to 'New' Labour in 1997 that returned a vaguely centre-left government to power in Westminster following the frustrations of an 18-year period in opposition also sapped the circulation of the radical left-wing press. Far from boosting circulation figures for the *Morning Star* (estimated to be around 13,500), and the magazines *New Statesman* (23,646), *Tribune* and *Red Pepper*, which are historically low, Labour in power has drawn the sting of anti-Conservative protest from many potential readers on the left. However in 2005 the readership of the right-wing

Spectator was rising (at 66,000), as it satisfied growing disillusionment on the right at the impotence of opposition (Greenslade, 2005).

In addition to not questioning fundamentals, much of journalism reinforces them through naturalization. Phenomena that by their ubiquity seem natural may be less likely to be challenged, because audiences are less able to conceive of things being different, if those elements of the *status quo* were ever questioned. In this way, after a government has announced its budget for the coming financial year, the wide-ranging political perspectives of the mainstream parties included in 'balanced' analyses of its fiscal policies do not conventionally question them from the perspective of an anarchist. Capitalism and anarchy are mutually exclusive, and indeed, sworn enemies, yet only an anarchist publication or website would bring to the discussion the fundamental rejection of ownership, investment and inheritance posited by the French anarchist thinker Pierre-Joseph Proudhon (1809–65).

Away from the political extremes, though, however valid an assessment this may have been in the past, McNair considered that by the end of the last century ever greater diversity of content and sources meant that the concept of newspaper owners imposing a 'dominant' ideology was outdated when it doesn't coincide with audiences' own experiences of life (1998: 29). This is consistent with the decline of deference since the 1960s: of individuals towards authority figures, from teachers and the police to politicians and royalty, and of the media towards those in authority or some branch of the 'establishment', particularly government (Pilger, 1998: 453). Paradoxically, in promoting popular culture above all else, even the British tabloid press, unrivalled elsewhere in Europe for its mass market exploitation of both celebrity and scandal, continues to defer to 'experts' (Pilger, 1998: 487), as long as judiciously chosen they can be used to support a story or an opinion.

If most of the press rarely question the tenets of the socio-political elite, where they do intervene most effectively in democratic debate is the centre ground: just as in election campaigns politicians target 'battleground' constituencies where relatively small numbers of undecided voters may 'swing' the result their way. Some argue that it wasn't 'The Sun wot swung it' for Labour in the UK in 1997 (2 May 1997), but that Rupert Murdoch's keen business sense had long previously detected that the kind of vigorous support his titles lent the majority of Margaret Thatcher's early policies had lost its resonance with the British public by the time of John Major's period in office. The change in the public mood, fuelled by the economic problems of the 1991 recession and an accumulation of political scandals around 'sleaze' had to be reflected in the newspaper unless it too was to lose touch with its public. Likewise, as the Conservatives' popularity waned, so did the support of all but the most vehement among the right-wing press, the *Daily Telegraph*, the *Daily Mail* and the *Daily Express* (McNair, 2000: 150–3).

On other issues, public opinion around the political centre may be more malleable. Hence the Blair government's reluctance to pursue both the euro, adopted relatively enthusiastically as the single European currency of 12 other countries in the European Union in 2002, and a national referendum on a European constitution agreed in June 2004 at Brussels by all its then 25 member states, in the context of fervently hostile press campaigns against them. Had the British press lined up as decisively against military action in Iraq in 2003, as they have done so consistently over the abolition of the pound sterling, the USA may have had to go into action without the UK.

Where the political battleground is over issues of which most individuals can have only very partial experience, such as the state of the health service, immigration and crime, their own inability to know decisively whether or not their own experiences are generalizable to the entire country, means they are at their most persuadable. The interests of those parties in opposition – and newspapers that support them – are usually best served by depicting the situation as bad and worsening, while governments will obviously want to persuade people that such situations are improving because their policies are working. Because both politicians and partisan newspapers readily perceive the power of individuals and their stories to illustrate issues far more understandably than bare statistics, such high profile stories as the 'War of Jennifer's Ear' in 1992 and the case of 'Mrs Dixon's Ear' in 2005 suddenly assume a national, if relatively momentary importance in the political agenda that is quite out of proportion to the actual problems encountered by those individuals in having medical operations postponed.

Quite apart from which issues are covered, there is also in today's journalism an equally disproportionate prioritization of process over policy. The course of recent history is littered with the political scalps of former ministers and their associates who were hounded out of office for procedural errors, rather than the legitimacy of their policies and principles. One of the most draconian Home Secretaries in UK politics, David Blunkett, was forced to resign in December 2004 because press revelations of an affair with a married woman exposed errors in his office over the handling of his mistress's maid's visa application (see page 10). The scandalizing of Blunkett's original socialist constituency of supporters by his firm policies affecting the lives of many on asylum, immigration and detention of terrorism suspects had proven a valuable source of copy, but pointedly not his downfall.

Kuhn rationalizes process reporting as 'easy' journalism, which can be undertaken most effectively by a clique of political reporters who move habitually within influential circles and 'corridors of power', without the need for specialist knowledge and with it the learning of a large amount of information that would be needed to examine policy issues in depth, or to operate convincingly as a financial or a medical correspondent, for example (2002: 66). British political reporting is often criticized for concentrating disproportionately on perspectives from inside the 'Westminster village' centred on parliament, the three 'main' party headquarters and the broadcasters' contribution studios in that London borough. There, an elite group of political correspondents perpetuates a spiral of charge and counter-charge among the most easily recognizable politicians, rather than making the short walk to Whitehall where the various ministries implement government policy, or travelling even farther afield in the country, where policies affect larger numbers of people.

A study by Loughborough University for the *Guardian* of the UK general election campaign in 1997 found that the greatest coverage across a number of different media was of the conduct of the election. At 32 per cent it decisively beat the main policy issues in the election: Europe (15 per cent) and 'sleaze' (10 per cent). The domestic policy areas of education, taxation, the constitution and privatization received only 7, 6, 5 and 4 per cent of the coverage respectively (Denver et al., 1998). It is natural that the media should want to cover the less routine elements of a campaign, and in the 2001 election the Deputy Leader of the Labour Party, John Prescott, provided them with spectacular pictures by punching a protestor. However, democracy may not be well served by the parties' actual policies being discussed only cursorily because of often momentary incidents providing more spectacle.

Similar criticisms are made of the White House Press Corps in the USA, who are also even less likely to initiate stories through investigation of policy outcomes, than to follow the news agenda of the president's press spokespeople (Fallows, 1997: 33–5). Ironically, although probably through expediency because they need publicity, politicians often share the same news values as the media, as evidenced by their willingness to stage events that will provide appealing copy or pictures that journalists can, in turn, most effectively sell to their editors. By extension, then, the media become participants in the story (Iyengar, 1997: 320–1) and sometimes the story themselves – any press partisanship being reflected in the nature of their intervention. Provoking reactions from politicians they oppose is as much a political act as physically campaigning for those the press support.

When press attention is hostile, or just persistent, it can be intimidating as well as politically disadvantageous. Hutton found that the revealing of Dr David Kelly's identity as the Gilligan source to the press was one of the factors placing him under the great stress that resulted in his suicide (2004: paragraphs 433–5). Similarly, the very public scandal surrounding the former Director of Public Prosecutions, Sir Alan Green, being caught kerb crawling in 1992, was said at his wife's inquest to have driven her to suicide. Harassment by large numbers of reporters from both the print and broadcast media can be very intrusive, and the 'pack' mentality among journalists competing for a story can lead to a feeding frenzy in which each latest development sparks a search for the next 'killer fact' to move the story on. Alia notes that it is, nonetheless, possible to sell newspapers without spreading misinformation or harming public safety (2004: 19).

The case for content regulation

In democracies there tend to be very few areas of content regulation in the press, either externally where an official body is imposed on the industry by government, or internally through self-regulation whereby it creates one itself. In some countries, issues around privacy and the right of individuals to reply to what they perceive as mistreatment by the press are managed by an industry committee, such as the Press Complaints Commission (PCC) in the UK (Harrison, 2006: 115–18). The PCC was constituted in 1990, in response to public and political outrage at what were widely perceived as excesses of the British press in the 1980s. Famously, in 1989 the then Minister for National Heritage, David Mellor, had warned newspapers they were 'drinking in the last chance saloon' and that actual regulation would be imposed on the industry if it failed to improve its practices. At the time, although public trust in politicians was shown in opinion polls to be very low, the same polls claimed journalists were trusted even less (Roberts, 2003: 18–19).

There had previously been a self-regulatory body for the UK press since 1953 (Alia, 2004: 70–1). The Press Council had been set up following a recommendation from a Royal Commission on the press in 1949, itself a response to the overwhelming support of the newspaper industry for the Conservatives in the 1945 general election. This was a democratic deficit demonstrably contradicting the public mood, which resulted in a Labour landslide. Subsequent Royal Commissions in 1961, 1965 and 1974 had failed to introduce either regulation or greater self-regulation, even though diversity of ownership was an issue for the Conservative government in 1965 and Labour fury at press partisanship was the catalyst in 1974 (Seaton, 2003: 27).

Towards the end of its tenure, the Press Council had enjoyed only narrow support, with the NUJ withdrawing from it in 1980 in protest at its ineffectiveness (Gopsill, 1999: 6), despite having previously lobbied for its creation. The industry's reluctant response was to recreate it as the PCC, with supposedly tougher powers to impose sanctions on its members, but the press were well able to exact vengeance on David Mellor shortly afterwards, bringing his political career to an abrupt end in 1992, by revealing secret 'romps' with Antonia de Sancha, for which he was said to have worn a Chelsea football strip, an attire modelled extensively, of course, in several tabloids. The effect of a stream of scandals involving Conservative ministers was devastating for the Major government, and the more 'sleaze' the press uncovered, the more keenly they searched for more.

A child born to a mistress, a homosexual 'outing' and the 'cash for questions' affair were among the big political stories uncovered by the press in the 1990s that without Thatcher as Conservative leader had begun to turn against the party. Although many people perceived the British press to be out of control, some were able to argue, as the PCC code required, a clear *public interest* in the revelations (as opposed to mere *interest among the public* in salacious details of famous people's private lives). Notwithstanding the importance of revealing real corruption where it exists, as over the receiving of money to ask questions in Parliament, Major had perhaps unwisely made morality a political issue by proclaiming at the party's 1993 conference that it would take the country 'back to basics'. In doing so, he made a virtue out of exposing any hypocrisy among the politicians at the top of the party in power (Tweedy and Barrow, 2002). The irony that remained undiscovered by the press until 2002 was that while in government Major was also having an affair with another Conservative minister, Edwina Currie.

Despite the political damage the British press inflicted on both Thatcher and Major, the inspiration for reviews of self-regulation by Sir David Calcutt was still that of individuals' rights to privacy, as opposed to press partisanship. It was in response to the first of Calcutt's reports (1990) that the PCC was created, while the second (1993) considered why the organization was failing to meet widely-held expectations of it (Roberts, 2003: 21). Latterly, judicial interpretations of such recent legislation as the Human Rights Act 1998 have begun to instil caution among the British press over personal privacy, where public outrage, political protest and even the perceived panacea of self-regulation have proven impotent (Tomlinson, 2002).

Not entirely reactive, such self-regulatory bodies as the PCC usually produce 'voluntary' codes that seek to modify the behaviour of their members, and a number are quoted extensively in Alia (2004: 192–207). Some refer to issues around 'balance'. The PCC, for example, allows newspapers to be partisan, but they 'must distinguish' between fact, comment and conjecture. The American Society of Newspaper Editors says the press should not 'abuse the power of their professional role' in such a way as to betray the trust of the public, but should apply an 'independent scrutiny' to the 'forces of power', including government. In Australia, the Country Press Association of New South Wales requires 'fair play' towards all persons and organizations, proscribing propaganda unless its source is indicated. The Spanish Federación de la Prensa Española concedes that the press is 'an important social tool' in the 'pluralism of a democratic state'.

The British experience over privacy suggests that if self-regulation were extended to cover issues of 'balance', 'bias' and 'impartiality', it would most likely be ineffectual in the absence of a real desire on the part of proprietors and editors to be 'fair' to all those engaged in democratic politics. Ending a centuries-old tradition of a 'free' press may simply be unpalatable in many territories, and not just to the press (McNair, 2000: 177). Even hard and fast rules over the relatively straightforward area of taste and decency may be difficult to defend in the context of almost unrestrained press freedom, where a range of approaches allow publication but restrict availability to youngsters. Those magazines containing material widely considered to be unsuitable for a family audience are confined to the top shelves of the newsagents, kept out of sight under the counter, only available by mail order or concealed by parental advisory notices.

Paradoxically, one of the most powerful and enduring images of the Vietnam War involved both nudity and violence, although the purpose of the picture was neither to titillate nor to excite as it depicted a young girl, naked, running towards the camera while fleeing the napalm raid on her village that was literally burning the skin on her back (Chong, 2001). Both shocking and upsetting to many, the political value of photographer Nick Ut's image resided in the way it caused people and politicians to confront uncomfortable realities of the war. Omission on grounds of 'taste and decency' would not simply have served to sanitize the page, but also to sanitize the war and to constrain articulation of the argument against the involvement of the USA in the conflict.

However, despite the difficulties this may create for editors, the press are rarely completely 'free' to always do as they please, and, like others who publish and broadcast, they are quite used to external regulation, imposed by legislation, that constrains expression in a number of respects. At one extreme of the taste and decency *continuum* lies obscenity, addressed in the UK by various statutes dating as far back as the Customs and Consolidation Act 1876, which prohibited the importation of indecent or obscene articles, and more recently by the Obscene Publications Acts of 1959 and 1964, and the Criminal Justice and Public Order Act 1994 which dealt more directly with material of any origin. Quite properly, child pornography is viewed more seriously by the law and in the manner of commonsense consensus considered in Chapter 1 there is no 'balancing' of the interests of paedophiles as if it were merely that they have a predilection which is not shared by others. Even those distributing and accessing such images via the otherwise relatively unrestricted Internet have been dealt with severely under the laws of several countries (Verhulst, 1998).

Press 'freedom' is also subject to *de facto* constraint by copyright, data protection and human rights legislation. Under defamation law, libel actions against any media organization can be expensive if lost. Although newspapers with sufficient resources to be untroubled by substantial awards against them of damages and costs in favour of a plaintiff could choose to publish and be damned, such considerations are certainly sobering influences on editorial decision making. Some individuals may be considered to be more litigious than others: for example while others may shy away from the exposure to the financial risk that mounting a libel action entails, the former Labour MP and anti-war campaigner George Galloway has won eight different libel actions against British newspapers, even when physical evidence against him had previously appeared to them to be sound. The former *Daily Mirror* owner, Robert Maxwell was known for his pre-emptive use of injunctions against other newspapers, which might otherwise have exposed the looming financial crisis that overwhelmed his publishing interests in 1991.

The argument, then, that press freedom to be politically partisan is somehow sacrosanct, while broadcasting, whether publicly or privately-owned, should be regulated in the interests of democracy is demonstrably tenuous.

The philosopher Onora O'Neill used the BBC's commemorative Reith Lecture series to call for greater accountability of the press, in order to restore public confidence in their output, arguing that press freedom should not be a 'licence to deceive' (2002). Responsibility is not necessarily censorship, even if it involves self-censorship, and if commercial broadcasters can aspire to political 'balance', then newspapers do not need to exercise their 'freedom' by deceiving their audiences any more than they need to print child pornography or incite readers to racial hatred.

The power exercised by the press should be accompanied by a responsibility not to distort the democratic process through deception – or, put another way, by misrepresenting reality for ulterior motives. Given the unlikelihood of self-regulation producing any more satisfactory a result than it has over privacy, it may be that regulation is necessary. In the UK, Ofcom has already been given an advisory role over press mergers being considered under competition legislation, and this role could be extended to content regulation of the press. One effective alternative is the use of public funds, as in Sweden, to provide three-year subsidies to support the development of alternative daily newspapers that provide different political perspectives but would otherwise be financially insecure and quickly cease to publish. While perhaps more palatable, this is an expensive approach. The continuation of similar schemes in Austria, France and Norway has been subject to review because of their substantial cost to the state (Murschetz, 1998: 291–313).

A cheaper compromise might exist in the granting of an automatic right to reply in the existing press, and this is widely practised via the correspondence columns of many newspapers. Such responses are rarely given the prominence, though, of the original article, and their inclusion may be as attributable to their entertainment value in stimulating debate, as to any editorial sense of 'fair' play. It is worth considering now, however, to what extent the press – and the rest of the mass media – actually have any effect on their audiences' perceptions. Could it really have been the 'Sun wot won it', or might it indeed be the case, as the truism implies, that (in a deliciously apposite payback for practising on them the deception perceived by O'Neill), people really do disbelieve what they read in the press anyway?

CHAPTER 4

In the Eye of the Beholder: Audience Perspectives of Balance and Bias

Audiences and the media

Whether bias in the mass media actually matters in a democracy may depend on the extent to which audiences are affected by it. As Denis McQuail observed, stopwatch-based analyses of broadcast output are of limited use without the contextualization that may be generated by understanding its possible effects on audiences (1992: 226). However, there is a considerable amount of epistemological uncertainty around audience behaviour, not least because so many competing theories have been articulated about it. In his *Mass Communication Theory*, McQuail capably distils the evolution of academic perspectives on audience behaviour over some 80 years into a detailed review of the wealth of literature on the subject (2005: 456–78). In essence, and necessarily relatively superficially, it is worth noting here that early claims made by academics, professionals and lay commentators about audience behaviour assumed that very simplistic relationships existed between content and effect, and that the media were so powerful that their audiences could be persuaded by propaganda into behaving as they wanted them to (for example Lasswell, 1927).

Later models of passive audience behaviour included that of the 'hypodermic needle'. This once popular metaphor for the relationship between 'omnipotent' media and 'lumpen, unquestioning' audiences considered it to be similar to that between a physical stimulus and a corresponding physiological response. It compared the injection of a drug into a muscle provoking an automatic reflex with the 'injection' of information into audiences' consciousness causing predictable and uniform reactions among them (Livingstone, 1990: 16–17). Popular beliefs about the media still suggest, for example, that the showing of violence on television makes people, particularly children, more violent, while the gratuitous showing of exciting toys and junk food causes children to demand that their parents buy the toys and feed them an unhealthy diet.

Although remaining superficially attractive to those (particularly laypeople) who would complain about what they perceive as any kind of irresponsibility or malice on the part of the media, from the late 1970s more persuasive academic perspectives have considered *individuals within* audiences much more diverse in terms of the readings they make of received texts and their responses to them (Livingstone, 1990: 62). We can observe this phenomenon ourselves: clearly, not everyone who sees gun crime on television automatically sets out to acquire a gun. Even children select particular items to demand from those on offer. Instead, alternative explanations of audience response include the 'uses and gratifications' model which suggests that as well as each being shaped by different circumstances and experiences (Katz, Blumler and Gurevitch, 1974: 24), different people are individually discerning: they make active readings of media texts according to their own beliefs and perspectives, and they use the media to satisfy their own differing needs, taking from them any content which provides some form of gratification, and being able to reject other content at will (McQuail, Blumler and Brown, 1972).

This area of media theory remains controversial, though. The opinion that individuals within audiences are not empty shells waiting to be filled with ideas (Curran and Seaton, 1997: 270) is certainly justified by numerous examples of audiences' resistance to media exhortations to behave in one way or another. In the USA, for example, the tide of newspaper endorsements of the Republicans – 78 per cent since 1948 – has not been accurately reflected in the 51 per cent average number of votes cast for the party (Bagdikian, 1997: 74). In the UK, despite the huge 'press deficit' in campaign bias, in which the *Daily Telegraph* was the only Conservative-supporting national daily in 2001, representing 7.6 per cent of total newspaper circulation, that party actually achieved a much larger 32.7 per cent share of the votes cast (McNair, 2002: 189–90). One of the most dramatic and durable mass rejections of a media message was the widespread boycott of the *Sun* newspaper by readers in Merseyside in north-west England, after its 19 April 1989 front page splash made unsubstantiated claims about the behaviour of Liverpool football fans at an away match at Hillsborough, where 96 of them died through crush injuries (Chippendale and Horrie, 1992). The fall in circulation in the city was so great that 15 years later, the *Sun* newspaper executives were still making public apologies to the people of Liverpool for the representation they had made of some of them.

Paradoxically, cultivation theory as articulated by Gerbner et al. over the last 40 years, and as recently as 2002 (pp. 19–42), describes an ability in the media to cultivate particular attitudes and values in audiences, from which actions may result. The heavier the use of the media, the greater the cultivation effect. Carey (1988) suggested that contextual factors may cause media effects to rise and fall in intensity, and indeed, when society is destabilized by such phenomena as crime, war and economic depression, people may collectively be more suggestible (McQuail, 2005: 462–4). An example may be the way Adolf Hitler was able to turn large sections of German opinion against the relatively prosperous Jewish community in the 1930s. Other relatively durable paradigms in modern thinking about the effects of journalism in various media include agenda setting. This recognizes that audiences cannot often be told what to think, but maintains that the media tells them which issues to think *about* as editors' news values transfer into the public's consciousness of social and political priorities (McCombs and Shaw, 1972: 176–87). This discussion of conflicting paradigms of audience behaviour being far from exhaustive, Street's more detailed review of studies of the effects on voting behaviour of the press and television (2001: 86–93) only serves to reinforce the uncertainty in this field. How, then, can we determine the implications of the plethora of often contradictory theories on audience behaviour for our study of balance and bias?

It is relatively easy to demonstrate very variable levels of compliance among audiences with advertising messages they may see or hear. Some advertising is very effective, and some is not, a phenomenon explained in part by Maslow's hierarchy of needs (1954), which distinguishes between the essential and the merely desirable. Unsuccessful advertising is ignored by millions: even though many of them may hugely enjoy a particular commercial or a combination of image and text, most feel unmoved to actually buy the product or service. By contrast, the huge sums spent on advertising, not least by political parties during election campaigns, do suggest that many in charge of marketing budgets consider their money well spent on the mass media. Where political advertising is confined to the print media (see Chapter 2), the role of the officially-sanctioned party political broadcast is perceived as an important one in incorporating broadcasting within the marketing mix.

If individuals within audiences were totally impervious to media content, in forming opinions and deciding between different possible actions, such effort and expense would be wasted. Many analyses of modern electioneering consider that the main campaign is fought on television. There, the party leadership and their favoured spokespeople assume greater visibility and, so, importance, than activists in constituencies (Ward and Walsh, 2000: 44–5). Furthermore, Schiller's reservations about individuals constituting 'active' or even 'resistive' audiences derive from widespread evidence of corporate and globalizing colonization of culture and cultural expression, occurring because most people are ill-equipped to filter genuine and benign content out from the false and the harmful (1989: 19).

The globalizing influence of corporate America is often overstated, however (Thompson, 1995: 14), and the Internet in particular has empowered many individuals with resistive and even subversive access to their own audiences, however diffuse. Websites, Internet streaming of original or semi-original content, blogging and podcasting (see Chapter 3) are all used extensively if unsystematically by amateur producers to complement the established media, and their output is often sought and consumed by others as alternatives to the more mainstream fare on offer through the more traditional channels and publications.

The apparently contrasting perspectives of Thompson and Schiller may both be partially correct in their assertions if critical autonomy in individuals – or, their ability to resist media messages – varies according to such factors as age, experience and education. Research by Brants and van Kempen found different levels of cynicism towards politicians in the Netherlands, between audiences of the public broadcaster NOS and those of the commercial channel RTL4. They attributed their findings to regular *NOS-Journaal* viewers being better educated than those of *RTL-Nieuws*. The latter were the more cynical at the beginning of the study, and watching the commercial channel's news coverage deepened their cynicism, while regular viewing of NOS had no effect on the other group. This phenomenon was explained by Brants and van Kempen as being due to cynicism among individuals within the NOS audience having already reached a natural plateau (2002: 180–1).

Advertising is not conducted in a vacuum, though, and other factors equally in accordance with Maslow's observations can be important here. One product being advertised may simply not have the appeal of another, or the rationale presented for purchasing it may easily be countered by more appealing advertising elsewhere. What appeals to one person may repel another (Starkey, 2004a: 164). The press endorsements of the Republican presidential candidates were overwhelmingly made through but a single medium, while other influences on the American public, such as television or radio, peer comment and their own life experiences, may have diminished the effect of the press. Those who disagree strongly enough with a newspaper's position on an issue to avoid buying it may do so. There is evidence of sufficient media literacy in the population for some, at least, to discern and, if necessary, discount what they may perceive to be biased reporting in the press. In Liverpool though, the rejection of the *Sun* was well orchestrated by agitators who found a public voice through such other media as the city's two local radio stations, as well as the newspaper's rival the *Daily Mirror*. Considerable peer pressure was brought to bear on those still inclined to buy the *Sun* to abstain, and newsagents were targeted by informal campaigns calling on them to remove the title from sale.

There is some evidence to suggest that education – and media literacy in particular, however acquired – can affect individuals' willingness to accept unquestioningly what they are told by the media. The academic discipline known as media studies, for example, grew from a desire to 'inoculate' children against potentially corrupting influences in the cinema identified in its infancy by Leavis and Thompson (1933). Theorizing the subject as it matured, Masterman perceived the development in school pupils of a 'critical autonomy' that they could apply to any media text as being a pedagogically worthwhile objective (1985: xiv). Even simplistic lay notions of media images provoking particular responses tend to concede that the danger of 'copycat' violence is most acute in the 'impressionable'. Consequently, those who use the power of the media, through newspaper columns or other instances of editorializing that foreground their own opinions, to argue against the teaching of media literacy, should understand that as a result they may appear to have something to hide from their own public.

Despite such efforts, and notwithstanding the existence of individuals who lack the critical autonomy of many of their peers, some degree of media literacy among wider populations is not a rare phenomenon, whether it has been taught or merely acquired. Research among American audiences appears to confirm that US voters' perceptions of news media vary according to their political positioning. Despite its slogan 'fair and balanced', the comparatively right-leaning Fox News, owned by Rupert Murdoch's News Corporation, is the most trusted news source among Republicans and the least trusted among Democrats. While CNN was once the most credible overall, rated so by 42 per cent of respondents in 1998, its credibility ratings fell dramatically to 32 per cent in 2004, mostly among Republicans and Independents. This biennial national poll of 3000 respondents conducted by the Pew Research Center for the People and the Press also suggests Rush Limbaugh's radio talk show is mainly popular with Republicans, while NPR is favoured by Democrats (2004). The centre's conclusion that American news choices are becoming more polarized may be persuasively attributed to the divisive nature of the 2003 war in Iraq, for which Fox News appeared to be overwhelmingly enthusiastic.

Bias, far from always being unnoticed, is sometimes so alienating to audiences that it can affect the commercial viability of an organization (Sutter, 2001: 432). Its potential effect on the 'bottom line' can be a sobering influence on partisan proprietors and editorial staff, who may choose to avoid extremes in order to prevent audience decline. However, there are different degrees of bias – such is the infinitely variable displacement away from a fulcrum discussed in Chapter 2 – and while audiences may on occasions react strongly and measurably to it, away from the extremes it may not merely fail to alienate, it may also be imperceptible. When a false representation is being given them by omission, incorrect emphasis or mischaracterization, how are individuals to notice it, unless they already have such prior knowledge of the subject or such resources to verify the representation as might be necessary to avoid deception?

As determining the existence of bias depends so heavily on perceptions, it may exist undetected where nobody perceives it and conversely be absent where it is perceived by some. Meticulous 'balancing' of one item by a journalist may be perceived as unfair by some in the audience, whose own readings may be biased. Extreme positioning of one person's perspective can make an otherwise quite reasonable representation appear outrageously unfair: for example, just as a conspiracy theorist might consider sceptical media to be part of the conspiracy, so those who perceive a malign Jewish domination of media control in the USA may appear to most other people as probably just victims of their own bigotry (see Chapter 3).

This is the difference between *production bias* and *reception bias*. The double hermeneutic of the producer's interpretation being subsequently reinterpreted by the receiver (Giddens, 1984: 284) is a further complication that renders establishing balance ever more problematic. Where reception bias affects audiences' ability to objectively evaluate production decisions, it will inevitably distort their perceptions of a text. Therefore, using audience perceptions as a means of measuring production bias can be very misleading. Their perceptions can be variously affected by their memory and their ability to comprehend the material, as well as the subjectivity inherent in any form of understanding (Gunter, 1997: 23–4, 128–9). Often, for example, common understandings of concepts can only be agreed by different individuals as a result of negotiation and, sometimes, compromise. A single meaning of the term 'subsidiarity' is widely understood among those who follow the politics of the European Union, but the word is lost on most Britons, who simply have not assimilated it within their own lexica. When negotiating meaning, some competing perspectives cannot be reconciled: as in the polarization of the popular and mutually exclusive descriptions of unorthodox combatants as to some, 'terrorists' and to others, 'freedom fighters'.

Using audiences in media research

These problems are particularly acute when choosing 'typical' members of an audience for any kind of academic study of their reactions to media texts (Gunter, 1987: 301–6), for producers hoping to validate their own work in the manner described by Burns (1977: 137) and also when 'representatives' of an audience are to be incorporated into the product itself, such as when compiling letters pages, editing online fora or producing broadcast debates (Amber, 2000: 149–50). The invisibility of mass media audiences presents those who would work with them with particular difficulties that do not apply to other groups in the cultural sectors: for instance visitors to a museum, cinemagoers and in short anyone who enters premises to see a play, an exhibition or some other literary or artistic work. They can be seen, physically counted and if necessary surveyed in some way that promises high levels of validity in the data collected. By contrast, listening to, viewing and reading the output of the print and broadcast mass media normally occurs away from the point of exhibition, being transmitted or distributed over great distances to audiences who cannot be seen or even individually counted (Starkey, 2004c: 3–6).

Broadcasters have consistently disagreed over the size and nature of audiences to their services, often routinely producing contradictory audience figures to sell advertising time or to justify public funding spent on their output. In the UK, the BBC and the commercial radio sector established a single company, Radio Joint Audience Research (RAJAR), to produce a 'gold standard' survey from 1992 on which they could both agree, and its findings were largely unchallenged until electronic metering of respondents by a second company, GfK, began to produce widely differing results (Starkey, 2003: 45–9). In other territories, including Belgium, even such traditional audience research methodologies as audiences completing listening diaries and researchers interviewing individuals about their radio listening have produced conflicting data because they have been implemented simultaneously by different survey companies with different sets of respondents (Antoine, 2003: 74–8). Using new technology offers few certainties: radio audience measurement meters cannot distinguish between actual listening and mere exposure to the sound of a nearby receiver, and years before their invention, Crisell noted that the act of listening may itself involve different levels of concentration (1994: 202).

Television audience measurement, often using electronic set meters to 'detect' viewing, has also been controversial, when the consistency of data has been disrupted simply by changing the sample of respondents surveyed or studies have found that individuals within audiences may not actually be viewing when the technology registers their presence in front of the screen (Starkey, 2004c: 16, 18–20). Meters cannot know whether a respondent has fallen asleep or is profiting from a commercial break to turn attention from the screen to another activity (Collett and Lamb, 1986). At least the press have the advantage of physical sales figures, which can be audited by an independent body after unsold returned copies have been deducted from the total distributed, but for the detail that simple paper counts cannot provide about the number and nature of the people who actually *read* each issue, they have to resort to surveying samples of the population in the editorial area and extrapolating audience data from their responses (Starkey, 2004c: 4–6).

The problems faced by producers in agreeing amongst themselves who is consuming their output, the nature of their audiences, and how to construct representative samples of them are also problematic for academic researchers interested in audience readings of broadcast and published texts. For such research to be convincingly generalizable to wider populations, samples need to be as representative as possible of those populations according to a range of different criteria. However, the industry research that attempts to measure audiences is routinely subject to both random and constant error (Starkey, 2004c: 3–25). Random error is introduced into survey data by maverick listening, viewing or reading by individual respondents, reporting consumption that is atypical for the section of the population they have been chosen to represent. Constant error derives from systemic faults in data collection, such as misleading base population data, inappropriate sample selection (Som, 1973: 278–80), inaccurate interpretation and misleading reporting of the results. The smaller the sample size, the greater the effect of any error on the data. Conversely, a point can be reached where increasing the sample size brings only limited gains in accuracy of results (Stopher and Meyburg, 1979: 93–8).

Even when a researcher has established a sample of the audience to study, their responses and how, in turn, they are reported remain epistemologically unstable. Some respondents may be unable or unwilling to accurately record their media consumption and their reactions in diaries, or to represent their readings faithfully in response to interviewing. This may be either for personal reasons or due to factors common to a demographic sub-population to which they belong. Because levels of concentration vary, some acts of listening, viewing or reading may be more accurate indications of typical audience readings than others, and some listeners may be better equipped to decode what they experience. For example, one survey found radio listeners in New York could only identify which station they were tuned into with 91 per cent accuracy (Frankel, 1969). Even without a political dimension to the research, the truthfulness of respondents can be difficult to verify. Sabo reported respondents overstating news viewing and understating cartoon watching, when surveyed. Radio listeners claimed to listen to 'cool' radio formats instead of politically incorrect 'shock jocks' (2002), because they were concerned about what opinions of them the researchers would develop.

Whether to trust respondents' responses may depend on their motivation for participating in a survey. Why does a person volunteer to a stranger to undertake what is often unpaid work, reporting on their readings of media texts, and taking care to do so according to that stranger's parameters? Reflexivity is the writing of the researcher into the research design and process, not a rare phenomenon in social scientific research, and it, too, may significantly distort academic research enough to raise important epistemological concerns about what the data seem to be telling us. Symbolic interaction theory suggests respondents will try to discern the motives behind the research, so in interviews, questionnaire surveys and focus groups the question/response transaction is itself a negotiation between the polarized positions of researcher and respondent (Blumer, 1969).

Merely becoming a research subject may alter the way individuals consume media products and so, simply participating in the research may 'taint' results. Even innocently, when asked by a researcher to provide reactions to texts, the respondent may listen, view or read more carefully in order to be able to respond 'correctly', than would otherwise have been the case. This has been recognized in controversies around anthropological research for some time. For example, groundbreaking studies by the anthropologist Margaret Mead (1901–78) were disputed by others who claimed the groups of people she observed and interviewed simply lied to her (Orans, 1996). Only an effectively covert approach to data collection, such as that used by Thompson (1966) to secretly observe the biking community featured in his controversial ethnography, can be relied upon to completely hide a researcher's motives from respondents. The Hell's Angels he studied did not realize he was researching their subculture, because the disguise he adopted was so effective he could move among them undetected.

Any interview, diary or questionnaire data collected may itself be located somewhere within Giddens's double hermeneutic framework (1984: 284). The interpretative nature of responses to texts may be misunderstood by us as researchers when we then interpret them. Respondent and researcher knowledge is often incomplete and their perceptions may be based on partial information. Finally, in creating a summative written text of multiple research data and findings, any researcher is therefore creating a 'representation' via a text that is itself probably worthy of close textual analysis.

One significant variable common to all approaches to audience data collection for academic research is survey size. Entirely worthwhile research into media consumption may dwell at length on small numbers of individuals, as did Domenget's description of radio listening by four retired people in France (2003, 141–54). Other researchers may recruit larger numbers of respondents to panels, in the hope that those panels will be sufficiently large and therefore 'representative' of wider populations to afford any conclusions greater generalizability. The purpose of research among audiences is often to provide intensive data about complex social and human phenomena in very specific contexts rather than to develop extensive conclusions (Deacon et al., 1999: 42–3). Even focus group research with perhaps half a dozen participants is routinely presented as meaningful (Livingstone, 1990: 107). Some of the data on audience perceptions discussed later in this chapter were collected by the author in an extended research project examining BBC Radio 4's *Today* programme during the 1997 UK general election campaign, and the epistemological issues raised above apply to these findings as much as to any others.

In the project, a panel of respondents were recruited mainly via the letters page of the programme journal, *Radio Times* (BBC, 1996). It would have been impractical to obtain data from the whole population of listeners to the *Today* programme, and any sampling of a population inevitably involves compromise. Asked if they would 'provide reactions' to coverage of the then forthcoming election, of the magazine's three million readers, a tiny percentage volunteered to supply data for the project via a self-completed questionnaire which asked for their opinions on general aspects of the programme and on specific items broadcast at peak times on predetermined days. In contacting the author, many of them chose to add critiques of politicians or of *Today* or even to write copiously about their own backgrounds, but all who responded were replied to and invited to join the sample.

At that stage, no further element of selection was used. Of course, this self-selecting sample may be better described as including *Radio Times* readers who were prepared to listen to *Today* for the purpose of this research. They may be distinct from the wider population of regular listeners to *Today* in some respects. The respondents were asked via the questionnaire about their listening habits, but if they wanted to conceal any atypicality about themselves or their listening, they could easily have done so. Without any corrective intervention (that is, initial researcher selection or subsequent exclusion by quota), the questionnaire sample, though modest, almost exactly matched the network's audience profile according to RAJAR, at least in terms of age (mean: 52.23 years), gender (45.16 per cent male) and region (highest density: south of England).

Several felt they should explain their interest – even though they were not asked to – and declared afterwards they had found the survey to be 'good fun'. A small number confessed to being members of a political party. All the respondents knew the researcher was asking about balance and bias, so in taking part they may have been artificially sensitized towards issues around representation, that they might not otherwise have queried. However, the listener reactions in the research could not otherwise have been gathered without their knowledge, as no form of covert data gathering could have been achieved over such a large geographical area and at such intimate times of the broadcast day as 7 am. In terms of eliminating reflexivity, it is doubtful whether in this case any form of 'decontaminating device' could really have concealed the researcher from the researched (Scott and Usher, 1993, 59).

A parallel investigation of audience perceptions in the same study involved those of the parties themselves. The three largest parties were approached immediately *after* the election, and asked for access to their media monitoring data for the period. The Conservative Party claimed it did not have any such data, while Labour admitted it did, but would not release it. The smaller and relatively modestly-funded Social and Liberal Democrats (SLD) (as the recently merged Liberals and Social Democrats were then called) admitted having kept monitoring data, and invited the author to their Westminster headquarters to view them on 19 February 1998. The SLD volunteer monitors' notes covered a number of different channels – both radio and television – and timeslots, from *Sunrise* (Sky News), BBC Radio Five Live's breakfast programme and *Breakfast News* (BBC1) to *Six O'Clock News*, the main breakfast-time commercial television broadcaster, GMTV, and the bi-media phone-in *Election Call* (Radio 4 and BBC1). Even an edition of *Farming Today* (Radio 4) had been monitored and a form filed away.

Spending the whole afternoon, largely alone and unsupervised, in the party's wood-panelled conference room with several large ringbinders spread out on the tables, the author was able to make whatever notes he wished about what he read – amounting to seven pages of notes – copying down all the interpretative material he could find about *Today* for later analysis and comparison with readings from other perspectives. He also read every 'media monitoring report' produced by the night team as part of the early-morning briefing for the 14 people most central to the running of the SLD campaign.

Most of this material related to evening and night-time broadcasting, and provided some evidence (if it were needed) of a considerable degree of media literacy within the party and a sense that they at least considered that media representation might have some effect upon the course of the election. One reference to the Brian Hayes phone-in on BBC Radio Five Live on 2 April, for example, noted a consensus of callers around the SLD as being 'irrelevant', and their sole supporter 'turning out to be an 11 year old'. Another referred to discussions having taken place with the *Today* programme and the *Nine O'Clock News* (BBC1) about the level of coverage the party was receiving.

Partial audience readings

Most of the 39 editions of *Today* were monitored for the SLD by a single
volunteer, who was in two immediately obvious respects atypical of their pool
of monitors: he often wrote his contemporaneous notes on plain lined paper
rather than on the forms completed conscientiously by his colleagues, and he
also used some shorthand to put information down quickly, suggesting he
might have been a journalist. If so, that might perhaps explain his greater
inclination to exert his own individuality in doing the work. It also appeared
that the intended readership for the contemporaneous material was limited,
perhaps even to himself. His identity was clearly visible, although because of
the terms under which the author was granted access, it is not reproduced
here. Often the writing, apparently produced under time constraints, was
hurried, and the time calculations in the margins were sometimes cryptic. In
general, though, there were methodological similarities with the contemporaneous notes the author had also been making of *Today* during the period:
descriptions of the programme content, who was speaking and what was
being said, with the remarks annotated on the texts or as brief summative
reports. On 23 April, for example, the monitor commented that the party's
live interviewee had a 'dry mouth', and on 24 April he observed that the then
party leader, Paddy Ashdown, sounded on radio like 'a bit of a character'.

On some occasions, he picked out 'key points' – probably for a wider
audience – observing for example an obsession with the Tatton constituency,
where the former BBC journalist Martin Bell was opposing the sitting
Conservative on an 'anti-sleaze' basis. One programme was a 'policy-free
zone', in another the 'Lib Dems' and Labour were 'badly discriminated
against', and a further comment criticized 14 minutes 'of Tories talking'
compared with less than one minute of either Labour or the SLD. In the time
calculations made within the notes, an interesting distinction was drawn
between party representatives 'talking' and parties being 'talked about' by
someone else, presumably including commentators and other politicians. The
timings were further explained by a separate annotation that circled figures
indicated 'wholly negative' coverage. A note written on 11 April recommended that the party make a written complaint to Tony Hall, then
Managing Director, BBC News and Current Affairs. The Conservatives had
been interviewed for 15 minutes, Labour had had less airtime and some
supportive voters, while the Lib Dems had had very little, but that was later
in the programme, after 08:30 'when audience declines sharply'.

Throughout, the log sheets revealed that the monitor was using a number
of parameters in his analysis: the duration of time allowed to representatives
from different parties, whether supportive voters were given airtime and the
scheduling of items as it relates to audience size. His readings were more
sophisticated than that, though, using simple discourse analysis methodologies (see Chapter 5) to quantify the lack of 'balance' he perceived at times.

The presenters' interviewing technique (see Chapter 5) was also scrutinized: the then Labour Shadow Chancellor, Gordon Brown, was described as having had 'an easy ride', for instance, and it was noted that his interview had been preceded by 'very sympathetic' comments by voters.

The monitor considered the effect not only of the allocation of airtime to express one's position, but also that of being talked *about* – that is, being characterized one way or another by an opponent, or by a commentator such as the BBC's then Political Editor, Robin Oakley or the then Head of Political Research, Bill Bush. Accusations of 'federalism' in any discussion of the UK's role within the European Union were perceived as requiring a right of reply in a comparatively prominent slot because of the negative connotations the word had acquired in the nation's wider political discourse before the election. One comment ran: 'If Europe is the story, Lib Dems should be given prime-time chances to defend their policies. Maddock wasn't asked about it. Oakley didn't mention what Paddy had said about it. Only Bill Bush mentioned what Nick Harvey had said.'

As being labelled a 'federalist' on air was widely considered harmful to a party's prospects, then it would almost inevitably consider being unable to challenge such a description as damaging to its interests, if the party thought there was a possibility of it having some effect on the audience. Certainly, in the opinion of the *Today* monitor, this seemed to be a cause for complaint on grounds of partiality. Without access to either Conservative or Labour monitoring of the same broadcasts, it is not possible for the author to establish whether they reacted in the same way to similar circumstances. It would be surprising, however, if they had not, particularly as there is considerable evidence that politicians or their representatives do indeed complain and make other representations to journalists in the hope of either getting redress for unfairnesses they themselves perceive or influencing future production decisions in their favour.

Notwithstanding the obvious existence of spin doctors, whose not always inglorious history is traced by McNair (2000: 122–7), there have been several noteworthy instances of politicians' own readings of broadcast texts provoking a public response, and sometimes precipitating other events in the unfolding of a nation's political narrative. For example, *Today* presenter John Humphrys cited a personal telephone call to the studio from the then Prime Minister Margaret Thatcher in 10 Downing Street (8 December 1988) as evidence of the programme's importance. According to his account, they were 'pretty pleased' with themselves and when she asked to be put 'on air' it was 'hard to say no' (BBC, 1998). Rather more fractious encounters are chronicled in Cockerell (1988), and one of the most public was the then Conservative Party Chairman, Norman Tebbitt's attack on the BBC's coverage of the 1986 bombing of Libya by the USA. Tebbitt's anger was focused on the BBC condemning rather than being equivocal over the UK's support for the American action, while other commentators perceived few differences between it and ITN's coverage of the same event (Miller, 1992).

The professional spin doctor, more commonly operating 'in the shadows', is paid to read media texts, judge their possible effects on the audiences who also – at least in part – constitute the electorate and where they perceive it necessary, intervene directly with both broadcasters and the press. Behind the public face of the British Labour Party's ideological and imaging transformation into the election-winning New Labour of the late 1990s and early 2000s were, among others, Peter Mandelson and Alastair Campbell. Their public notoriety, fuelled by the media's interest in political processes and personalities, stemmed largely from their effectiveness as an interface between the party and individual journalists – some of whom complained of 'bullying' tactics being used to affect coverage. The irony of a powerful, influential profession complaining it has been individually or collectively bullied lies not only in the unlikelihood of media power being wielded unchallenged in a democratic state, but also in the role of the media in both men eventually losing jobs in public office: Mandelson, later a Member of Parliament, then a European Commissioner, twice resigning from the Cabinet, and Campbell's 2004 resignation as chief press secretary to Tony Blair following very public rows over the Gilligan affair (see Chapter 1).

In some respects, though, both angry politician and spin doctor are merely seeking a right to reply when their readings of texts suggest to them they could be better represented in the media. Such a right is rarely given by newspaper editors, unless serving some editorial purpose of their own: for example, stimulating a positive audience response that, in turn, the editor hopes will increase circulation or ratings, or perhaps in avoiding a possible libel action. In some territories broadcast regulation does establish a right to reply – following a regulator's adjudication over a complaint, for example. In the UK, Ofcom (2003–), the Broadcasting Standards Commission (1997–2003) before it and first the Broadcasting Complaints Commission (1981–97) have occasionally found in favour of complainants and required the broadcasting of an apology. These have almost exclusively been traders, though, criticized in consumer programmes for alleged malpractice in business, rather than politicians or even pressure groups that feel they have been misrepresented.

Regulatory bodies may not be the only guarantors of 'fairness' in some instances. The right to reply, if not actually guaranteed, can seem within an aggrieved party's reach where a media organization voluntarily appoints an ombudsman, even if that person's autonomy may be restricted. The international Organization of News Ombudsmen (ONO) includes approximately 45 members worldwide, ranging through national and regional, state and privately-owned press and broadcasting organizations, but coverage is sporadic: in Canada, for example, CBC appointed its own ombudsman in 1989, while among the country's press, in 2005 only the *Toronto Star* had one. In 2004 the *New York Times* joined around 35 American titles with ombudsmen – out of 1400 dailies – and some, such as the *Orlando Sentinel*, invite readers to participate in editorial board meetings.

A notable exception among the otherwise resolutely partisan British Press is the *Guardian*, which appointed a 'readers' editor' to 'represent' readers who consider a misrepresentation to have taken place. Ombudsmen though, like regulators, vary greatly in the speed and enthusiasm that they are able to bring to individual complaints. Certainly, few political parties consider such processes likely to neutralize editorial bias against them, and being uncompromisingly a newspaper of the left, the *Guardian* is unlikely to print much more positive coverage of the political right as a result. Furthermore, the majority of its readership would find such a seismic editorial shift unpalatable, as they choose the newspaper because of, not in spite of, its intrinsic left-wing bias. It is unlikely that such a change would go unnoticed, given that most readers, individually, read a partisan newspaper's output from a particular perspective about which the editor and staff routinely make judgements. In this way, partisan media may well satisfy their core audiences most, when the expectations of reception bias are fully met by the effects of production bias. It is in the case of regulated broadcasting (see Chapter 2) that wider audiences' reception bias is more likely to conflict, Tebbitt-style, with any production bias that may exist.

Research among the *Today* 'audience'

Notwithstanding the caveats above about the selection and interrogation of any sample for the purposes of academic and practitioner research into audiences, the author's 1997 study did produce some interesting data about how individuals can respond to broadcast stimuli. When asked, the sample proved reluctant to attribute much bias to *Today*'s presenters, but individual respondents often 'read' the same programme items differently, according to their own political positioning. This aspect of the research seemed more significant than might be expected, because the self-selected panel collectively shared a number of characteristics with the wider population of Radio 4 listeners.

As individuals they were, of course, highly self-conscious. They had, after all been invited to be introspective and 'provide reactions'. Some spontaneous self-justifications, either demographic or experiential, were offered in response to the original call for participants, as follows:

> I ... will be a first-time voter at the general election, but I have been extremely interested in politics for several years.

> I consider myself to be reasonably politically aware and always vote in elections. However I am something of a floating voter and do not always vote for the same party. I am not a member of any political organisation.

> As a background to my qualifications for this work, I can inform you

that I was a former Labour Leader of Liverpool City Council so I have a good knowledge of electioneering.

As an articulate man whose heart and upbringing was in the Rhondda Valley – son of a miner (dead at 46) – and a habitual Labour voter – as my father's family flirted with Communism – I feel I have a unique outlook on the sway of the South Wales Valley constituencies.

I would like to give my reactions to election coverage by those opera-loving twits on Radio 4, who seem to exist in a media bubble so far removed from real-life, not unlike the grey man [then Prime Minister John Major] who carps on about how hard life was in Brixton. I am a 48 year-old man who has been out of work for 12 months and subjected to the ordeals of Jobcentres, Job seminars, Job Clubs and the other measures used by government to conceal the social divisions of Britain.

Clearly, for the purposes of making production decisions most broadcasters' notions of 'typical' listeners are in essence reductive, ignoring as they surely must such extra layers of identity and experience as listeners' political careers, any exposure of their fathers to the grim realities of mining or any unsophisticated antipathy to opera. In practice, in addition to the sample's close demographic match to the wider *Today* audience, there were similarities of political positioning, too. Although the percentages of votes cast nationally for Labour, the Conservatives and the SLD in 1997 were 44, 31 and 17 respectively, an under-representation of Conservative supporters in the sample, which voted 42, 10 and 32 per cent respectively, suggests similarities with the BBC's own analysis of the Radio 4 audience as being broadsheet readers, 'particularly the *Guardian*' (Bunker, 1996).

With focus group research often being conducted with much smaller numbers, and the fact that the sample was not, then, wildly unrepresentative, this could mean some responses mirrored those of substantial numbers of the *Today* audience. None of the respondents cited anything heard on *Today* as a specific reason for changing or not changing their voting intentions over the seven-week campaign, although 16 per cent thought their votes had been affected by something they had heard on the programme and several referred in their answers to general party policies or presentation. However, of all the British media covering the campaign only one respondent identified election coverage (in the *Guardian*) as being influential.

Many responses suggested high levels of both media and political literacy. For example:

I heard nothing from Major or Blair to bring me back to the Conservative agenda. [voted for the Referendum Party]

I am a socialist and there was no realistic alternative, but I had to think about it. [voted Labour]

... the infighting and sleaze in the Tory party and then as Labour's policies began to [sic] those of the Tories I decided to go for common sense and honesty ... [had voted Conservative in 1992, intended to vote Labour then changed to Liberal Democrat]

... mainly during last week of campaign JM gave impression of telling the truth – more human – rather than TB's almost false bonhomie and man of the people act – form over substance. [had voted Conservative in 1992, planned not to vote in 1997 but finally voted Conservative]

I got heartily fed up with the personal abuse/lack of cohesion/dignity shown by the two main parties. Paddy Ashdown was impressive throughout, as was our local candidate. [had voted Labour, then voted SLD]

I believe in socialist, rather than capitalist principles (so why am I voting Labour?) [a Labour voter]

Some explanations were disarmingly honest in their simplicity, for example:

Nothing changed my views, if anything, the campaign made my [sic] more than ever not to change. I could never vote for any other party. [voted Conservative]

I am a member of the SNP. [voted Scottish National Party]

Yet, a small number of responses were so sophisticated as to be confusing, such as:

This vote is heartfelt and tactical. [a SLD voter]

Rather than passively 'receiving' the programme as broadcast, some questioned such editorial decision making behind the programmes as agenda setting and choosing interviewees. For example:

On the whole, very even-handed except that undue prominence was given to Eurosceptics in the numbers of them selected for interviews.

Bearing in mind the first two weeks of the six-week campaign were given over to the 'sleaze' factor, once that was out of the way I felt *Today* was as balanced as these sort of programmes can be.

Two weeks spent deliberating over the 'sleaze' factor – this was media hype at its worst. It was obviously going to come up, but after a couple of days the programme should have switched to the real election issues.

When asked directly if they agreed with the suggestion that *Today* was politically biased overall, only 15 per cent of respondents agreed, while 61 per cent disagreed. This result may to some extent have been affected by loyalty towards the programme or its presenters, and an unwillingness to directly accuse them of bias when asked bluntly to do so. Where the questionnaire later asked the same respondents for more detailed responses that majority was quickly eroded. As expected, and depending on respondents' reasoning and political positioning, some contradicted each other, as follows:

Balance retained throughout.

Unbalanced – Labour politicians were constantly challenged about future policies but Conservatives were very rarely asked to account for their failures and record of 18 years in government.

I found the few programmes I did listened [sic] to were left-wing inclined.

I feel that I didn't hear a lot of Lib Dem items in the time frame I listened.

Not much measured sensible debate from Conservatives although there were several sensible contributions from other two parties, apart from all emphasizing their own battle cries. [voted Labour]

I'm afraid one's answer is somewhat coloured according to one's sympathies. I welcome the aggression if it takes that to get an answer – but I don't like a Green getting picked on! – if there ever are any!"

It may be that the subjectivity behind such judgements is so content-sensitive that even heard from apparently broadly similar positions, different individuals make highly individual readings of the same texts. Some respondents even contradicted themselves, although their readings may simply have been irrational. The first of the two examples below was a Liberal Democrat voter who, when asked directly, disagreed that the programme was biased but then later commented that:

The only bias I can generally detect is towards opposition to the party in power *because* they are the party in power, not necessarily because of their policies. Possibly Ashdown had a slightly easier ride.

> Quite well balanced. Appeared to favour Lib/Dem and possibly Labour, but ... from the content of the programmes rather than from the interviewers.

That individuals within audiences should be capable of such contradictory responses seems to defy logic, but also confirms initial suspicions that caution would be appropriate in interpreting them. Another respondent disagreed very strongly when asked directly if the programme was biased, yet later not only went on to identify bias in favour of the 'two big parties' but also attributed it to the ' ... power they have to put pressure on the BBC'. This suggests other ways in which audience readings of bias may be problematic: not only does understanding of what constitutes bias lack universality, but individual readings that confirm or deny the presence of bias may wrongly attribute reasons for it.

The small number of respondents who did characterize *Today* as biased overall were more likely by a ratio of 3:1 to be opposition supporters than to vote for the incumbent Conservatives. There are clear similarities between their readings and the quantitative data in Chapter 7 showing that the programme gave more airtime to Conservatives than to any other party. Several commented on the relative absence of minority parties from the programmes (see Chapter 7), and interestingly these were not mainly supporters of minority parties: the majority of them were Liberal Democrat and Labour voters. Such comments included:

> The minor parties could have got more coverage, otherwise very balanced.

> For Cons, Labour and Lib Dems it was very balanced. My main grouse, as you would expect, was NO GREENS (or any minor parties), NOT ONCE – the electorate never had a chance to know anything about us.

> It was mainly concerned with the two main parties with very little coverage of others.

> Generally well balanced with views from all parties, although I seemed to listen to more Tories than Labour or Lib Dem. Don't remember any minority parties except SNP and Referendum Party mentioned.

Several respondents commented on the adversarial nature of political interviews (see Chapter 5), and among them several suggested any accusations of bias might be attributable to the polarization of broadcaster and politician, as follows:

> ... the interviews with political figures are equally rigorous and ... the interviewers should actually be *tougher* with them about answering the

question set. It might seem like political bias, but it's because the politicians don't answer the question. [voted Labour]

I would not say that any of them are basically biased – though all of them can head in that direction if interviewing a difficult politician – and particularly, they can react against a patronising attitude from either side!

... the programme is fairly balanced notwithstanding the presenters pursuing politicians in a vigorous manner.

Incumbency in government was cited as a likely cause of confrontation, by some of those who did perceive bias in the programme, and one Labour voter commented that:

Any interviewer must push Govt Ministers of the day into explanations of ongoing policy. Perhaps we have had a Conservative Govt for so long that interviewers often appear to support the Opposition.

If interviews do polarize interviewer and interviewee, that predominance of Conservative politicians may account for one of their voters commenting that: 'I do feel that when I do listen, the presenters are left wing'.

When asked to rate the five presenters individually, respondents were even less prepared to accuse them personally of bias, than they were to criticize the programme overall – perhaps they were wary of possible litigation – although the denials were most unequivocal over James Naughtie and Sue MacGregor. For example, Naughtie was: 'more even handed altogether – quite difficult, sometimes, to know what he does think'. Depending on their perspectives, respondents offered a number of sporadic, often contradictory perspectives on the five, such as:

Too 'chummy' with Conservatives. Argumentative/interrupts with Labour/Lib Dems/Scot Nat.

... the person more acceptable to the Conservative hierarchy and can be trusted not to be too aggressive towards them.

She takes a subtle critical stance with Labour MPs but appears to give Conservatives the benefit of the doubt.

Politicians were constantly interrupted so that either any real information was lost OR in the case of Conservative politicians, they just 'talked over' the interruption with whatever comments they wished to make. [voted Labour]

> [He] frequently allowed Conservative politicians to end interviews with as long as two minutes, uninterrupted party political broadcasts. [voted Labour]

> I think they did their best to be balanced and to give people a fair hearing, but they were too easy-going with Bill Morris of the TGWU who was very evasive and got away with it by being charming.

Some respondents were even conscious of paralinguistic elements within the discourse (see Chapter 5). For example:

> ... his opinion shows more in the tone of his farewells – ironic if he doesn't like them, incredulous if he's got nowhere, polite if he agrees with them – but he usually has a go at most people.

Few respondents thought any presenter favoured Labour: bias, if perceived, was usually towards the Conservatives. One attempted to position herself at the political fulcrum:

> Not being politically dedicated, I think I am reasonably objective, and I am amazed at the number of Conservatives who say it is very left-wing biased and vice versa.

> I feel [John Humphrys] is confrontational which can be misconstrued as being politically biased, depending on who he is interviewing.

> Picking over the minutiae. i.e. a comment made months earlier by an unsuspecting Politician which probably is negligible, and then blown up out of all proportion by John Humphrys, in particular.

Another considered the three main presenters, James Naughtie, Sue MacGregor and John Humphrys 'extremely skilful and professional'. She thought Humphrys was 'not so much biased as opinionated ... allows more of himself to come through', then cited his interview with Labour leader Tony Blair (08:10, 28 April 1997) as undermining Blair's credibility and describing it as:

> ... probably the most significant single interview on *Today*. It certainly confirmed for me that the Labour Party was no longer socialist, not one I wanted to support.

Her response certainly accords with (but couldn't wholly account for) Labour's falling opinion poll lead during the campaign: a possible effect of the scrutiny to which he and his party's policies and previous record in office were subjected by the broadcast media.

Despite their different party allegiances, though, only one respondent sought to defend the politicians, while only one other found fault with the interviewers:

> Generalist interviewers ... often seem to bring poor briefings to interviews. Then they cling to trite popular beliefs despite being given contrary information which could be taken up.

More commonly, respondents blamed the politicians for the coverage of the campaign, as below:

> Sometimes the attacking, negative campaigns, especially the Conservative one, made it difficult to actually get information of policies. [a Labour voter]

> The campaign was too long so the same ground was covered too many times giving the impression of harassment.

Comparing audience responses

In the *Today* research, some of the most interesting findings arose from respondents' readings of the *same* items. Rather than comparing overall impressions of a series of programmes, which can lack the rigour of a more systematic approach, here they were all asked in advance to listen at specific times on specific days, and report back via the questionnaire. One such item, at 08:10 on 27 March 1997, was in the recorded stimulus/live response format (see Chapter 5), beginning with a brief clip of the popular entrepreneur Richard Branson commenting on the election campaign as a 'disinterested Briton overseas', followed by a live interview with the then Conservative Deputy Prime Minister Michael Heseltine responding as an 'interested party caught up in the action'. Paradoxically, the 'disinterest' attributed to Branson in the presenter's live cue might be hard to appreciate, given the size of his business interests in the UK, but less controvertible was the latter's anchoring of the discourse in the realms of 'sleaze'. This was a key issue in an election in which only about a third of all media stories generally were mainly about a party presenting its policies to the electorate (Denver et al., 1998).

The item considered a sitting Conservative MP who had admitted taking undeclared cash from Harrods owner Mohamed Al Fayed to advance his interests in Parliament and consequently had withdrawn his candidacy in the election. A former Conservative respondent who voted Referendum in 1997 commented that the programme was 'anti-Conservative at this stage', but added that the item would be of most benefit to the Conservatives. This right-wing perspective contrasted sharply with the reaction of the majority, typified by the following responses:

Showed the arrogance of the Government. Morally bankrupt.

Sleaze is a serious matter and an embarrassment to the Tories.

Points out even more strongly how empty and incompetent the Tories have become.

[Will] adversely affect Tory chances – Mr Heseltine very evasive and keen to blame media/Labour Party for stories.

Michael Heseltine is so hilarious now it's time for him to go, the fact that he blames the 'Labour' *Sun* for Tory indiscretions is ludicrous. A 'Labour trick' – oh dear!

Confirms my total lack of respect for Conservatives.

When asked which party would gain most electoral advantage from the item, the sample indicated the opposition parties rather than the Conservatives by a ratio of 11:4 – and of the opposition parties they mostly identified Labour. The minority view among respondents unsympathetic to the Conservative message was that the granting of airtime to Heseltine was beneficial to him, because even though it was not one of the Conservatives' preferred issues, he at least had an opportunity to articulate his own perspective. This is evidence of an ability in some listeners to assume reactions in others that are dissimilar to their own.

Asked to comment on the likely effect of the item on the election, their views were diverse:

Reinforced diehard Tories' vote – maybe alienated some wavering Tories.

Little or none except perhaps on a purely local level.

Further swing away from Tories if it has an effect.

Provided there are no more allegations or counter-allegations against Labour I think Labour will gain.

Reduced anti-Tory feeling.

Possibly none.

Because 'sleaze' was a negative issue for the Conservatives, Heseltine seemed keen to change the agenda: after 1 minute 45 seconds asserting it was not a 'real issue', and after 5 minutes 50 seconds complaining that the *Sun* had

deliberately raised the issue in support of Labour. The conduct of the interview was interpreted in a variety of ways by different respondents who all
voted Labour:

> Heseltine dominates conversation and is very difficult to interrupt, even
> by Humphrys.

> Again all very polite – let them chunder on, but they had nothing new
> to say.

> Interviewer stuck to subject and would not allow Mr Heseltine's diver-
> sionary tactics, but this is within his brief to clarify Conservatives'
> involvement with cash for questions.

> John Humphrys didn't press Mr Heseltine over the delaying of closing
> Parliament so that the Downey Report could be published; I felt he
> should have.

> Michael Heseltine for once spoke in a fairly measured way. Unusual for
> him on the *Today* prog. He was able to get in virtually no attack on
> Labour until the end. He seemed to engage in damage limitation rather
> than attack or electioneering.

> Very probing with Michael Heseltine who didn't cope very well. Lost
> for words and stumbling – he tried to get onto more 'comfortable
> territory' but wasn't convincing.

> The relative positions of Michael Heseltine and Richard Branson meant
> that Michael had a great opportunity and time to put his point of view.

> Deputy PM was unable to shift discussion away from sleaze.

That such a variety of readings, some of them contradicting others, should be
made by a group of listeners with some broad commonality of perspective,
confirms the polysemic nature of broadcast speech.

There are clear similarities between the data above and the various ways
in which broadcasters and publishers allow their audiences very limited
opportunities to interact with their output. Where audience reactions feature
as part of the content, other individuals within those audiences engage in a
reflexive reinterpretation in which they re-read the readings of others. The
earliest examples were the letters pages of newspapers and magazines,
followed by television and radio programmes featuring written or phoned-in
comment. As the Internet developed as a popular interactive medium in the
mid-1990s they quickly spawned official message boards, on which, for
example, viewers and listeners to radio and television programmes can

comment on what they have seen and heard. The obvious constraints of time and space physically limit what can be included in the letters page or the built programme, whereas the cyber equivalent has the potential of a virtually unlimited capacity, subject only to the size of the server storing the data.

Whereas websites often seek to create the impression of unlimited access, the editorial role in choosing what is included and what is not is more easily apparent where there is only room on the page for a certain amount of text, or time in the programme for so many letters or callers (see Chapter 5). Where message board contributions are genuinely uncensored except, perhaps, over matters of taste and decency or to avoid a potential libel, postings may well reflect wider audience reactions to the broadcast texts. The *Today* message board featured 9500 postings as this book went to press, many of them widely differing readings of the same programme items, depending on each correspondent's positioning. Other well-resourced BBC sites, such as *Question Time* (BBC1) and *The World at One* accommodate only selected postings, characterized by the sites as being a 'representative' selection of responses received.

Whenever audience 'reactions' diverge – or even contradict themselves – in their apparent readings of broadcast and published texts, they may be more or less effective as justification of 'balance'. Broadcasters sometimes use roughly equal numbers of responses for and against an item to defend their approach as 'about right' as if in themselves they prove the existence of balance (Schlesinger, 1987: 171). However, if a more systematic analysis should demonstrate that the complaints come more frequently from one side of the issue fulcrum, patently they do not.

Furthermore, it is as difficult to *measure* reception bias as it is to measure production bias, however easily we may both define and identify them. Given the numerous caveats with which the collection of any audience responses should be considered, their use in any analysis of balance and bias is extremely problematic for practitioner and academic alike. The difficulties for broadcasters in determining the size and identity of their audiences both cause and resonate with problems facing academics in finding appropriate social actors to contribute to their own research into consumption. So, the problems of knowing audiences are compounded by those of reading them in such a way as to produce valid data and to draw meaningful conclusions from them. Drawing attention to these epistemological concerns is not, however, a rationale for restricting research into audiences over validity and generalizability, but one for proceeding with caution both in conducting that research and in interpreting it. Part of that caution may require a greater emphasis on production bias, and the following chapter considers 'balance' in the kind of discourse articulated by the media.

CHAPTER 5

Broadcast Talk and the Printed Word: A Balancing Act

Discourse and bias

Production bias, where it impacts on audiences, lies mainly in the discourse articulated by a broadcaster or a publication, and it is to discourse that we now turn our attention. In the case of print, as also in television and the Internet, the discourse assembled by the originator normally consists of a combination of words and images. On radio, as on television, words may combine with other diegetic and non-diegetic sounds to create meanings, either intentional or unintentional, in the perception of individuals within audiences. Rather than struggling with the contradictions inherent in reception bias (see Chapter 4), it is in the encoding of meaning through the mass media that we may most effectively identify bias and, conversely, seek something approaching 'balance' in the representation of 'reality'. This is no simple task: we have already considered how 'balance' must be determined between an infinitely complex number of positions, and 'impartiality' would require broadcasters to accurately position themselves at a fulcrum more elusive than simply a mid-point between left and right (see Chapter 2).

Speaking on *Today* (08:52, 22 March 1997) about the topical light entertainment programme *The News Quiz* (Radio 4), *Times* columnist Alan Coren joked that 'grown men with tax-deductible suits' were monitoring the dialogue, ensuring each joke is 'not only of equal length, but of equal comedy'. If Coren's arbiters of positioning in broadcast humour existed, the difficulties facing them would be considerable. Determining how 'funny' a joke is would necessitate consideration of in whom the amusement is to be measured, and how representative they might be of the wider audience. Although his point was meant frivolously, it suggested that what should matter in discerning political bias in comedy is how amusing it is. That would be to deny the polysemic nature of language. In fact, a statement may not be at all funny, yet it may nonetheless effectively make a political point even within the context of a comedy programme. To underrate its impact, then, because the humour is lacking, would be just as misleading as to ignore many other aspects of the discourse being presented.

Between 1984 and 1996, the latex puppet-based satirical television sketch show *Spitting Image* (Central) both portrayed and played a role in British politics – just as its various reincarnations have done in such other territories as France, where *Les Guignols de l'Info* (Canal Plus) still features in prime time. Likewise, such unrelated but stylistically similar series as *DC Follies* in the USA have also influenced political processes elsewhere, following the tradition of irreverently sending-up the political establishment begun by such early television classics as the 1960s series *That Was the Week that Was* (BBC) and the 1970s *National Lampoon* radio and television shows in the USA, but traceable to the early political cartoonists of the mid-nineteenth century.

Several relatively well-informed commentators have attributed the failure of the SDP-Liberal Alliance to make much impact on the British general election of 1987 to the merciless *Spitting Image* portrayal of the Liberal Leader David Steel as a miniature politician in the SDP leader's breast pocket. Even more effective in shaping events may have been the broadcasting of the programme's 1992 general election special on the *eve* of the poll, rather than after the polling stations had closed, as had previously been the practice. By caricaturing the incumbent Conservative leader John Major as a grey, boring man pushing peas around his dinner plate, yet ultimately a very safe choice, compared to the risk to the country represented by the wild-eyed, flared-nostriled Labour challenger, Neil Kinnock, a likely message being encoded by the programme and conveyed to its prime-time audience for subsequent decoding was that voting Labour carried more risk than voting Conservative. Paradoxically, bias hunters might wonder why, according to Lewisohn, British political satire 'works best' when the Conservatives are in power (2003).

Satire is not only found in discrete contexts that are billed and widely understood as such. Entertainment sequences, such as *Saturday Night Live* (NBC), a British version entitled first *Saturday Live* and then *Friday Night Live* (Channel 4), and such celebrity chat shows as *The Late Show with David Letterman* and Jay Leno's *The Tonight Show* also reach far larger audiences than rival programmes produced by news and current affairs departments and have regularly included political satire among their comic repertoire (see Chapter 2). The then upcoming socialist comedian Ben Elton's weekly monologue on *Saturday Live* and *Friday Night Live* would regularly include sustained rants against the Thatcher government, without any 'balancing' right-wing commentary offered to counter it, either immediately afterwards or later within the same programmes.

The partisan nature of such conservative American radio and television talk shows as Rush Limbaugh's is not in question, and the sustained anti-liberal rhetoric they unashamedly voice would seem preposterous in territories where broadcasting is regulated over 'balance' (see Chapter 2). Limbaugh's daily show (EIB), syndicated to hundreds of US radio stations and available over the Internet, is a powerful cocktail of extended monologue, interviews, caller interaction and actuality – to which, if of Democrat politicians' speeches, for example, Limbaugh is not averse to adding scathing commentaries. A regular target for the pressure group Fairness and Accuracy in Reporting, many of Limbaugh's views on such issues as climate change diverge dramatically from widely-shared consensual understandings in the scientific community, and in an effort to counter the political imbalance represented by Limbaugh and others, Air America Radio, 'The Liberal Talk Radio Network', began offering such 'alternatives' as (Jerry) *Springer on the Radio* in March 2004. By the end of its first year, though, the programming was being syndicated to only 54 stations, and it faced an uphill struggle to match the impact of conservative talk radio.

To assume though, elsewhere, that banning overt presenter polemic, Limbaugh-style, in itself guarantees 'balance' would be quite wrong, simply because of the wide range of discursive elements which constitute any broadcast on radio or television, as in the text-based media. In phone-ins, panel discussions and even music and lifestyle programming, the potential for partiality over matters of political controversy is great, and it is very hard to scientifically prove or disprove whether 'balance' has been achieved. Despite McQuail's reservations (see Chapter 4), the one physically measurable dimension in broadcasting is time: a stopwatch is all that is required to reduce programmes or programming elements to finite durations which can then be added or subtracted, multiplied or divided at will. In their content analysis of Dutch elections, for example, Brants and van Kempen studied discursive elements of talk radio involving politicians and journalists and considered the distribution and average length of soundbites (2002: 177–9).

Qualitative judgements about which of those minutes and seconds counted might counterbalance another – and whether they do so in whole or in part – are much more difficult to make, and may inevitably depend upon one's own perspective. Whatever methodological approaches to discourse analysis one chooses to apply to a text (see Montgomery, 1991: 139), particularly in the case of political discourse, context must be a consideration. Fairclough's discussion of tensions between his own and Bourdieu's approaches acknowledges this (1995: 176–84). However, an issue being problematic is not a valid rationale for not mentioning it, and many of those qualitative judgements are raised in this chapter.

Beyond the obvious time and party label analysis, different academics have developed a variety of approaches. McNair's chronology of content studies detected a trend away from attempting to 'prove' the existence of bias to rationalizing 'the factors involved in the production of journalistic accounts of the world' (1994: 38). He considered much content analysis to reveal a tendency in the media to reflect the interests of the advantaged over those of the disadvantaged (McNair, 1994: 34). Where analyses become more dependent on qualitative issues, though, production bias becomes more difficult to distinguish from reception bias (see Chapter 4). However, some methodologies may be more transferable across different ideological perspectives: despite right-wing condemnation of the Glasgow University Media Group's findings (including 1976), their methodology was perhaps less unattractive to right-wing opinion than some public pronouncements may have suggested. McNair describes the Conservative Party's subsequent use of 'comparative content analysis' by its own Media Monitoring Unit to produce the so-called 'Tebbit dossier' about BBC coverage of the US air strikes against Libya in 1987 (1994: 68) (and see Chapter 2).

That the discourse articulated in otherwise straightforward reporting should cause controversy is hardly surprising. Reporting the news routinely presents would-be impartial journalists with discursive issues that are difficult to resolve. On 16 July 2004, in its 8 am news bulletin, BBC Radio 4 reported the outcome of two by-elections at Leicester South and Birmingham Hodge Hill in the English Midlands. The bulletin led by stating that the Liberal Democrats had 'defeated Labour ... and come close to winning another [seat]'. The interpretation of these two results compares well with the kind of scenario popularly envisaged as choosing to consider a glass to be either half full or half empty. In the opinion of Labour and their supporters the glass may certainly have been half full because they had previously been widely predicted to lose both seats at the end of what the media were only days before calling 'Blair's worst week'.

In fact other interpretations of the same result that were given airtime – but not headlined – included disappointment for the Liberal Democrats at not taking both seats, and an early indication that the Conservatives' new leader Michael Howard was failing to mount a successful challenge to Labour in advance of a general election being widely predicted as less than a year away. Later in the bulletin, Labour spokesman and Health Secretary Dr John Reid called the night's results 'a score draw with the Liberals'. The bulletin writer's dilemma, if indeed the dilemma was ever perceived, was whether to characterize Labour's result optimistically or pessimistically. The choice was problematic because choosing optimism would be to associate the bulletin with Labour, while choosing pessimism would be to position it with the opposition.

Effectively, in the manner explained by Fowler, the headline articulated a representational discourse from a 'particular ideological position' (1991: 11). This runs counter not only to the BBC's Charter requirement of 'impartiality', but the ethos observed by Schlesinger, among others, as central to the internal discourse of the Corporation's production staff. As they went about their work they rationalized their practices using a repertoire of justificatory terms: objectivity, balance, responsibility, fairness, freedom from bias (1987: 163, 203–4). The 'inferential frameworks' identified in broadcasting by the Glasgow University Media Group as favouring establishment positions and assumptions (see Chapter 1) provide the syntax (or grammar) of reporting, while the lexicon (or vocabulary) used draws on a 'stockpile of common assumptions and beliefs' (Burns, 1977: 203). Particularly when institutional and peer pressure legitimizes careless use of language, 'neutrality' in discourse is hard to achieve, because as Masterman observed, innocence and transparency of meaning are not inherent in many forms of mass communication. The media are unavoidably 'impregnated with values' and they 'actively shape' their content accordingly (1985: 27).

Inferential frameworks revolve around 'common-sense discourses, imaginary scenarios and popular metaphors', creating and recreating popular paradigms used in a 'public forum' by politicians and the press alike with 'decidedly detrimental effects for the articulation of progressive political positions' (Garton, Montgomery and Tolson, 1991: 116–17). The 'bully script' to which media discourse frequently reverted in discussing industrial relations in the UK in the 1970s and 1980s compares with more contemporary examples from the 1990s and the following decade as the 'sleaze script', which perpetuated the impression that publicly exposed evidence of corruption in the Conservatives in office was symptomatic of a more widespread phenomenon, and the 'spin script' around which accusations of superficiality were frequently levelled against the subsequent Labour government. Other common patterns of discourse could be described as the 'soft on Europe script', the 'tough on crime script' and the 'economy, stupid, script'.

Similarly, the lexicon of political discourse draws consistently on words and phrases that through the development of metaphor and metaphorical transfer become key signifiers in certain contexts. For example 'the Tartan Tax', meaning the cost to Scottish voters of devolution of power to their own parliament, and a whole panoply of pugilistic terms which often dominate copywriting in election periods as one party 'makes advances in the polls' and another is described as 'in retreat': successes and reverses made not least in party 'battlebuses'. Often, the use of such linguistic shorthand, rendering complex issues more manageably, actively misrepresents 'reality'. If not actually calculated to affect the political process, resorting to such patterns of discourse may be attributable to journalistic dependency on a 'discursive reserve'. Somewhere within the journalists' own psyche there may be a set of values or assumptions that makes one position rather than another seem evidently the more reasonable (Ferguson, 2000).

Achieving 'balance'

Even the apparently innocuous can be highly problematic. For example, in reporting the weekly Prime Minister's Questions in the House of Commons, the phrase 'the prime minister had a difficult time at the despatch box' may really be more contentious than intended, particularly if its most likely interpretation may not be palatable to the prime minister's party, which might prefer to put a different complexion on the event. Its preferred reading of the 'difficult time' may be that the prime minister gave a robust performance under heavy, but ineffective fire from the opposition. Within the party political arena, the kind of broad consensus otherwise commonly found around such issues as racism and pressures on the environment (see Chapter 1) will almost always be elusive.

The choice of language can easily introduce unwitting or 'clumsy' bias. The political advantages of incumbency in government are particularly evident in election periods when journalists choose to positively identify candidates as the 'prime minister', the 'president' or 'the secretary of state'. On *Today* in 1997, listeners were repeatedly reminded of John Major's status as 'the Prime Minister' rather than the equally correct, but politically more neutral 'Leader of the Conservative Party'. In 2005, Labour politicians were reinforced in office as the 'home secretary', the 'foreign secretary' and so on, where more neutral descriptors were readily available. Although Labour won in 1997, and *Today* is but one programme on one network, it should be remembered that the party's poll lead fell, rather than rose, over the seven weeks of the campaign. With less value-laden possibilities at their disposal, for 'impartial' broadcasters to systematically choose language which is more likely to favour one party, can be seen as negligent or malign, depending on one's perspective. Certainly, such a policy cannot easily be interpreted as even-handed.

Operationally, always being 'fair' to everyone may, however, be impossible. Clause 13(2) of the BBC's Licence and Agreement requires the organization to broadcast daily 'an impartial account' of the 'proceedings in both Houses of Parliament'. Yet, even with the introduction of the digital television channel BBC Parliament, allowing round the clock retransmission of pictures and sound from the Palace of Westminster, some selection is inevitable if both chambers, together with their various committee meetings, are to be covered other than very superficially. In the UK neither cable nor satellite broadcasters have made provision for the kind of simultaneous coverage provided in the USA by C-Span, C-Span 2 and C-Span 3, just as in France, La Chaîne Parlementaire, and broadcasters in many other territories, each provide but a single relay from their various legislatures.

On British radio, no analogue or digital frequency having been allocated for continuous coverage of either house, the imperative is 'satisfied' by the digests *Yesterday in Parliament* and *Today in Parliament* (both Radio 4), and because lengthy unedited coverage is relatively unpalatable, except during moments of heightened interest, a television equivalent is *The Record* (BBC Parliament). The impossibility of 'reporting the day's proceedings' in the two Houses without some editing is obvious. The (almost verbatim) transcript published daily when parliament is sitting, *Hansard*, runs to hundreds of pages in each edition, and even contemporaneous transmission of both Houses and associated Committees would, at times, require several dedicated channels. To produce a 15 to 30-minute report, including audio, clearly involves sifting, prioritizing, selecting, editing, summarizing, paraphrasing and, effectively, positioning and repositioning the fulcrum around which an 'impartial' representation attempts a still highly problematic balancing act.

Consequently sometimes difficult editorial decisions have to be made, and Gunter, for example, examined in detail contentious research findings from television news coverage of parliament that seemed to prioritize Conservatives when in government. He attributed this to the then prevalence of Conservatives in parliament, together with the broadcasters' natural desire to hold the governing party to account for its actions and the need to reflect internal dissent within the party itself (1997: 60–2). However, it still represented a marginalization of other parties that risks turning mere incumbency in government into a hegemonic domination of the media that excludes alternative voices to their detriment.

That content-regulated broadcasters attempt at all to present 'an impartial account' of any aspect of public controversy, however, is a conscious act of legitimization of the notion that such a thing may be possible. The 'record' of events, be it *Yesterday in Parliament*, a documentary or a bulletin is routinely produced and broadcast. If there were anything wrong with it, it may be assumed one or other of the parties would have complained by now, or at least, complaints from one or more quarters would be more frequent, more strident or more effective. There is, however, no sustained campaign to end political reporting in democratic states on the grounds that it is inherently unfair.

This oxymoron, then – impartial reporting – is routinely naturalized by journalists and broadcasters as a given of the trade, and wider society is expected to endorse its manifestations wherever they are published or broadcast. The reporter's version of events and ideas is presented as the 'correct' reading, and the expectation is that both the audience and the broadcaster should unite around it (Hood, 1980). In this way, media discourse routinely presents itself as unbiased, legitimizing itself as a transparent presentation of 'reality': rarely if ever introspective and seldom inviting its audiences to question its veracity. When, on occasions, politicians challenge their 'impartiality', broadcasters routinely mount a robust defence that often displays an unshakable confidence in their infallibility. The notion that the BBC, for example, and those whose work constitutes its output are all impartial is to the BBC's Charter, the *Editorial Guidelines*, and the NUJ Code like a creed is to a collection of holy scriptures.

Religious adherence sometimes requires denial of imperfection in the creed, lest the whole edifice of beliefs, scriptures and institutions should come tumbling down as a result: in this case the edifice is either the BBC or the concept of broadcast journalism as 'professional', or both. Adherents rarely tolerate criticism of the creed: for example, the late Brian Redhead, a former *Today* presenter, expressed great indignation (whether real or synthetic) when the then Conservative Chancellor of the Exchequer Nigel Lawson accused him of being a Labour Party supporter all his life. Redhead's response was to interrupt him, calling for 'a one-minute silence, now in this interview ... for you to apologise for daring to suggest that you know how I vote ...' (18 March 1987). With belief often comes doubt: when broadcasters express public confidence in their practices, behind the scenes there may actually be greater preparedness to recognize failings than can be readily confessed (Wells, 2003a).

How, though, is the content-regulated broadcaster to meet expectations of 'balance'? On an instructional level, some practical advice recognizes 'complete impartiality' to be 'like perfection', something to strive for but practically unattainable, so although bias is inevitable, it should never be surrendered to (Boyd, 2001: 200). Others suggest 'fairness' might be achieved by avoiding 'moral judgements', serving the audience and having 'as wide and varied a background as possible' (McLeish, 1994: 92–3). A common approach is the credit–debit model in which a critical piece at 8 am on Monday might be countered by a reply the same time the next day, thus achieving 'balance' 'over a period of time', rather than within individual bulletins, so both sides of an argument may reach the same audience even though 'on consecutive days' (Chantler and Harris, 1992: 39).

'Balance over time' is the essence of the BBC's own policy: its former *Producers' Guidelines* described 'accurate, robust, independent, and impartial journalism' as the 'DNA of the BBC' (2004a, Chapter 2: 3). However, not all issues span the political spectrum, and covering them may promote certain groups and perspectives over others that are left out of the debate. For example, television and radio coverage of the battle for the leadership of the Conservative Party, after the Thatcher resignation in 1990, was hugely dominated by talking Conservative heads confessing allegiance to one candidate or another. Opposition parties received little media exposure during the period, and the Conservatives' standing in the opinion polls subsequently recovered significantly. One can only guess how much this recovery in Conservative fortunes was due to the change of party leader or to the amount of exposure the party received in the British media. In 2005 the phenomenon was repeated when the Conservative leadership was again contested, following the resignation in opposition of Michael Howard, and won by David Cameron. Certainly, such rises in the party's popularity would appear to contradict the often articulated belief that divided parties are unattractive to the electorate: before the election of John Major, the Conservatives had been split into the three camps around the three leadership contenders, and in 2005 there were two.

It might therefore be to a party's advantage to manufacture a row, to gain disproportionate airtime to match the range of views it represents. The French phrase '*avoir la parole*' (or 'to have the floor') neatly conveys being able to articulate one's opinion. Van Leeuwen identified 'having the floor' as an aspect of political interviews in which each participant vies to dominate the other in an attempt 'to silence the other and to assert the self' (1999: 67). Paradoxically, a discussion involving two viewpoints within a party could allow that party twice the airtime it might have had in a confrontation with another. In 1990 and 2005 a range of Conservative views were being expressed, so that party 'had the floor' for longer.

This and other dilemmas must be confronted by the broadcaster wishing to remain true to the creed of impartiality. The *Producers' Guidelines* also distinguished between 'professional judgement' and 'personal opinion' – the former being allowed, and the latter not (BBC, 2004a, Chapter 2: 4). Differentiating between the two, though, is more problematic than they suggested, not least for Gavyn Davies with his 'different view' from that of the government over the Gilligan affair (see Chapter 2). While they may in theory be antitheses, in practice the distinction between them might be better described as blurred. In the absence of content regulation, and without consensual codes of ethics, Fink identified in the USA what he called a 'credibility gap', to be filled only by each journalist assuming an individual responsibility for ethical behaviour, just as 'Aristotle put on each individual the burden of personal responsibility for virtuous conduct' (1988, 13). Because most regulators will only intervene *in extremis*, though, that responsibility should extend to all but those who openly declare any allegiances and partiality.

Production bias in political positioning

The difficulty for content-regulated broadcasters in trying to balance two opposing interviewees – and therefore the positions they have been invited to represent – is not just to give them equal airtime, so neither side feels disadvantaged in the encounter, but also to present each one with the same level of challenge. When playing 'devil's advocate' in the questioning, this means presenters shifting their own positions from one side of the debate to the other: paraphrasing on each occasion the opposing position, as convincingly with one interviewee as with the other, lest they be accused by one of them of greater sympathy with the opponent. Done effectively, over a suitably short period of time, this approach positions both the presenter and the programme *between* the two positions, rather than exclusively on one 'side', and they are both more likely to be perceived as 'balanced' in the short term.

This has long been a common approach in the content-regulated broadcast media over issues including but not restricted to party politics. More recent examples include such public controversies as those over the MMR vaccine (see page xix) and the ordination of gay bishops. However, despite often heroic efforts by the BBC to 'balance' strongly-felt beliefs on the inclusiveness of the church, on other occasions where either the law or widely-shared notions of common decency render certain positions difficult to espouse even through liberal 'enlightenment', the clergy have also attacked the BBC, alleging bias when accusations of child abuse being sanctioned by the church were treated with less equanimity (Gledhill and Sherwin, 2003). Often there are logistical, technological or format-related factors which complicate matters (see pages 106–9), but in most issues, *appearing* to 'balance' competing perspectives is not impossible, although it often requires some deft footwork by the individual broadcaster.

Regular 'devil's advocacy', though, directed at a single target – as in the calling of a government to account rationalized by Gunter (see page 98) – can seem to position broadcasters some distance from the political fulcrum. Not calling the opposition to account on equal terms can readily seem to be bias against the one without any counterbalancing against the other. Consequently, it can seem to position them and their programmes within a debate or on a particular 'side', often provoking such accusations of bias as Norman Tebbitt's in 1986 (see Chapter 4). A change of government, if the same broadcasters persist with equal vigour in their 'calling to account', might then seem to reposition them on the other side of the fulcrum. Individuals within their audiences may be surprised to hear broadcasters of whom they may previously have approved changing 'sides' and adopting positions they had previously seemed to oppose.

Regular espousal of particular positions and the challenging use of rhetoric in order to convey them by those who consider themselves to be professional equivocators are remarkably common. In fact, taking a position, as Reith did most dramatically in 1926 and having a 'different view' over an issue, as explained so catastrophically by Gavyn Davies in 2003, rather than reflecting a 'balance' of views, is very common in current affairs broadcasting in many countries, despite any legislative and regulatory controls that might be in place (see Chapter 2). Audiences will make their own readings of the texts before them, many of them quite reasonable in essence. At various times over recent years, *Today*, for example, could reasonably have been read as opposed to the war in Iraq, disapproving of four-wheel-drive vehicles being driven in towns, and sceptical about GM foods, yet equivocal about gay bishops. Conclusions such as these would be generously supported by a close textual analysis of the choice of items and contributors made by the programme's editors, the way in which topics were introduced and how the presenters dealt with interviewees. Many *Today* listeners would find it hard to imagine either John Humphrys or James Naughtie regularly berating members of a different government for not having invaded Iraq.

This is because repetition of common approaches and positions over time are bound to become naturalized within the context, and so they begin to define the context. There would be considerable merit in an academic study that compares the positions taken by *Today* and the nightly television news and current affairs magazine *Newsnight* (BBC2) on a range of topical controversies, through the discourse they articulate. Despite Schlesinger's institutional observations that 'an absolute distinction between fact and comment is philosophically dubious' (1987: 247), there is no suggestion here that content-regulated broadcasters necessarily indulge in the extreme mixing of news and comment, the selective reporting and the misrepresentation of fact that cherished, if fanciful, notions of freedom of speech have allowed to persist in the press in many territories (see Chapter 3).

It would be unusual in the UK, for example, for the *Sun* to suggest that the euro might be a positive benefit to British business, or for the *Guardian* to consider whether perhaps there are more asylum seekers coming to Britain than might be practical. Producing rhetoric to order may be a far less challenging task for journalists when they have proprietorial and institutional backing for such clear and entrenched perspectives on public controversies as underpinned the notorious jingoistic *Sun* headline 'Gotcha', used to report the sinking of the Argentine warship, the *General Belgrano*, by Britain, with the loss of 323 lives (3 May 1982). The partisan press feel little need to conceal their bias. The positioning of the short-lived *News on Sunday* (see Chapter 3) was immediately apparent from such headlines as 'Giant tax dodge for the rich' and 'Horrors of the hunt' (18 October 1987), as well as 'Murder: NHS savaged – more lives could be lost' (25 October 1987), while such inside stories as '[Tony] Benn's vision of a brave new world' and 'Nurses are casualties on hospital battlefield' (25 October 1987) served to reinforce the front-page polemic. There is no obligation on the letters editor, either, to reflect a range of views, unless the inclusion of some alternative perspectives is seen as a means of provoking 'target' readers into a response.

However, some democracies have decreed that broadcasters using the finite resource of broadcasting spectrum should feel a greater obligation to the proper working of democracy, particularly when, in the case of the BBC, they are funded by compulsory licence fees. Yet, broadcasters and the programmes they produce and present may reasonably be considered by audiences to hold their 'own' sets of political beliefs, because those audiences are encouraged to make such readings by positioning both 'on air' and 'off air'. An extreme example is the way in which *Today*, in asserting its independence from government and robustly defending the Gilligan report, positioned itself as a firm believer in the alleged 'sexing up' of the dossier by Number 10. On 26 June 2003, in the prime 08:10 slot following the main news bulletin, the programme indulged itself with a 12-minute line-by-line rebuttal of Alastair Campbell's responses to the Foreign Affairs select committee the previous day. In it James Naughtie 'interviewed' the BBC's then Head of News, Richard Sambrook about what Campbell had said. Far from subjecting Sambrook's line to the kind of rigorous cross-examination for which *Today* is renowned, Naughtie merely invited him to answer points raised in brief clips of Campbell's evidence to the committee. It is worth noting that there are few individuals or organizations that are publicly criticized and can organize their own detailed and uninterrupted defence on *Today* or elsewhere on the BBC.

However, positioning is rarely so obvious. More commonly, live interviewees appear on that programme alone – leading politicians often make that a condition of their taking part – so any confrontation is between interviewer and guest. If a programme regularly challenges ministers with interruptions and at least feigned disbelief at their answers and doesn't separately treat their critics in the same way, it will be read as being anti-government, and not only by Alastair Campbell. Often, before an interview, a programme will use pre-recorded material as a scene-setter: a package, one or more voice clips from an opponent or a collection of authoritative challengers, arranged in a brief but confrontational discourse often aimed at wrong-footing the live guest by demonstrating the presence of dissent. Typically, *Today* presenters will use a succession of gentle, open questions in the scene-setting material to elicit the points they then wish the main interviewee to answer.

The practicalities of broadcasting topical material to tight deadlines, within rigorously enforced programme structures do, of course, impact on programme content. However, the systematic application of certain formulae such as this to the routines of programme making also impact on their nature, and then inevitably on how their output is perceived. The set-up described above actively positions the programme and the programme makers with the preceding material in opposition to the live guest who follows. The stimulus material, linked by the presenter, becomes assimilated within a discourse he or she is perceived to be actively constructing as part of the confrontation, much in the same way as quoted or cited material in an academic work is used for affirmation and reinforcement. This argument, or thesis, readily appears to be the presenter's own, and the presenter, together with the programme of which it is part, as well as the institution which facilitates its dissemination, become closely associated with the argument and the political positioning it represents. In effect, this is institutional polemic: the broadcaster – that is, the presenter, the programme or even the network itself – becomes associated with a particular position, to the detriment of others.

Institutional polemic in broadcast discourse also results from such other structural elements as the bringing together of a number of people with differing views in a debate. The choice of panellists for such weekly topical discussion programmes as *Question Time* (BBC1) or *Any Questions* (Radio 4) in the UK represents a *de facto* positioning of the panel, and therefore, the programme. Out of, for example, four or even five panellists, it might be expected that at least one of them is a fairly robust defender of the government's line on most of the issues discussed: perhaps a loyal back-bencher or a minister bound by the collective responsibility of Cabinet membership. Imagine, though, the despair in Downing Street on discovering that, yet again, the 'Labour' voice is to be that of the long-standing dissident left-winger Tony Benn, or a nouveau-malcontent such as Robin Cook (1946–2005) or Clare Short who both resigned from the Blair government over Iraq in 2003. (Chapter 7 includes a detailed case study of panel composition on an entire season of *Question Time*.)

The callers heard on radio and television phone-ins are, of course, selected behind the scenes before they are granted limited access to the airwaves, and this act of selection contributes to the construction of the discourse the complete programme articulates. Even when both sides of a controversy are represented by equal numbers of callers, between them given equal amounts of airtime, there is no guarantee that one set of callers are equally effective advocates for their position as the others. Even the most adept players of 'devil's advocacy' rarely treat them with equal measures of latitude and antipathy, and there are, of course, controversies on which equivocation is not an option. Racism is one example in which, if not common decency, specific legislation prevents us from giving currency to the most extreme of opinions (see Chapter 2). Few interviewers or phone-in hosts are going to advocate child pornography either, even to provoke a reaction when the phone-lines are quiet. However, these are only marginal issues in many communities, whereas the reasons for going to war, the decision to vaccinate one's child with MMR and the acceptability of genetically-modified crops (or 'Frankenstein food') are far more central to political debate.

Production bias within texts is further complicated by contextualization of internal diegeses by the external diegeses within which they are situated. An example is layers of meaning resulting from the external activities of 'impartial broadcasters': the newspaper column in which he or she condemns GM foods, the appearances on other, even satirical programmes which involve criticism of one position or another. A journalist's known personal friendship with the Prince of Wales, for instance, may well compromise his ability to adjudicate in any debate in the UK between monarchists and republicans. The Gilligan allegation on Radio 4, about Number 10 'sexing up' the September 2002 Iraq dossier, was re-read and so reinterpreted by audiences when Gilligan named Alastair Campbell as the individual responsible in an article he contributed to the *Mail on Sunday* on 1 June 2003. Once this new allegation was picked up by other media, Campbell's anger was directed at the BBC, as the context for the original single-sourced claim.

More generally, if newspapers have known party allegiances or frequently articulated opinions on specific issues, by being closely associated with them broadcasters may be compromising the impartiality of their 'on-air' work. The Kelly affair was the catalyst for a subsequent ban on BBC journalists making unvetted contributions to other media (Baldwin, 2003) – an activity which cost former *Today* editor Rod Liddle his job (Wells, 2002) – but why should it have taken so long for the Corporation to realize that opinions expressed in other contexts will affect readings made by the public of its own broadcasts? Just as in London the Metropolitan Police were accused in 1999 of institutional racism, and have striven with varying degrees of success ever since to both eliminate racism and show their working practices are now beyond reproach, so broadcasting organizations bound by rules over impartiality may have to work harder to reduce institutional polemic that positions them as intrinsically biased in audiences' perceptions. Furthermore, just as the public sector is subject to scrutiny by the Audit Commission, one solution might be that broadcasters could also be independently audited in terms of their ability to achieve 'balance' – as in Australia (see page 31).

Discourse in interviews

Like political perspectives, political interviews are heterogeneous, consisting of several related and unrelated phenomena that both systematically and chaotically can result in disparate performances and positionings. This heterogeneity is not confined to any one genre, as Fairclough observed about both print and broadcast media (1995: 86–90). Because the interview is such a common element of broadcast journalism, it follows that much of the balance to which programmes aspire must be attempted within (if not necessarily throughout) their interviewing. It would be an oversimplification to characterize interviews as merely 'hard' and 'soft' as they are in essence both structurally complex and polysemic. Interviewers are themselves variables and may be considered to subject their interviewees to varying degrees of scrutiny. Skills trainers often overestimate the ability of individuals to interview 'fairly', avoiding expressing their own opinions or getting drawn into argument (McLeish, 1994: 37).

In practice, few interviews may be 'neutral' – devoid of value beyond the superficiality of 'A talking to B about C'. Interviewees may represent an institution or be speaking from an individual perspective, but they must inevitably adopt a position in relation to the subject. That position may be defensive if, for instance, A's position is calculated to 'balance' that of B. A negotiation takes place, either before or during the encounter (or both), as to the different parameters within which the discussion is to take place. The discourse may then confine itself to the subject or even stray beyond a declared or previously agreed agenda. It is worth noting that the 'oppositional' voice of most interviewers will raise questions only from within a particular paradigm: for instance, there is rarely any questioning of orthodoxy from the standpoint of the anarchist. Most journalists are themselves positioned within that orthodoxy: for example, it would be unusual for a budget speech to be followed by a discussion of the positive and negative aspects of capitalism. Certain positions are not challenged, certain questions are not put, and certain perspectives are, thus, excluded from the representation offered.

Yet, on 17 April 1996 the then Conservative Party chairman, Dr Brian Mawhinney, still found a question from Sue MacGregor on *Today* about a possible leadership challenge to John Major to be inappropriate, calling it 'a ludicrous and indefensible question', adding that it was 'that kind of smeary question' which also annoys the public. Subsequent press coverage, including reported reactions from readers, backed MacGregor, but far from the neutral encounter, or simple conversation, as interviews are often depicted, Mawhinney's analysis highlighted the polarization of competing paradigms or vocations: journalists and politicians need each other – the one as raw material and the other as a conduit to the electorate – but the relationship is often an uneasy one.

What, then, is the political interview: an innocuous exchange of questions and answers or a ritual of attack and defence? It is most transparent when live and therefore broadcast without editorial alteration, as the interviewee's comments cannot be taken out of context. It will usually be preceded by a short introduction – or 'cue' – in which presenters set up the encounter by establishing the topic, the parameters for the discussion and what previously known information they consider relevant. The agenda-setting nature of the cue is not, though, always uncontroversial, and interviewees may dispute the nature of the questioning at will. If live, their objections will be heard by their audiences. For example, on a live link from Strasbourg, Robert Kilroy-Silk, then a United Kingdom Independence Party (UKIP) Member of the European Parliament (MEP), complained in an interview with Krishnan Guru-Murthy on *Channel Four News* (19:38, 27 October 2004) of 'sloppy journalism'. Because of the time delay, the exchange had become awkward and stilted, with both men repeatedly speaking at the same time, then both pausing. Then Kilroy-Silk asserted that Guru-Murthy kept asking him three questions at once, and interrupting when he was unable to instantly provide three answers. He declared he wouldn't evade the questions and would answer in full, but he needed to be given time to do so.

Freedom to dissent from editorial decisions, as did Mawhinney and Kilroy-Silk, is more limited in many of the other contexts within which interview material is used, including those that are text-based. Where interviews are recorded and then subsequently broadcast 'as live', the acknowledgement in the preceding cue material that the interviewer 'spoke earlier' to the subject is discretionary. What is rarely ever admitted is whether the encounter is being broadcast exactly as it happened or in edited form. Editing can be totally invisible to audiences, not only in text-based media, but in audio and video too. An aspect of the widely-proclaimed 'professionalism' that under-pins many claims of 'balance' (see Chapter 1) may be to avoid altering meaning or placing material 'within an unintended context' (McLeish, 1994: 31–2), but as 'professional' edits are not apparent, the listener's belief that no change of meaning has taken place in a recorded interview is necessarily an act of faith. Given the likelihood of differing readings of media artefacts (Hall, 1981: 67), the possibility does exist that meanings that remain unaltered to the person who edits may however be changed meanings to those who listen.

Interviewees who would dissent from the discourse in a subsequently written cue are unable to make such dissent apparent to the audience. Editing and using interview material in packages can produce new juxtapositions, as can the selective use of 'soundbites' – even when motivated by 'innocent' producer creativity – which can create new meanings, intentional or unintentional. So the potential here for production bias is considerable. Recorded interview material is often used as a stimulus to precede a live response in the form of a main, live interview that might be of a considerably longer duration. The live interviewee is free to agree with or refute at relative leisure any points made by those who went before. Now silenced by their temporal and physical displacement from the continuing discourse, they cannot intervene to develop their own earlier argument or reiterate their position, so a very unequal status is accorded to the different individuals involved in such items.

Multiple interviews, be they live or pre-recorded and then perhaps edited before being broadcast 'as live', feature a number of interviewees, normally each of them being present because they have differing views they have been invited to articulate. This creates particular problems over 'balancing' their conflicting interests in such a way as to minimize criticism of the item on grounds of 'fairness'. Not everyone can have the last word. There are obvious similarities to the 'round table' discussion programme, and characteristics of such examples of that particular genre as *Any Questions* (Radio 4) and *Question Time* (BBC1) may be heard. The rules of a formal debating society may be implemented to some degree, although the time and attention span imperatives in radio and television mitigate against over-cumbersome procedures, however well-motivated.

In so-called 'two-ways' between presenter and reporter, it is not uncommon for the whole exchange to have been planned by the interviewee, whose suggestions as to what the questions might be are much more likely to be taken up by the presenter than in an interview with someone other than a colleague. The reporter has a clear agenda in terms of what information and comment can be offered to the programme and the questions merely provide a framework within which they can be smoothly delivered. It is precisely the semblance of relative informality in a two-way which often allows reporters to indulge in greater speculation than would be appropriate in a report. It would be counterproductive, though, for the presenter to encourage the reporter to be indiscreet in the way a politician might be pressed to reveal more than he or she intended. Both are likely to respect each other's editorial judgment. However, it was in just such a two-way that *Today* broadcast Andrew Gilligan's early morning allegations about the Iraq dossier (see Chapter 1) and erroneous speculation that an explosion at the 1996 Olympic Games in Atlanta had resulted in 41 fatalities. Previous and subsequent news bulletins in the same programme restricted themselves to the correct figure of two fatalities (27 July 1996).

Remotes, such as Kilroy-Silk's, place distances between interviewer and interviewee that are only superficially surmountable through modern communications technology. Direct eye contact between interviewer and interviewee is impossible, as is communication through body language. If circumstances allow, the only opportunity for informal contact before and after the interview is verbal – as links are being established and tested, before engineers or studio managers cut them again after the piece. On radio, when interviewees' voices are of studio quality, they are likely to be in a contribution studio or an outside broadcast vehicle at a convenient location, or using ISDN lines which deploy digital/analogue converters and high-quality lines to bring studio quality sound from less permanent locations. The converter (or codec) needed at the remote end is, however, expensive and it needs to be *in situ* before the interview can begin. ISDN is, therefore, unlikely to be very useful in getting immediate reactions from individuals early in the morning at short notice.

Even with its inherent lack of studio quality and susceptibility to crossed lines (to which neither landlines nor satellite feeds are immune) the telephone offers the broadcaster an unrivalled technological flexibility. Early morning contributions can often be more easily secured if the interviewees have only to pick up their own telephones, but on television the absence of live pictures is sorely felt. The technical characteristics of the telephone balancing unit required at the interface between the telephone line and the studio sound mixer do, however, alter quite significantly the power relationship between interviewer and interviewee with the presenter's voice often automatically 'ducking' the phone line (McLeish, 1994, 139). Rarely is it otherwise considered acceptable to lower the voice of an interviewee in this way, so the interviewer may be heard more clearly.

Items may be ended abruptly by the quick fading (potting) of a guest's microphone, but only during a telephone interview is the presenter accorded an automatic right to talk down the interviewee. If both should speak simultaneously, the voice of the interviewer prevails. It is not even possible for the interviewee to persist with the '… if I can just finish this point …' with which so many live studio interviews are punctuated. It is simply not heard or understood: so often, the remote or telephone interviewee is at a particular disadvantage, especially if in a multiple interviewee situation against others who do have eye contact with the presenter and the ability to send and receive body language signals that will not be apparent to the listener ('I want to interject …', 'It's my turn'). The remote or telephone contributor may also suffer from inferior audio quality heard 'down the line', perhaps mishearing words or points that are made by others. Such broken or delayed responses may be misinterpreted by audiences as hesitation, uncertainty, ignorance or evasiveness, perhaps negatively so.

In addition to physical and technical arrangements, other factors determining the nature of the broadcast interview include the power relationship between interviewer and interviewee in an exchange that is sometimes likened to the swapping of gifts. Each gift – be it question or answer – demands a reciprocal response, as two partners become bound by a debtor–creditor relationship (Goody, 1978: 23). Conventionally, the presenter is supposed to set the agenda. With a running order to follow if live, or a completion deadline to meet if it is recorded, he or she will have planned a number of questions. The wearing of headphones or an earpiece receiving communications from the control room, the presence of cameras, microphones and crew, the running order and script, as well as the presenter's role in linking the programme, all convey to the interviewee just who is 'in charge' of the event. Television talk shows often deliberately position such interviewers as Jay Leno authoritatively behind a desk, while the guest walks on and is seated by the host on a lower easy chair into which it is relatively easy to slump. The interviewee has been invited into the broadcaster's world, to be heard by the broadcaster's audience, only to have such privileges terminated at the end of the item. The presenter is part of a team, a collective, masters of the local environment, while the interviewee is in unfamiliar surroundings, is alone, physically isolated from any peer group, and being 'managed' in terms of where to sit, how to sit, when to speak and when to stop speaking.

The media interview is in essence then an unequal encounter as it is constituted. How the interviewee chooses to deal with this inequality resides on a scale ranging from quiet, cooperative complicity to annoyed disruption of the conventions such as the Mawhinney outburst or even a flamboyant 'walk out'. Any disruption of the normal relationship can result in confrontation, as can any attempt to subvert it by the interviewee: the broader public context of the broadcast interview means this can be no ordinary chat. Most media commentators assumed Brian Mawhinney's criticisms of his 1996 interview were made in a genuine loss of temper. Equally, though, it could have been another example of the 'indirection' found by Harris in over 60 per cent of politicians' responses in her research: diverting attention from uncomfortable issues (1991: 76–99).

Interviewees are increasingly accused of subverting interviews as evasive action. In a former, less combative age, such encounters were gentler, less adversarial than today, interviewers asked polite, deferential questions, seldom insisted their interviewees follow their agenda and even allowed them to rehearse (Bell and van Leeuwen, 1994: 129). This may have resulted in greater transparency of the material broadcast – being subject to less mediation or representation. Whether those interviewers better justified the trust of their audiences, though, as representing them effectively as their 'proxy', is doubtful. Today's interviewers are 'far more demanding' (Bell and van Leeuwen, 1994: 145–6) often displaying the 'crusading spirit' identified by television producer Allan Martin, as 'a sense of justice, of what is wrong, and what needs changing' (quoted in Bell and van Leeuwen, 1994: 133). Often, they will repeat questions remaining unanswered to their satisfaction, question contentious claims and, sometimes, push the interviewees too far. This is the 'rudeness' of which some commentators, including politicians and the public alike, can complain (see Chapter 4). Even the veteran British radio and television interviewer, Sir Robin Day (1923–2000) considered that rudeness had become more common in media interviews, claiming he was never so rude as his successors, John Humphrys and Jeremy Paxman (Hay, 1996: 85).

As robust posturing by experienced politicians becomes more common, interviewers often attempt to further legitimize their authority or mandate as the audience's proxy, by inviting them to telephone, e-mail or text in questions they would like to be put on their behalf. The impression thus generated of 'empowerment' of the listener is rarely, if ever, accompanied by any transparency in the process of question selection: of presumably large numbers of questions received, very few are used. Those that are have been subjected to mediation of the pool of questions proposed, yet, without any knowledge of the selection criteria, audiences may falsely construe notions of them as being the most popular or the most 'important' ones asked. The technique is often reductive: simplifying subjects and representing them on the audience's level (Wilby and Conroy, 1994: 132).

The visual codes evident in television interviews – such as framing, spatial relations, and walking in and out – are of course absent on radio. Other codes that are common to both media include atmosphere (background sounds), voice quality (a 'telephone' sound denoting remoteness from the studio), music (in packages) and the presenter's spoken cue (or scene-setting) material. The latter can be the most important of the anchoring devices used to establish context, while the structure given to the encounter by the way the questions are formulated and the dialogue is controlled punctuates the material and indicates the terms of reference within which the content is to be read. If interviewees object to this mediation being imposed upon the content of the interview, they are likely to want to subvert the process either overtly or covertly.

Of course, in the interests of balance, interviewees on all sides of the fulcrum should expect similar treatment: perhaps a 'balance' might be achieved by subjecting the claims, opinions and record of every politician who is interviewed to an equally rigorous examination. This, though, is particularly problematic when one party has been in office for a long period, as none of the other opposition parties could be reasonably challenged on its own record. Evenhandedness would require the interviewer to feign an amnesia that would exclude questions about the recent past and so permit no party's record to be examined.

Questions and answers

Discourse analysis of broadcast interviews must recognize the unequal power relationship between interviewer and interviewee as the one attempts to control the encounter while the other either accedes to or resists that control. Interviewer discourse consists largely of the preceding cue material and then the questions asked, but another measurable within it is the *latitude* allowed to the interviewee to respond between interviewer interventions. While interviewees 'have the floor', they are free to articulate whatever discourse they please, until the interviewer intervenes, either cooperatively or correctively. Cooperative action by the interviewer may be simply asking another question, agreeing in some way or adding information. Corrective action is where the interviewer seeks to reassert control, perhaps in the form of a question designed to focus the interviewee on a particular point, or to attempt to move the agenda forward or in a different direction. Most controversially, corrective action by an interviewer interrupting an interviewee can signal dissent, and *Newsnight* presenter Jeremy Paxman famously put the same question to the then Home Secretary Michael Howard 12 times, before eventually expressing his dissatisfaction with the answer and moving on (22:30, 13 May 1997).

Such systematic textual analyses of interviews as those in Chapter 7 require clear methodologies for categorizing questions and measuring latitude. The greater the sophistication of question analysis, the more it can avoid reinforcing superficial notions of 'hard' questions and 'easy' ones. The advice of instructors on 'good' question technique (McLeish, 1994: 41–8), and the theorizing of the process by academics (Bell and van Leeuwen, 1994, 148–57) suggest a range of pragmatic but neither exhaustive nor mutually exclusive categories by which questions can be classified. So it is worth considering them in some detail here, beginning with McLeish's categories. On the simplest level, choosing to ask an *open* question such as 'What will happen to taxes?', rather than a *closed* one such as 'Will you raise taxes?', can in itself allow an interviewee more latitude. Generally, being more insistent in the framing of a question, rather than asking for impressions or feelings, can be more corrective than cooperative. Bull's survey (1994) of political interviews on television found the closed question to be the most commonly used type. However informed or naive the question, few experienced politicians will answer a closed question with 'yes' or 'no' if they do not wish to, or resist the opportunity to take the initiative and speak according to their own agenda if allowed, attempting to seize control – and some greater latitude – for themselves. Unfortunately for them, audiences readily perceive an unwillingness to answer 'yes' or 'no' as evasive.

Multiple questions – such as asking all at once 'Which taxes are going up, why and how do you feel about that?' – can be unclear and allow interviewees considerable freedom to ignore the awkward parts of them and focus on those they would rather answer, particularly as listeners will soon forget exactly what the question was asking. Their corrective potential is inherently low, particularly when muddled questions are 'clarified' to little effect by the interviewer, adding further layers of confusion, indirection and so, latitude. *Non-questions* may be either corrective or cooperative, depending on their nature. They don't begin with the usual interrogatives, 'what', 'when', 'where', 'why', 'how' and 'who', but they are mere statements put forward by the interviewer for confirmation or rebuttal by the interviewee, or as prompts to begin talking on a subject: for example 'taxes will be going up'.

Bell and van Leeuwen's categorization of questions offers greater sophistication because they consider the interviewer's motives behind each question. Firstly, they say, *soliciting opinion* is inherently cooperative, lacking in challenge, and typified by the opening 'What do you think of ... ?' The interviewee's views are being sought and it is usually clear they are valued. Sometimes, the interviewer might of course be playing a longer game: soliciting the interviewee's opinion now in preparation for a more searching follow through later. *Checking* questions are less cooperative and may also be corrective, as they demand only affirmation of specific facts or opinions.

Usually closed, they will seek a polarized response, as in 'Are interest rates coming down then?', to which the only response without risking seeming evasive may be 'yes' or 'no'. *Challenging* questions share some characteristics with checking questions, and their inherently confrontational nature means they are often asked correctively. The interviewer contradicts or confronts the interviewee, who in turn may need to dispute assumptions in the question.

Bell and van Leeuwen identify *entrapment* questions as best demonstrating the power of the interviewer, being 'unanswerable challenges', that is, assertions with which guests 'can neither agree nor disagree without losing face' or 'contradicting themselves'. They are often used correctively, but the consequences of their use can be dramatic, because the inequality of the conflict can be particularly damaging (1994: 155). The MacGregor question, which provoked such an angry response from Brian Mawhinney fits this description: his party had previously unseated its then leader in similar circumstances, so was it about to do so again? The existence of the possible precedent could not be denied, and to denounce it as wrong then would be to undermine the current leader, who had risen to power as a result: Mawhinney was trapped. The risk to the interviewee is huge: a split-second calculation must be made as to the appropriateness of the response: what psychologists might term 'fight or flight'.

Release questions are deliberately cooperative. They are intentionally soft, often jocular and very common after confrontation or entrapment. Their use locates individual politicians as limited resources in a pool of 'talent', whose contributions will be sought by the programme in the future. As is a common convention of narrative structure, they offer a return to equilibrium, and even very tough interviews often end with an opportunity for interviewees to re-establish their authority, rather than leaving angry – but the catharsis they offer comes at a price, in that interviewees who accept this verbal olive branch may readily seem to accept and endorse any confrontation that has preceded it. When an interview ends without release – as in Anna Ford's *Today* interview with the then Conservative Chancellor of the Exchequer Kenneth Clarke (08:10, 16 September 1996) – the resulting disequilibrium can spell trouble. Following an exchange for which the then BBC Director General John Birt later apologized by letter, Ford ended the item with the words: 'So you are not going to elevate the debate?'. The contrast with the more usual expression of the interviewer's thanks at the end of an interview was startling. Allowed no immediate chance to reply to Ford's rhetorical statement – his microphone was off and her co-presenter had begun the link into the next item – in one Parthian shot, Clarke's whole contribution had been typified as low in tone. Ford had dealt Clarke a premature *coup de grace*, preventing a return to equilibrium and unleashing forces that then surfaced in a number of different media. The party's subsequent official complaint to Birt called Ford's question '…a disgraceful lapse from impartiality into blatant editorialising'.

Most question types can also be *leading* in nature, if they are loaded with assumptions, quite possibly incorrect, that the interviewee must either accept or deny. Inserted into the interview, they can have a corrective effect. A classic example is 'When did you stop beating your wife?' Feeling the need to deny the allegation in the question can disadvantage the interviewee, who might have to come 'off message' to do so. It further constrains the interviewee, causing further loss of latitude, and it can actively position an interviewer on an issue, who seems to be accepting the premise in it. The techniques of checking, challenge, leading and entrapment are best used carefully if interviewers wish to limit the latitude afforded to experienced interviewees and wring out of them anything controversial enough to make headlines.

Despite the professional advice given in training, it seems unlikely that many broadcasters consciously plan interview questions according to the labels given them above: structuring the interviews in advance while keeping a tally of leading or entrapment questions, carefully 'balancing' multiple questions against ones that are open. However, classification does provide useful tools for subsequent textual analyses, both quantitative and qualitative, considering the role of questions asked in achieving or compromising balance. The ratio of soliciting and checking questions to those that challenge or entrap might suggest how difficult the interviewer intends the interview to be for the interviewee. The presence or absence of release questions can be considered too. Mere classification and counting of the question types, though, does ignore the possibility of levels of difficulty within categories, and somehow this must be addressed.

How, though, could different broadcasters with different personalities, in different moods at different times and with different subject matter to ask about, avoid the charge of 'lapsing from impartiality'? In reiterating the importance of 'professionalism', Australian television interviewer Paul Lyneham told Bell he treated his interviewees equitably, seeking to put to everyone 'the hardest and most robust line of questioning that their opponents, were they there, would put to them'. He also acknowledged the need to provoke public contempt (albeit temporary) from supporters of those he antagonizes (Bell and van Leeuwen, 1994: 175). Institutional contexts place constraints on professionals that 'contribute to the shaping of output and the form of the final product' (McNair, 1994: 57), and ignoring the combined effects of deadlines, resources and organizational structures would be to produce distortions of our own. However, individual journalists are necessarily implicated in the production of meaning, and bear at least some responsibility for any production bias that occurs, through the application of their own perceptions and understanding of how stories should be reconciled with 'consensual' ways of perceiving 'reality' (McNair, 1994: 57).

On a paralinguistic level, presenters may further position otherwise less value-laden scripts and *ad libbed* material by their use of tone, expression, mannerisms and other vocal signifiers, including laughter, sneers or sighs. For example, in practice a rising intonation may well simply denote a question – or it may instead be an expression of surprise or even irony. A laugh may connote much more than innocent amusement. Even former BBC Chairman

Gavyn Davies was reported to have considered John Humphrys' tone to be repeatedly 'inappropriate' on *Today* (Wells, 2003b). Paralinguistic elements can combine semiotically with more innocent syntactical and lexical contiguities to add further and complicating layers of meaning, such as the feigned naivety of Jonathan Dimbleby, saying 'should Iraq come up' in trailing that evening's *Any Questions* just two days after the release of the Butler Report on the role of the intelligence services before the 2003 Iraq War (Radio 4, 07:59, 16 July 2004). As barely an edition of the programme had been produced without discussing Iraq since before the conflict began, this was pure theatre, but hardly music to the ears of a government keen to put behind it what was likely to be an electorally-damaging issue.

In summary, the unlikelihood of any media discourse being value-free compounds the difficulties we explored earlier, in achieving a 'balance' that might be universally supported by protagonists and interested audiences alike. We have assumed so far, that except in particular circumstances where legislation or common sense preclude journalists from aspiring to achieve a 'balance' in reporting controversial issues, it is in the interests of democracy for them to do so. In turning our attention now to a number of supranational contexts, we may have to further compromise our understanding of 'balance' as an ideal, in order that democracy itself may survive.

CHAPTER 6

Mediated Imperialism: International Journalism in the Global News Market Place

International media

As McLuhan noted in 1964, it was radio that first contracted the planet to 'village size' (2001: 334), not simply because it was invented before television – Gutenberg's printing press predated the first 'wireless' transmissions by 450 years (see Chapter 3) – but also because of the technical characteristics of short-wave transmissions. While the press could soon print quickly and in large quantities, the distribution of its paper product over long distances was subject to the considerable delays inherent in geographical displacement and the corresponding transport infrastructure until electronic transmission of facsimile pages allowed the development of remote printing. The *International Herald Tribune*, founded in Paris in 1887 as the European edition of the *New York Herald*, was first printed in London in 1974, in Zurich in 1977 and in Hong Kong in 1980, and it is now printed in around two dozen different locations in more than 180 countries. Even now, though, international print distribution is highly dependent on the consent of national governments for publishers to operate presses, use transport and retail publications. Without that consent, getting printed material into a foreign country presents considerable logistical difficulties. Smuggling bibles into Eastern Europe during the Soviet era was a very risky, though laudable activity: in economic terms, demand far outstripped the limited supply because of the constraints of authoritarian regimes that for ideological reasons banned the promotion of Christianity.

Even in the Western democracies, the cinema newsreel was beset by delays in both production and distribution. Although *Pathé's Animated Gazette* launched in 1910, gathering and processing footage, then post-production, duplication and distribution all conspired to delay the arrival of images and sound in auditoria. So the newsreel lacked immediacy, and like print it required official consent: smuggling huge reels of film into restrictive territories was not an option open to Pathé News or its imitators. High frequency or short-wave radio, though, crosses national boundaries with relative impunity: radio waves in that part of the electromagnetic spectrum are reflected back to earth by the ionosphere, starting at 60 kilometres above the surface, so that transmissions directed towards the horizon can effectively be 'bounced' around the curvature of the planet, redirected by the ionosphere down to potential audiences whole continents away. Wireless telegraph, consisting of encoded messages rather than speech, was used as early as October 1917 by Russian communists to proclaim their victory and invite potential revolutionaries in Europe to rise up against their own governments. Speech radio soon followed, and the Czechs were among the first to experiment with this phenomenon: Radio Prague claims to have begun international broadcasts in a mix of English and Esperanto in 1924.

Radio Moscow's short-wave service began in 1925, and in that year the Dutch began tests from Eindhoven, which in turn became regular broadcasts in 1927. The BBC's first experimental broadcasts to the British Empire from Chelmsford, England, started on 11 November 1927, and its Empire Service began on a permanent basis on 19 December 1932. The value to the nation state of being able to communicate directly with people in other lands was soon realized, and other international broadcasters quickly emerged: Vatican Radio among them, on 12 February 1931. Nazi Germany developed an extensive system of radio broadcasting for propaganda purposes, in addition to broadcasts on the long and medium-wave bands for neighbouring countries, targeting a new short-wave service at the USA in 1933 and rolling out other specially-tailored services for different continents until the outbreak of war in 1939. Some countries were much slower to launch 'official' stations, although private short-wave broadcasters preceded their state offerings: the Voice of America (VOA) launched in 1942 and Radio Canada began broadcasting in 1945 (Heil, 2003). The BBC's reliance on English in its international broadcasting ended on 3 January 1938, when its first foreign language service began, in Arabic, closely followed by the launch of a European service in French, German, Italian, Portuguese and Spanish.

Television transmissions, however, because of the different characteristics of the frequency range within which they are broadcast, rely upon virtual line-of-sight coverage. Once over the horizon they pass undeflected through the ionosphere and into space, so it was not until 1962, with the launch of the Telstar satellite, that even the first broadcaster-to-broadcaster signals were sent across the Atlantic. This early satellite technology enabled the sending and receiving of programme material over long distances, but not the direct-to-home (DTH) transmission over distant frontiers that could enable governments to target whole populations way beyond their own frontiers, afforded by radio. Home satellite reception began in the late 1980s, as enthusiasts bought expensive equipment designed to intercept signals intended for distribution to cable network headends. A big enough dish in the footprint of a geostationary satellite can pick up signals and relay them to receiving and decoding equipment, no matter for whom they are intended. Unlike short-wave radio in the early twentieth century, the development of satellite television was commercially driven, so in the true DTH market which developed in the 1990s, among the first channels to win small but appreciative audiences were the Discovery Channel, MTV with its first continentally-branded variants for Europe (1987) and Asia (1991), and CNN, the burgeoning American cable news channel based in Atlanta, Georgia.

Partly because of the much greater cost of television production, and partly because even the cultural imperialism of the early twentieth century had become widely unacceptable by its close, satellite television as an international manifestation of the nation state has been slow to develop. Enjoying its historical legacy from the days of the Empire, the BBC World Service, as the General Overseas Service (formerly the Empire Service) was renamed in 1965, continues to be funded by the British Government through a direct grant from the Foreign and Commonwealth Office (FCO) that amounted to £225 million in 2004–05. Neither the Thatcher nor Major governments of the early 1990s were politically inclined to invest public money in developing a parallel operation on television. So BBC World Service Television (now BBC World) was launched in 1991 and it forms part of the Corporation's commercial entity BBC Worldwide. Although broadcast free-to-air, like the subscription-based international entertainment channels BBC Prime, BBC America and BBC Canada, it must earn its own income from such sources as advertising, sponsorship and carriage rights from cable distributors.

While satellite television lacks the global equivalent of Swiss Radio International, Radio Nederland or Radio Australia, notable exceptions include the Voice of America television (named Worldnet until 2004) and Deutsche Welle TV, each offering a 24-hour service of news and information programming in a range of different languages. Other countries broadcast internationally, but limit themselves to their native languages, as in the case of the Spanish TVE Internacional, the Dutch BVN (Beste van Nederland) and the Francophone channel TV5, run jointly by France, Canada, Switzerland and Belgium since 1984. Far removed from the revolutionary zeal of the Russian revolutionaries of 1917, the imperialism of the British in the late 1920s or the aggression of Hitler's Germany, television's late development as an internationally broadcast medium has cast it in the role of commercial venture, rather than state instrument.

McLuhan's second observation about radio's role in creating the 'global village' was that it has been a far from homogenizing influence (2001: 334). Only in territories where political oppression has created an appetite for 'free' news and information from the 'outside world', have international radio broadcasters such as the BBC World Service won sizeable audiences other than among diasporic audiences of business travellers and expatriates seeking a link with home. Estimates of the World Service's global weekly audience in 2004 suggested 146 million (BBC, 2004b), but in most territories such numbers are inevitably spread very thinly. As the medium has developed, a progressively widening range of alternatives and the attractiveness of music and entertainment services have conspired against the mainly speech-based international stations. Radio's greatest strength may be its ability to cheaply redefine itself according to the tastes and needs of national, regional and local communities, often attracting the largest audiences when at its most relevant and apparently personal (Crisell, 1994: 13). In terms of content, shared experience, language and presentation style, local radio can exploit particularly advantageous synergies with the lives of individual listeners.

Until the development of Digital Radio Mondiale (DRM) in the mid-2000s the sound quality of short-wave transmissions was very poor, even in comparison with those on long and medium wave, which travel much shorter distances. This matters less in the case of speech radio, but notwithstanding the popularity of the late John Peel on the BBC, only the most poorly resourced of people would choose to listen for long periods to music broadcast via an analogue short-wave signal from across the world. Because the ionosphere quite literally rises and falls in line with the rotation of the earth, the 'bounce' of signals reflected by it lengthens and shortens around the clock. Listening for continuous periods requires retuning regularly to different frequencies in different parts of the band, as in turn particular transmissions on them become audible and then inaudible. Even as DRM becomes more widely exploited for international broadcasting, and the relatively expensive receivers fall in price, coverage will be subject to continuous change. Agreements reached with governments and broadcasters have allowed the BBC to reach some distant audiences via local relays, even using the technically superior transmissions on FM. In some cases, such as Singapore, these are on dedicated frequencies, and in others these are carriage agreements under which stations rebroadcast BBC content, including news bulletins, within their own scheduled programming. Otherwise, short-wave listening has in most territories long been confined to enthusiasts, many of them more interested in discovering transmissions that are new to them, rather than actually seeking to listen to the content.

DTH satellite television, with its potential for cross-frontier broadcasting, quickly developed into a fiercely competitive market, and the proliferation of a vast range of channels even in such relatively underdeveloped regions as the Middle East and South East Asia means few will ever reach the mass audiences traditionally achieved by domestic terrestrial channels. Even as the European Union (EU) has grown, pan-European broadcasting has failed to win large audiences, largely because of linguistic and cultural differences, as demonstrated by the 1998 transformation of NBC Europe from a channel of repackaged American NBC talk show and documentary programming aimed at Anglophones across the continent, into a German cable station majoring on 'youth' programming themed mainly around computer games. Both Eurosport and EuroNews use common pictures but simulcast different language soundtracks, so the services are customizable within individual markets, but they both suffer from the absence of any onscreen presentation this entails. The EU's channel Europe by Satellite is merely a service of 'feeds' to traditional broadcasters.

So, despite the economies of scale and the relative logistical simplicity of broadcasting to whole continents with a single radio transmission or satellite footprint, some of the most effective examples of international broadcasting have been those which have targeted specific communities from across borders in order to further particular political ambitions. This specificity may be far more expensive on a *per capita* basis, but in times of military action or diplomatic impasse they can seem like money well spent. The propaganda broadcast in Europe by both sides in the Second World War was greeted with differing degrees of enthusiasm and scepticism, depending on the context. De Gaulle gave hope and purpose to French civilians and resistance fighters alike, while the credibility gap was so great between Lord Haw Haw's claims of German advances and the confident denials of that other consummate orator and broadcaster, Winston Churchill (1874–1965), that Joyce was greeted in Britain with widespread derision (see Chapter 2).

With the post-war drawing of an 'iron curtain' across Europe, the armed standoff that was to characterize east–west relations through the cold war that lasted until the early 1990s severely ratcheted up the intensity of cross-border propaganda being broadcast (Critchlow, 1999). From Russia, the political centre of the Soviet bloc of totalitarian communist republics, both Radio Moscow and Radio Peace and Progress 'broadcasting the voice of Soviet public opinion' together targeted the Western democracies with overt propaganda. From a weekly total of 284 hours in 33 languages in 1946, by 1950 their combined output had risen to 533 hours a week in 38 languages. The Eastern European states controlled by Russia had their own propaganda stations, Radio Prague among them, whose weekly output more than trebled to 412 hours by 1950 (Bumpus and Skelt, 1986: 43). Whereas the end of the war had destabilized the Voice of America – considered by some to have outlived its initial wartime remit – the growth of Soviet external broadcasting secured it: in January 1948 President Harry S. Truman (1884–1972) signed the 'Smith-Mundt Act', resurrecting America's overseas propaganda effort and guaranteeing funding for the rapid expansion of VOA infrastructure in Europe.

Further American involvement in the developing propaganda war in Europe was initiated by the CIA, although such is the nature of the organization that the connection was first publicly revealed by the *New York Times* in 1967 (Cone, 1998: 148–46). They recruited political refugees as announcers on a number of parallel foreign language services branded as Radio Free Europe (RFE), opened on 4 July 1950 for Eastern Europe, and Radio Liberation launched for Russia on 1 March 1953, before being renamed Radio Liberty in 1959 (Mickelson, 1983). Powerful transmitters in West Germany beamed dedicated RFE services into Czechoslovakia, Romania, Hungary, Poland and Bulgaria. As listening to these stations was outlawed in the communist bloc, reliable estimates of their audience reach are difficult to obtain, but the 1956 Hungarian uprising, brutally suppressed by the Soviet authorities with the loss of between 10,000 and 20,000 lives, may have been attributable in part to the influence of Radio Free Europe. Certainly, their broadcasting of uncensored news and comment from Western perspectives was not appreciated by the Soviet authorities, who interpreted it as anti-communist propaganda, and they committed considerable resources to jamming the signals using their own transmitters to broadcast noise on the same frequencies, in an attempt to make the programmes if not always inaudible, certainly unpleasant to listen to.

America's determination to communicate Western ideology to the eastern bloc was similarly demonstrated in 1951 by its dropping of 11 million leaflets on the Czechs from war-surplus hydrogen-filled weather balloons carried across the iron curtain by westerly winds. Radio's ability to penetrate the eastern bloc was not only more reliable than the wind, but also more effective. The iconic leader of Polish resistance, Gdansk shipbuilder and later President of the newly liberated Republic of Poland from 1990–5, Lech Walesa (1943–) wrote that 'without Western broadcasting, totalitarian regimes would have survived much longer', for they encouraged independent thought where it was forcefully banned (Nelson, 1997: xi).

There are many other examples of targeted cross-border broadcasting for political purposes, including the Farsi service of the VOA, beamed into Iran both before and after the overthrow of the Shah in the Islamic fundamentalist revolution of 1979. Radio Liberation added such other languages as Armenian, Chechen and Azerbaijani to address new audiences on the southern and eastern fringes of the Soviet empire. The thrice-weekly programmes of communist North Vietnamese Trinh Thi Ngo (1931–) or 'Hanoi Hannah' were broadcast by Radio Hanoi to American GIs supporting the South Vietnamese against the Viet Cong during US involvement in the Vietnam War from 1964–73. Ngo's broadcasts consisted of reports of unfavourable comment from around the world on America's involvement, detailed lists of Americans killed in action and their bereaved families, reports of anti-war protests in the USA and elsewhere, together with speeches, poems and songs by prisoners of war (POWs), deserters and antiwar activists. Initially the music was Vietnamese, but it changed to American chart hits in order to increase its appeal.

More recently, the USA targeted communist Cuba, controlled since 1959 by Fidel Castro (1927–), with Radio Martí. Broadcast from Florida since 1984, by the US Office of Cuba Broadcasting, the Spanish-language programmes consist of music and news, but given widespread suspicions about the organization's links to the CIA, Castro supporters feel justified in reading them as propaganda, aimed at destabilizing the regime. While the medium-wave radio signal crosses the Straits of Ronda, the corresponding TV Martí, again because of the technical characteristics of television transmissions, is broadcast from either aeroplanes flying off the Cuban coast or an air balloon 10,000 feet above the Florida Keys. The Havana government attempts to prevent both services being received on the island, systematically jamming them with as much zeal as the Soviets had done before them.

Jamming may seem unfair to those who profess to believe in democracy and freedom of expression, but there are similarities with the closing down of satellite relays, as in the case of the Lebanese television channel, Al Manar (see Chapter 2). On acquiring Star Television in 1993, Rupert Murdoch closed down its relay of the BBC, in order to appease Chinese sensitivities over the Corporation's criticism of their record on human rights (MacGregor, 1997: 146). The USA jammed Hanoi Hannah and Britain used a 10,000-watt transmitter at Rochester in Kent to jam Radio Northsea International in a virtual game of cat and mouse from 15 April 1970 (see Chapter 2). RNI changed frequency several times to avoid the jamming, which followed it up or down the medium-wave band until the month after the general election, when the radio ship set sail for the Dutch coast. The most recent attempts to circumvent jamming by Cuba of TV and Radio Martí include simulcasting by satellite because the high directionality of the receiving dish makes blanket jamming of satellite transmission difficult and ordinarily authoritarian regimes wishing to prevent access by their citizens to channels they deem to be undesirable would have to resort to the unpopular step of banning dishes altogether. While the VOA achieves almost worldwide television coverage via eight different geostationary satellites, getting signals into Iran is a particular concern for the US government's International Broadcasting Bureau. Ironically, despite Iran introducing a loosely-enforced ban on privately-owned dishes in 1995, the US suspected them of finding a pragmatic but less unpopular solution to the problem in 2003: getting Cuba to use its sophisticated jamming technology to interfere with the VOA uplink to the Telstar 12 satellite (Carter, 2003).

Globalization and resistance

Despite McLuhan's reassurances about the 'global village' not being a homogenizing influence on societies (2001: 334), more alarming culturally apocalyptic predictions have tended to characterize more recent theorizing of the mass media, not least because the world has changed significantly since 1964 (McQuail, 2005: 254–6). Many commentators have detected in constraining influences on public service provision in broadcasting, to the advantage of a burgeoning commercial sector, synergies with the increasingly international ownership of newspaper and magazine titles discussed in Chapter 3. Typically, fears of globalization focus on the growing influence of multinational conglomerates based in a small number of capitalist Western democracies where power is becoming concentrated in the hands of a few key players. Cartels dedicated to the furtherance of their own interests operate in a number of political and economic spheres and the USA is most frequently cited as the main beneficiary of the process, consolidating its position as the world's largest economy, to the detriment of sociological and cultural hetero-geneity wherever in the world it remains. A hard core of anti-globalization activists often steal headlines from more moderate protestors by clashing violently with those they regard as their opponents, in a wider battle of ideologies that seems unlikely to be resolved in the near future.

Paradoxically, alternative perspectives on globalization accommodate some more positive assessments of developments in the mass media (McQuail, 2005: 256–8). Some societies are inherently more resistant to change, because their local cultures are for practical or linguistic reasons more impervious to cultural osmosis than others (Street, 2001: 176). Although American music, values and programming principles have been widely exported through radio, the medium has a long history as a resistive and even democratizing force for communities as diverse as Hutus in Rwanda, the Kurds repressed by Saddam Hussein and tin miners in Bolivia (Hendy, 2000: 194–205). Some key initiatives among Latin American people use community radio to promote economic development by promoting local identity and facilitating communication centred on common goals (Chaparro Escudero, 2002: 89–93). Local radio reinforces local identity and language in some of the poorest parts of Africa (Ba, 2003: 124–5). Some territories, including Cuba and Iran, erect physical barriers against what they perceive to be imperialist influences, even, as in the case of North Korea, reducing their citizens' experience of the outside world to a bare minimum, and preventing all but very rare access to them by foreigners. Yet, among the most interest-ing are those societies whose resistance to globalization fits an adaptive model, which actually draws inspiration from some globalizing influences and uses it to reinforce their own distinctiveness. This is exemplified by the experience of CNN: an American news channel using satellite transmission and, in many locations, further cable relays to reach as global an audience as politically-motivated physical barriers and, of course, such financial constraints as third-world poverty, will allow.

From its beginnings as a single cable television news channel in 1980, CNN has evolved into the CNN News Group, with a dozen or so brands also using radio and the Internet, from CNNStudentNews.com to CNN Airport Network, CNN Money and CNN en Español. CNN International is produced in London and Hong Kong, but it also features such programmes produced at its world headquarters in Atlanta as *Larry King Live*. As part of McChesney's 'Holy Trinity' of the global media system (2000: 91–100) – Time Warner, Disney and News Corporation – CNN is situated within Time Warner's multi-million dollar portfolio of film, publishing, cable systems, television networks and interactive services. Imbued with American values and perspectives, Fox News and MSNBC followed (on 7 and 15 July 1996 respectively), but with its wider distribution and greater brand recognition, CNN International would appear to be a prime suspect among the world's globalizing influences, and well placed to influence access to information in the territories where it can be viewed. The CNN brand first came to widespread attention on the first day of the 1991 Gulf War, when around the world domestic newsrooms relayed CNN's Peter Arnett commenting from his Baghdad hotel room on the first shots to be fired in the conflict, in the absence of their own correspondents from the Iraqi capital (MacGregor, 1997: 12).

However, despite the spread of satellite dishes and increasing cable penetration, by 2005 the channel's daily reach among international air travellers surveyed in 25 major airports was a mere 12 per cent (EDR, 2005). The relatively cosmopolitan nature of the sample polled might suggest that the channels' reach must be far lower among more general populations, particularly in those countries where the cost of international air travel is prohibitive. The international business community is clearly an attractive audience for CNN to sell on to its advertisers, but the globalizing potential of the operation in its current forms appears very limited. Most viewers, particularly those in lower socio-economic groups, encounter television news within the mixed diets of more general channels, rather than on dedicated services (BARB, 2005), so while national services retain their editorial independence their resistive potential against globalization is high.

The impact of CNN has been further diminished by adaptive behaviour elsewhere in the world. Using many of the conventions of style and content of the developing genre, and each bringing their own distinctiveness to the mix, its imitators include Fox News and MSNBC but also Canal 24 Horas run by the Spanish state broadcaster TVE, the Italian RAINEWS24, BBC News 24, BBC World and most notably Al-Jazeera. Of the non-Anglophone channels listed here, only Al-Jazeera has achieved a high international profile, aimed as it is at the Arab world and capable of adopting particular editorial stances that are robustly independent of Western capitalist opinion. Its direct international competitors, Arabic News Network (ANN) and the full-service channel Middle East Broadcasting Centre (MBC), began operations in London, circumventing the censorship of certain of the Arab states, but somewhat incongruously being subject to British broadcasting regulation (see Chapter 2). A curious feature of MBC's commercial breaks was the statutory inclusion of regular spot advertising encouraging viewers to write to the Independent Television Commission in London with any complaints about taste and decency, matters of fair treatment and so on. A particular feature of ANN's editorial policy has been to avoid criticism of the absolute monarchy (Miles, 2005: 27) which has ruled Saudi Arabia since its formation in 1932, and which is widely considered sympathetic, although very different in character, to the Western democracies and the United States in particular.

Based in Qatar, with more than 30 bureaux in the Middle East and elsewhere, Al-Jazeera proclaims on its website to be 'free from the shackles of censorship and government control'. It was launched in November 1996 with a start up grant from the emir of Qatar, but its failure to breakeven through advertising and content sales in subsequent years led to its continuing dependence on the emir for support. On 15 July 2004 the channel launched its own code of ethics, espousing very similar values to those discussed in Chapter 3 – including 'balance, independence, credibility and diversity' – and promising to 'present diverse points of view and opinions without bias or partiality' (Al-Jazeera, 2004). It began the English-language website in 2001, planning to launch Al-Jazeera International in 2006.

Not only does Al-Jazeera reflect particular Arab values and perspectives, but its ability to scoop Western news media with such 'exclusives' as video and audio recordings from the most hunted fugitives from the US military has led to bitter accusations of partisanship. Conversely, the direct hit on Al-Jazeera's Baghdad office on 8 April 2003 as American forces entered the Iraqi capital was seen by many commentators as revenge for hostile coverage of the war, and the showing of footage of American casualties and captured service personnel. The channel's Iraq office was closed down by the Iraqi interim government in August 2004 for presenting a 'negative image' of Iraq, and in 2003 two of its reporters were banned from the New York Stock Exchange for 'security reasons'. Nevertheless, criticism has not all been from the same direction: many Muslim viewers complained about the channel's inclination to interview Israeli officials: a reaction very easily construed as reception bias, if their reaction means they consider Israeli perspectives on conflict in the Middle East to be unworthy of inclusion. More positively, as well as promoting divisions between the Arab world and the west, Al-Jazeera might also have become a democratizing influence in the Middle-East. The Lebanese politician, Walid Jumblatt, commented on 3 March 2005 that the first free elections in Iraq since the 1950s, seen around the Arab world on the channel, might have given some impetus to those seeking democratic change in some of those territories. Mass public protest in Lebanon, just a month later, was an unexpected manifestation of a growing desire for the country to resist Syrian occupation and instead control its own destiny.

However, the most effective wielding of influence over television news across international frontiers is that which uses the newspaper model discussed in Chapter 3. Just as News Corporation owns or has interests in apparently domestic titles in a number of territories, the development of apparently national brands, such as Sky News in the UK and Ireland, allows multinationals deeper penetration of national markets. Because production occurs in London, with presentation largely by British journalists, Sky News is widely perceived in the UK as British, with most viewers being only rarely compelled to confront the channel's foreign ownership, with its implications for influence and control. It is widely perceived as a British channel, as much a part of the domestic broadcasting landscape as the BBC and ITV, and not as a homogenizing, anti-democratic or malign influence any more than a purveyor of either American or Australian imperialism. The reasons for this are twofold: the UK is a highly-regulated broadcasting environment, and television and radio broadcasters either based or uplinked to satellite from within its boundaries are subject to content regulation (see Chapter 2). Sky is also a commercial operation and Rupert Murdoch an astute businessman in whom most inclinations to influence events in foreign countries are subordinate to the profit motive. While various explanations for his newspapers' switching their support to the Labour Party in 1997 accommodate backroom deals with the party leadership, the advantages of government feeling obligated to friends in the press and mounting exasperation with the equivocation of the Conservatives under John Major, most credible is the desire not to be out of kilter with a dramatic swing to Labour among his readership.

Others have adopted this model, among them CNN News Group, with its German channel n-tv. Linguistic differences aside, its success lies in its ability to better adapt output to satisfy local taste and news values, in the same way that in January 2002 Fox News overtook the domestic version of CNN in its share of the US market. CNN's difficulty in retaining its appeal at home, while establishing and maintaining broadly common editorial standards across a number of interrelated brands, is that perceptions of its output abroad are different to those in the domestic market. Elsewhere CNN's concept of impartial journalism is often perceived as pro-American, but compared to Fox it may not seem pro-American enough (Sabbagh, 2005). Al-Jazeera's motive, in launching its own English-language international service, was inevitably to counter any influence of CNN among Anglophones. The world and its peoples may – in the near future, at least – be simply too heterogeneous to succumb completely to globalization.

Imperialism and the media

What, then, are the implications of mediated imperialism – and resistance to it – for our discussion of balance and bias? The essence of imperialism lays in a belief that one's own country, society, economic system or religion is at least in some way superior to those that are indigenous to other parts of the world. The motivation behind wanting to extend its influence may be either offensive or defensive, but it is keenly felt and the various initiatives in international broadcasting discussed earlier in this chapter are frequently accompanied by other more and less subtle activities that share common goals. However unattractive colonial powers may have seemed to conquered peoples in previous centuries, even in educated societies the benefits to others of 'civilizing' less well-developed countries, their infrastructure, legal systems, attitudes, beliefs and living conditions, were rarely disputed. Just as such resistive acts as the American War of Independence (1775–83) and the transformation of the British Empire into a mutually supportive yet relatively democratic collective known as the Commonwealth in 1931 were symptomatic of changing attitudes, relatively few people in the Western democracies today still harbour strongly felt notions of superiority of race, religion or culture. Today imperialism is mainly driven by commerce. It is not so much Western governments that are implicated in the most destructive of practices in the African continent, but multinational companies.

However much 'impartiality' might be an ambition of CNN International, and no matter how much the state-owned international broadcasters might attempt to construct a more 'balanced' worldview for consumption overseas, the essential dichotomy here is that on many issues there is rarely a 'common-sense' perspective around which large percentages of the global population may unite (see Chapter 1). Whether intentional or not, because of global heterogeneity, somewhere in the world the editorial positioning they may consider to be an 'impartial' stance is likely to be perceived as biased. The notion that there could be a single 'common sense' worldview on everything is plainly a nonsense, however much we might hope for others to share our own values and understandings of humanity, and there are few signs that diverse perspectives are converging very much, even through the spread of literacy, the gradual raising of living standards in the Third World, sudden economic growth in China and the influence of the United Nations and non-governmental organizations (NGOs) in underdeveloped regions. Symptomatic of this is the refusal of the USA, alone among the world's great-est polluters, to sign up to the 1997 Kyoto Protocol on preventing climate change, despite compelling evidence to suggest considerable merit in its strictures on the production of greenhouse gases.

Instead, there is a cacophony of competing perspectives, some more widely shared than others. These may be at their most diverse, in the post-9/11 world, over such issues as the 'war on terror', religious fundamentalism and the right of countries to intervene militarily in others in the absence of specific acts of provocation, even though such international conflicts as those over the disputed territories of the Middle East, the six counties in the north of Ireland that the Protestant community calls Ulster, and Kashmir among many others, have been sources of tension for decades rather than years. These different perspectives are reflected in different ways in the discourse presented by different media texts, and assessments of balance and bias in both production and reception will naturally be affected by them. In today's language, reporting of the American War of Independence might from the British side have characterized George Washington (1732–99) as a terrorist, but Americans of the day would have been more likely to acclaim their commander in chief, the man who was to become the first president of the newly-independent USA, a freedom fighter. Equally, the British could have termed their ill-fated attempts to resist the colonial uprising he led as a 'war on terror', so disruptive were such incidents as the 1773 Boston Tea Party which preceded the outbreak of armed conflict.

The articulation of media discourse by those who would be perceived as impartial by a worldwide audience is particularly problematic. Just as a victory in an armed conflict will be widely welcomed at home, portraying it as such internationally is to invite criticisms of bias from the losers. Reporting of the 1982 Falklands (Malvinas) War by the BBC World Service had to recognize that part of the target audience was in Latin America, yet even the Corporation's domestic services were subject to often vehement criticism in the UK that they were 'unacceptably even-handed' (MacGregor, 1997: 134). Informed commentators still represent the World Service in such terms as playing 'a vital role globally as a source of impartial international news' (Born, 2004: 9), but such issues as war, famine and atrocity polarize world opinion to such an extent that 'balance' is virtually impossible. Just as small victories in the American War of Independence, Vietnam, the Falklands (Malvinas) will have been acclaimed by various sides as great triumphs over dangerous evils, and derided by others as murderous acts against humanity, so other events mean different things to different constituencies within the worldwide audience. While the 9/11 attacks on the New York World Trade Center were widely perceived in the Western democracies as an unwarranted slaughter of innocents and Yasser Arafat was moved to publicly donate blood as a sign of solidarity with surviving victims, in some Arab streets they were a cause for celebration. The Chechen rebels who took 1000 schoolchildren hostage in the town of Beslan on 3 September 2004, with the subsequent loss of more than 300 lives, apparently also felt that what the USA has elsewhere termed 'collateral damage' among civilian populations is justified, in their wider struggle against Russian domination of their homeland. Similarly, to the sick and starving of several regions of the world, including but not restricted to the highly-profiled continent of Africa, most of the material concerns of the Western democracies probably appear either irrelevant or obscene.

Despite the inevitability of conflicting perspectives, seeking complete impartiality over such contentious issues is simply not on the agenda of most international broadcasters or publishers. Describing the 9/11 victims or those killed and injured in the London suicide bombings of 7 July 2005 as 'combatants' in a wider struggle or mere 'collateral damage' would have devastating consequences for both the BBC and CNN alike, in terms of public reaction in the west, even if done to 'balance' mainstream perspectives on them at home with the opinions of those who would construe them as acts of resistance against modern-day crusaders, globalizing forces or decadent blasphemers against religious fundamentalism. The discourse of international current affairs, while recognizing need in the Third World, is unlikely to completely postpone discussion of economic activity, technological advance, sport or leisure activities until such time as all poverty has been eradicated and as matters of interest or controversy they cease to be irrelevant to large numbers of people on the margins of existence.

So, notwithstanding their best intentions, the international media are not impartial. They may broaden their terms of reference to accommodate alternative perspectives, but at least *in extremis* they are infused with the values and perspectives of their hosts and paymasters, and the discourse they present routinely reflects this. The FCO grant that sustains the BBC World Service, the advertising on CNN, BBC World and others, the Qatari emir's support for Al-Jazeera and the necessity for a service to be based somewhere, all conspire against the notion of independence from outside influence – sometimes in their audiences' perceptions, sometimes in practice and often in both.

Partisanship and public interest

At times, though, partisanship can be highly desirable, and just as in the specific circumstances explored in the introduction to this book, there is sometimes a compelling case for bias based on national interest. The influence of domestic and foreign proprietors can be fiercely anti-democratic (see Chapter 3), skewing for instance the debate in the UK over greater integration within the EU, as most of the country's national newspapers vie to be the most eurosceptic. At others, though, it is 'balance' that can be the more dangerous, to the extent that it can seriously challenge the notions of 'ethical' journalism that normally underpin it. For sometimes national interest lies in bias, as might in some territories the interests of semi-autonomous regions within nation states.

While Fox News was criticized by left-wing commentators for its unquestioning – even jingoistic – support of the USA in its 2003 war on Iraq, the BBC broadcast many hours of unfavourable comment and conjecture about Britain's involvement from a range of different people, including two high-profile members of the Cabinet who resigned over the issue, Robin Cook and Clare Short. In this case, broadcasting dissent, just as the *Daily Mirror*, *The Guardian* and *The Independent* editorialized vehemently against the UK's involvement in the conflict, was politically challenging but it had only a limited effect on the government's morale, the conduct of the war and the willingness of the armed forces to follow orders. The BBC's lack of restraint over Iraq contrasts sharply with its coverage of the Falklands War, a subsequent *Panorama* (BBC1) having unearthed evidence of its excluding critical perspectives because they were not in 'the national interest'. Interviews with bereaved relatives of service personnel were not broadcast, and critical phone-in callers wanting to say the war was not justified were not put on air (Born, 2004: 383–4).

Imagine, though, the possible effect of covering dissent in a more equal conflict, such as the Second World War: if in 1939–45 the BBC and the press had 'balanced' their coverage, presenting the decision to resist Hitler as a simple 50–50 choice in the manner of the more recent media debate about MMR (see page xix), the effect on morale might have been devastating, as the population struggled through six years – possibly more – of deprivation, fear and loss of life. The wartime slogan, 'Careless talk costs lives' might have been proven correct, if ignored by journalists bent on critical discussion of tactics and motives, logistical difficulties and the likely effects of such events as the bombing of the German city of Dresden in February 1945. If Britain's war effort had not benefited from a focused national response to German aggression the UK may not have been saved from invasion by the Nazis and so the media would have influenced events for the worse. In the event, the BBC's national and international services, like ABC in Australia, were far more patriotic. The morality of war as an issue was contextualized by the certainties of a strongly-held belief in self-defence – a belief the author noted as common among service padres in the British armed forces in the aftermath of the Falklands War – and so the thousands of victims of the British bombing of Dresden were not discussed, the morality of the first use of an atomic bomb by the Americans at Hiroshima on 6 August 1945 was hardly considered and even news about earlier devastating military reverses was suppressed in the interests of the war effort (Crook, 1998: 209–17).

If in 1940s wartime Britain all but a few voices at the margins were overwhelmingly patriotic, was latter-day dissent over Iraq a form of treachery? For broadcasting his anti-British propaganda, William Joyce ('Lord Haw Haw') was hanged for treason (see Chapter 2), paying the ultimate price for his partisanship. Would an inquisitive reporter, a combative interviewer or a crusading editor have suffered the same fate, if not immediately silenced by government or popular reaction? To what extent should journalists be ethically troubled by the impact their reporting or non-reporting might have on their home nation's war effort, and where does this leave any obligations towards diverse audiences spread over whole continents? The answers to these questions may lie in international law (although it is inevitably vulnerable to conflicting interpretations), and more specifically the way following the Second World War the victors subjugated the vanquished to trial for war crimes at Nuremberg between November 1945 and October 1946, and later as several of those who had initially evaded capture were tracked down and brought before other *ad hoc* courts. In trying a range of top Nazis and prison officials for their roles in the conflict, 'just following orders' was not accepted as a defence from prosecution for crimes against humanity. Playing a role in a propaganda machine, that is, being complicit in the perpetration of a great evil irrespective of its impact on humanity, then, certainly lacks the principled clarity of dissent, should circumstances demand it.

Often, though, moral dilemmas lack the certainties inherent in Hollywood-style struggles between obvious good and great evil. The other side of the wartime censorship coin discussed by Crook was the BBC's deliberate under-reporting of the holocaust and the atrocities Hitler was perpetrating against the Jews who fell under his control (1998: 192–208). Whether due to anti-Semitism in the British establishment, or a desire to avoid alienating German or Arab listeners to the BBC's overseas services, this was a glaring omission. Perhaps even Joyce would have been appalled by the Nazi concentration camps, had he visited them, as were many of the German people when the slaughter of six million Jews became apparent as the war ended.

When newspaper proprietors intervene in democratic processes in order to resist European integration, and to defend the pound sterling in the face of moves to adopt the euro, they may feel the stakes are high and be driven through passionate belief that they are in some way saving the country and its sovereignty from being overrun by foreigners. Others may consider their concerns relatively minor or even suspect that their motives are more subtle.

Consensus around the point at which a government policy turns from merely unwise or wrong to bad or even evil will inevitably be hard to achieve, opinion in peacetime rarely becoming as polarized as in wartime.

Inevitably, perspectives are affected by ideology – and among worldwide audiences, ideology varies dramatically. The set of beliefs, values and attitudes inherent in the apparent logic of Western capitalism, tempered as it is by various shades of religious belief from Christianity to the widespread agnosticism of the self-proclaimed intelligentsia, is constantly being updated and renegotiated in response to events and changing attitudes. However, as the world seems an ever-smaller place, through advances in communication technology and transport infrastructure, competing ideologies range in their ability to co-exist with Western capitalism from the grudging acceptance of socialism and neo-communism to the uncompromising jihadism of extreme Islamic fundamentalism. Embracing the world of different perspectives and expectations this entails would make 'impartiality' even more difficult to achieve. It is difficult to conceive of a viable editorial policy that would balance the defence of the nation against the interests of those whose ambition is to destroy it. Even condemning all violent action, by whomsoever, would be interpreted by some as a dangerous appeasement of evil.

So international broadcasters and the owners of newspapers published in countries that are foreign to them will inevitably best accommodate ideologies which resonate the most with their own beliefs and interests. The Voice of America will not call the 9/11 victims 'combatants' and the BBC will not label the London bomb victims 'collateral damage'. Rupert Murdoch's newspaper interests in the UK will maintain their fervent resistance to the euro, even though the relevance of the pound sterling to a naturalized American of Australian origin is hard to surmise. Their output will be construed by many to be as colonial in nature and intent as the early broadcasts of the BBC's Empire service, and by some as malign in purpose as Radios Martí, Free Europe, Northsea International and others were perceived by those governments that sought to jam them. For it is the very heterogeneity of international audiences that makes a global 'balance' – even if 'balance' were achievable in practice – not only impossible but except in the most fanciful of aspirations, also ultimately undesirable.

CHAPTER 7

Case Studies:
Balance and Bias in Practice

So far we have considered a range of different factors implicated in the media-tion of 'reality' into a representation that is broadcast or published to individ-uals within audiences. They range from the readily quantifiable – such as duration and frequency of appearance – to such easily controvertible issues as selection, emphasis, perspective and paralinguistics. Underlying them are moti-vational issues around ownership and regulation, as well as the relationship between production bias and reception bias. Whatever the wider contexts, it is in broadcast and published texts that production bias can be observed, yet specific examples have necessarily been used only sparingly to illustrate broad principles. The textual analyses in this chapter use quantitative and qualitative data from the public domain to examine a number of 'tangibles' within media representations of controversial issues from the mass media. The very nature of exemplar material means that some of the following approaches may be appropriate for use in other contexts, for further research and subsequent debate. They will not, however, be exhaustive, and readers may want to develop and adapt other methodologies for their own purposes.

Mainstream current affairs television:
Breakfast with Frost

The BBC ran almost all of the 500 editions of *Breakfast with Frost* on its main full service channel BBC1 on Sundays, from January 1993 to May 2005, before its replacement with *Sunday AM* which, despite the change of presenter, a faster pace and a smarter 'look', dispensed with few of its prede-cessor's practices. The transmission time of *Breakfast with Frost* was subject to occasional change, particularly in the event of important sporting occa-sions that the channel wished to cover, such as the London Marathon, but most of the programmes in its final season began at 09:30. Occasional relief presenters, such as Peter Sissons, would be drafted in to cover any absences of the eponymous presenter David Frost, but the programme traded largely

on his centrality within it and his ability to attract world-class interviewees
from presidents and royalty to international sporting champions, in addition
to the more routine players in UK politics. Although occasional pre-records
and more often live links were used, most contributors joined Frost live on
set, which encouraged a semblance of informality with its coffee table, comfy
chairs and sofa. Guests walked on off-camera, during news bulletins, weather
forecasts or brief videotaped (VT) inserts, and only very occasionally was
there any studio audience or relocation of the programme as an outside
broadcast.

Frost's 'fireside chat' approach was sometimes compared unfavourably
with the argumentative style exemplified by Jeremy Paxman on *Newsnight*
and John Humphrys on *Today*. However, the programme often scooped the
other Sunday political programmes, regularly being quoted in subsequent
television and radio news bulletins, and the following day's newspapers. It
may have been Frost's friendly but professional cordiality that helped secure
the high profile guests, as much as his 1960s role in *That Was the Week That
Was* (see Chapter 5) or his long and distinguished career as a television
presenter in both the UK and the USA. Crucially for the BBC, in a timeslot
when the commercial channels were running imported or repeated children's
or youth programming, Frost could deliver audiences of up to three million
(BBC, 2005b). This was a programme that could provide sustained popular
coverage of current affairs without being marginalized, as is the case of the
Daily Politics at lunchtimes on the second channel BBC2 and *This Week* late
on Thursday nights on BBC1. However disarming, neither the focus on
personality, nor the feigned informality should detract from the programme's
importance as a representation of current affairs and events on the world
stage and in the narrower context of the UK.

Following the opening welcomes, previews and a news bulletin, most
programmes began with a review of the Sunday newspapers, with two or
three guest reviewers commenting on press items of their own choosing.
Typically these were authors, journalists and editors, but also television
presenters, spokespersons for pressure groups, and such 'wild card' guests
as those the programme identified in the final season as 'the lyricist' Tim
Rice (24 October 2004), 'the social campaigner and actress' Vanessa
Redgrave (27 February 2005) and 'the millionaire entrepreneur and poet'
Felix Dennis (14 November 2004). Many reviewers were politicians: either
current or past representatives of their parties or such less publicly politi-
cally-active figures as 'the former Conservative Deputy Chairman and best
selling author' Michael Dobbs (23 January 2005). Frost's informality –
which can be read as inconsistency – naturally led to some past or present
political affiliations being undeclared. For example, 'the writer and broadcaster' Giles Brandreth who appeared twice in the season (19 September
2004 and 29 May 2005) had previously been Conservative MP for Chester
between 1992 and 1997. On other occasions Frost would declare affiliations, for example proclaiming Tim Rice to be a 'lyricist and one of the

Tory party's most famous supporters' (10 April 2005), and reminding viewers that Matthew Parris was 'a journalist and former Tory MP' (1 May 2005), even though when appearing separately to be interviewed on 10 October 2004 he was colourfully described only as having 'just returned from covering the Afghan elections'. Often Frost's tendency towards frivolity downplayed political affiliation, as if on a current affairs programme it could ever be a lower order consideration: for example 'David Mellor, broadcaster, former cabinet minister, classical music aficionado and Britain's answer to Errol Flynn' (20 March 2005).

Deciding here which reviewers had party affiliations that might be apparent to reasonably politically literate individuals within the *Breakfast with Frost* audience is of course problematic. The notoriety of Margaret Thatcher as prime minister between 1979 and 1990 probably assures recognition in most Britons of 'the writer and broadcaster' Carol Thatcher as her daughter and so indicates at least some past influences on her political perspectives. How many outside the constituency of Chester would necessarily relate Brandreth to the Conservative Party is inevitably unclear. A count of those in the final season – in which for the purposes of this analysis Brandreth, Rice and others in similar circumstances are included, while Thatcher junior and, giving them enormous benefit of the doubt, journalists and editors are not – reveals some striking results about the selection of reviewers provided with this important mainstream platform from which to promote their own perspectives.

Ten such Conservatives appeared in the slot, compared to only five from Labour and none from any of the other parties. The Member of Parliament (MP) Diane Abbott was included in Labour's total, even though Frost felt inclined to point out 'her opposition to the war [in Iraq]' and revelling in her credentials as one of the party's 'awkward squad', strongly resistant to control inside and outside the Commons by the party whips, she herself commented 'I'm a fierce critic of Tony Blair' (17 October 2004). Paradoxically Felix Dennis was not included above even though he confessed to 'speak as a Labour Party supporter', because mere support for a party was not a criterion for inclusion and few reviewers were as candid as he. Also excluded above was Amanda Platell 'journalist and former advisor to (former Conservative Party Leader) William Hague' but included was Trevor Phillips, 'Chair of the Commission for Racial Equality' who was also previously active in the Labour Party, representing it as a candidate for London Mayor in 2000 (both 6 February 2005). The inclusion of twice as many Conservatives as Labour representatives – in a way which over a whole season would be undetectable to all but the most assiduous of viewers, yet is a significant factor in the discourse presented by the programme – was disappointing, when the producers could have attempted to construct a more careful 'balance' between them and reflect other shades of party political opinion.

Casting Giles Brandreth and another former Conservative MP, Ann Widdecombe, as the two reviewers on the same programme (19 September 2004) can hardly have been an attempt to 'balance' a very broad range of political perspectives. There was little attempt to 'balance' the item with others in the programme, either, as the other contributors were the then Iraqi Foreign Minister, the then Ulster Unionist Party leader, David Trimble, the then Liberal Democrat leader Charles Kennedy and the former BBC Director General, Greg Dyke. The Dyke interview was one of his first after the Hutton Report (see Chapter 1), and he articulated at length his perspective on the controversy, adding that he didn't think there was 'an honourable peace to be made now' between him and the Labour government. Perhaps sensing an absence of 'balance', Frost commented that he would 'let Tony Blair answer next week'.

So, admitting that balance may not necessarily be achieved within a series of similar items, such as the press reviews, or within whole programmes, to what extent was a 'balance' of contributors achieved over the whole series of programmes? Counting appearances of interviewees who were then or had previously been representatives of political parties, over the whole final season there were 31 Conservatives and 30 for Labour: an almost exact balance between the two principal contenders for government in the 2005 general elections. The Liberal Democrats appeared on eight occasions and various other parties on a total of 12.

While the balance of actual appearances between Conservatives and Labour over the series might appear admirable, duration and placement were less even. Labour were twice as likely to feature in an extended final 'showpiece' item before the closing news headlines as the Conservatives, often trailed in advance during the programme as a major feature: Labour benefiting from 15 such placements to the Conservatives' seven. The New Year interviews with party leaders Tony Blair (9 January 2005) and Michael Howard (16 January 2005) were also of unequal durations: Blair's lasted nine minutes longer than Howard's. A second run of party leader interviews during the 2005 election campaign also featured Blair (1 May 2005) and Howard (24 April 2005). Using the categories identified in Chapter 5, of questions asked of the two, another disparity of treatment emerges. Frost was twice as likely to ask Howard a challenging question than Blair, asking him 22 such questions to Blair's 11, whereas he asked Blair seven entrapment questions – mainly over Iraq – and Howard none. Of course, the topics and approaches of the two interviews varied, as did the kinds of responses: it was over his party's policy towards immigration and asylum that Frost pressed Howard most challengingly. He was more likely to solicit Blair's opinion than he was to solicit Howard's – asking him six such questions to Howard's two – tending to more readily assume a Blair victory rather than a Conservative future, and in the process naturalize opinion poll predictions of such an outcome.

Televised panel debate: *Question Time*

Question Time began in 1979 and was hosted for its first ten seasons by Robin Day. Transmitted on BBC1 in various mid-evening timeslots typified by its scheduling in the 2004–05 season at 22:35, this peripatetic topical panel debate is one of the channel's few remaining regular concessions to the BBC's PSB commitment to mainstream peak-time current affairs programming. It has been presented since 1994 by David Dimbleby, following a brief period under the stewardship of Peter Sissons. Two of the most pertinent issues around 'balance' are the membership of the panel and the topics discussed. Unlike on *Breakfast with Frost*, the governing party is inevitably at a disadvantage in terms of representation: even if it had a seat at the table each week, it would be only one voice in four or five, so given the likelihood of questioning from the studio audience that is hostile to government policy, it simply could not achieve the share of voice that even a system of proportional representation would give it in parliament. However large the government majority in parliament, its voice is a minority one on *Question Time*. Winning elections among the wider electorate achieves for a political party no greater status on an individual programme in this series than is accorded to its main opposition, the third largest or even minority parties and other 'wild card' participants – such as actress Jane Fonda (9 June 2005), 'comedian and writer' David Baddiel (14 April 2005), 'human rights campaigner' Bianca Jagger (7 July 2005) and 'author and academic' Germaine Greer (9 December 2004) – each of which may be given equal opportunities by the presenter to 'have the floor'.

An analysis of the 31 editions of the programme in the 2004–05 season recorded in the UK venues reveals that only 26 featured front-bench members of the government or Labour politicians closely associated with most of the government's policies. Given that the single most discussed issue on the programmes was the 2003 decision to invade Iraq, it is surprising that on four occasions the Labour representative was either Clare Short (25 November 2004, 6 January 2005, 16 June 2005) or Robin Cook (21 April 05): the two highest-profile former members of the government to resign over the issue. Apparently unaware of any irony in his words, in previewing the week before the third Clare Short appearance, the experienced political journalist and commentator David Dimbleby even promised she would 'be there for Labour'. Similarly, that other prominent dissident Labour backbencher, Diane Abbott, appeared 'for' the party on 17 February 2005. Before five of the 31 programmes were recorded, then, the producer could easily have anticipated that on the subject of Iraq at least, there would be nobody on the panel who would convincingly articulate the government's perspective. Except in the four 'special editions', recorded in Miami (28 October 2005), Shanghai (10 March 2005), Paris (26 May 2005) and Johannesburg (7 July 2005), it was discussion of Iraq and various other aspects of government policy that dominated the programmes. There were only infrequent digressions on to, for example, the leadership of the Conservative Party. Yet, on such occasions as 25 November 2004 there was no pro-government voice on the panel to represent it. So, in discussing in that edition the issue of the proposed introduction of identity cards in the UK, all the panellists were against the policy.

In the same edition, Dimbleby asked the audience – regularly billed on-air as a politically representative cross-section of public opinion – to show their support or otherwise for the policy, and then proclaimed the result of their show of hands to be 80 per cent against. This was a surprising result, as was noted on the programme, because wider opinion polling had found *support* for ID cards nationally to be in the region of 80 per cent (MORI, 2004). Given the importance of the audience in such a programme (suggesting questions to be put to the panel, providing reactions and voicing opinions) occasional contradictory evidence such as this – that they are not necessarily as representative as is claimed – is also problematic for the programme in terms of the discourse articulated by it. It was the anti-Americanism of large numbers of the *Question Time* studio audience that provoked a public apology from the then Director-General Greg Dyke for the programme broadcast two days after 9/11 (Hodgson, 2001). Such opinions from the audience as one that 'everyone hated America' were met with an 'unprecedented' number of complaints about the programme from viewers, who clearly did not feel that their views were being properly represented by those who had gained access to the venue.

Discerning the positioning of prospective members of any audience is not an exact science, and only the most naïve of producers and panellists will expect all of them to be truthful in the selection process (Clark, 2000: 124). It seems highly likely that in addition to people with a party affiliation, there will be many single issue activists who will perceive gaining access to the programme by lying about their voting intentions as a reasonable means to an end. In a separate study, Ross found that participants in the BBC's *Election Call* phone-in programmes thought the politicians they interrogated would not influence them, but they hoped their own contributions might influence the votes of other 'ordinary people' in the audience (2004: 789). The disparity between opinion poll support for government policies and disproportionately disapproving *Question Time* audiences may well be accounted for by such phenomena.

Another reason might simply be that invitations to join the studio audience of such programmes as this attract uncharacteristically cynical or, read another way, unusually politically literate people, particularly given the greater effort required to attend a recording rather than merely switch on the television to watch its broadcast. As political commentators note falling levels of participation in elections and referenda in Western democracies (for example Bartle, Atkinson and Mortimore, 2002: 280–5), public interest in current affairs is now challenged by the unprecedented plethora of alternative programming offered in the multi-channel media environment. By contrast, when *Question Time* began, in the UK except in a small number of cabled areas viewers' television choice was restricted to three terrestrial channels and the videocassette recorder was but a developing technology, not quite ready for mass commercialization via the high street. If now only the most politically-motivated of viewers are watching, despite the programme's mainstream scheduling, the studio audiences may be drawn from an increasingly rarefied pool of potential participants.

The questions submitted by the studio audience and selected for use on the programme betray not only high levels of political awareness, but often political motivation. For example, there is little neutrality in 'Why does it take a celebrity chef to force the government to admit the current funding for school meals is totally inadequate?' (31 March 2005) or 'As (Chancellor of the Exchequer) Gordon Brown has lost confidence in the Prime Minister, should he copy Germaine Greer and walk out?' (13 January 2005). The leading nature of both questions suggests some positioning of the questioners in opposition to government policy, but the intertextual reference in the second to Greer's high profile exit from the *Big Brother* house deliberately confuses the visibility of friction on the 'reality' television series with hostile press comment on the relationship between the two men, which was not borne out in their continued public expressions of mutual support before and after the 2005 general election.

It is not just government that may feel underrepresented on *Question Time*. Although there were usually frontbench Conservatives on the panel, (with the notable exception of the 10 February 2005 edition from Belfast), minority parties were rarely included. This was in part due to the producers' desire to seek higher ratings by including the popular 'wild card' personalities drawn from outside mainstream political debate. The last edition before the 2005 general election was an extended 'special' in which the leaders of the three 'main' parties were each featured individually in a sequence beginning with Charles Kennedy and clearly climaxing with Tony Blair (28 April 2005). The three other party leaders accorded airtime during the campaign appeared as ordinary panellists in the first and third programmes respectively (6 April 2005 and 14 April 2005).

The range of individual viewer reactions to the programme is at least suggested by edited e-mails received during and after the broadcasts and posted on the programme's official website. Inevitably, although many will reflect the views of larger numbers of people, some will be more maverick. For instance, on the question of panel representativeness, a correspondent 'from Oxford' asked 'Where is the balance in a Tory, a New Labour and three people to the left of New Labour?' (24 February 2005). Because this feedback is compiled from e-mails, as opposed to being even a monitored bulletin board, viewer reactions on it have been filtered by editorial staff who chose what to include and what to exclude. Despite the headline 'What you've said' and the encouragement on such pages to 'find out what you had to say' about each programme, smaller print acknowledges the limitations of the process and claims that the comments below it 'reflect the balance of opinion we have received'. The small number of viewer responses included during the 2004–05 season suggests that only a tiny minority make it on to the page. Yet, despite the inevitable praise for the programme, and approval for panellists, there were usually negative responses too, criticizing the representativeness of the panels, the appropriateness or effectiveness of individual panellists, the topics discussed or even the expense involved in taking the programme overseas. Often respondents contradicted each other, achieving on the page a two-dimensional 'balance' of sorts and suggesting similar effects of reception bias to those reported in Chapter 4.

The essential problem in determining whether *Question Time* achieves a 'balance' in any wider sense lies in the large number of criteria by which this kind of programme would need to be fully evaluated. Beyond the relatively straightforward issues of who is on the panel, how long they are allowed to 'have the floor', what subjects are discussed, the constitution of the studio audience and the representation of viewer reactions on the BBC's website, lie other, less easily measurable criteria. The intensity of negative or positive audience reaction to a point of view, woven into the discourse articulated by the programme in the manner discussed in Chapter 5, is difficult to quantify, because it manifests itself in a variety of ways. They include such mass responses as applause, cheers, boos and so on, approving or disapproving comment by individuals invited by the presenter to ask a question or to respond to a panellist, and also non-verbal communication caught by the cameras as they focus on individuals who are speaking or as cutaways. A cynical or doubting expression on one person's face, the shaking of a head or the shouting of rebuttal (even if off-microphone and so, barely audible) can seriously undermine the effectiveness of what someone else is saying at the time, and malicious direction could easily seek to systematically detract from one or more contributors to the benefit of others.

There remains the question of what positions, in striving to achieve balance, that 'balance' should be between. As we have seen, a 'balance' of opinions on the panel may not reflect that in the wider electorate, just as the opinions voiced by the studio audience may be generally unpalatable to the larger television audience, to the press, to people who do not watch the programme (but subsequently hear or read reports about it) or even to more distant constituencies of opinion overseas. It may be that 'balance' should simply be between government policy and opposition to it – a straight 50–50 – or perhaps government policy should be presented as just one of a range of alternatives. If there are too many alternatives, though, and each one is given little positive airtime, policies supported by a parliamentary majority would be substantially underrepresented in electoral terms.

It is not difficult to imagine such programmes as *Question Time* conducting wider systematic polling to sample broader public opinion on a range of issues, before deciding how different perspectives on those issues should be represented 'on air' and online, and there may be a strong case for such a strategy, likely as it would be to reinforce such a programme's legitimacy in the way it chooses to represent issues and opinions in the future. It would then be the job of the producer to select panellists more likely to reflect public opinion on the most topical issues of the day, that of the presenter to apportion airtime between individual panellists and members of the audience accordingly, and that of the director to ensure that cutaways to supportive or negative individuals reinforce this 'balance' as well.

Today and UK general elections in 1997, 2001 and 2005

Although – or perhaps *because* – it is broadcast on radio, *Today* has long been firmly established as the BBC's flagship daily news and current affairs programme. A former Conservative Party Director of Communications, Hugh Colver, rationalized its very high profile as being due to the fact it is the programme with which many of the country's top politicians begin their day.[1] Donovan (1997) chronicled its development from an initial proposal by Robin Day in July 1955 to its 40th anniversary in 1997. Originally it was conceived as a 'morning miscellany' of items ranging from political interviews – only mildly challenging by twenty-first century standards – to daily keep-fit exercises and a religious slot. Despite such early pro-establishment attitudes as exemplified by Jack de Manio's towards anti-war protestors (see Chapter 2), by the 1980s the BBC in general and *Today* in particular had begun to attract more criticism for attacking government than for supporting it. However, Donovan quotes Conservative interviewees – their party then in power – as denying the existence of any *systematic* bias against them in the programme. His discussion of balance (1997: 201–6) suggests that by 1997 it had become less controversial than during the early to mid-1990s: a phenomenon that he attributed to 'both the Tory leadership and ... BBC culture [being] less partisan and more consensual in approach' (1997: 201). In other words, Margaret Thatcher's confrontational style and big parliamentary majorities were succeeded by the equivocation and relative instability of John Major's premiership. Informally-derived perceptions do not exclude the possibility of bias being systematic but simply not apparent, nor of its being present but sporadic.

In democratic states it is inevitable that in the heat of an election campaign the question of balance should become even more crucial. Gunter identified election coverage as a prime focus of research into media balance over 50 years (1997: 56). The BBC and other broadcasters recognize this heightened interest, as does parliament, which has passed legislation to increase control of broadcasting immediately before and during polling. Because of the loophole in the Representation of the People Act 1983, Section 93 (see Chapter 2), it really dealt only with the margins of broadcasting: the constituency-based debates in off-peak slots, which are more typical of local stations than the networks as the more parochial nature of the often little-known issues and candidates render them of only marginal interest to a national audience. The Political Parties, Elections and Referendums Act 2000 relaxed the rules on absent candidates' consent, but placed the onus on regulators to ensure 'balance' and 'fairness' overall during election periods. The BBC's stated policy was already to aim for 'fairness', which they clarified in a 1995 revision of the then current 1993 *Producers' Guidelines* as giving: '... due weight to the main parties and to any party contesting a substantial number of seats and with substantial proven electoral support'.

In 1997, as in 2001 and 2005, *Today*'s general election coverage largely ignored all but what they repeatedly called the three 'main' parties – Conservative, Labour and SLD (later Liberal Democrats) – choosing to promote their interests over those of all the others seeking election by according them the vast majority of the airtime available. The *Guardian* identified no fewer than 168 'parties' as fielding candidates in 1997, many of whom were represented by one solitary 'joke' candidate or someone seeking publicity for a campaign on a single issue (ranging from the All Night Party to the West Cheshire College in Crisis Party) and clearly no realistic attempt to represent them all in a national programme would have been either practical or deserved. The BBC's approach to the regional parties, the Scottish Nationalist Party (SNP), Plaid Cymru in Wales and several in Northern Ireland, was that regional programming on such other BBC networks as Radios Scotland, Wales, Cymru and Ulster would properly reflect regional interests and issues. However, in 1997 the Referendum, Natural Law, UK Independence and Liberal Parties each fielded sufficient candidates (at least 50) to merit their own Party Election Broadcasts on national radio and television. In 2005 the United Kingdom Independence Party (UKIP) and George Galloway's party, Respect, each had a national presence in the election.

In defining 'main' parties, the BBC could have considered membership, funding or some other criterion, such as political representation in the previous House of Commons, in which the 'first past the post' electoral system tends to disadvantage even the third party. Figure 7.1 shows the frequency of appearance of party representatives in the 1997 programmes. (*Excluding* news bulletins on the hour and the half-hour and the four editions of *Yesterday in Parliament* covering the proceedings between the calling of the election and the proroguing of parliament on 21 March 1997, because these are considered later in this case study.)

This simple enumeration does not consider the duration, context, scheduling, content or outcomes of appearances, but merely their occurrence. This caveat is of some significance, because an 'appearance' in this count could amount to an extended 'set-piece' interview with a party leader lasting up to 20 minutes, or be a brief audio clip of just a few seconds, such as those accorded to the 'others' in the table: what were called 'minor parties' in reporter Lance Price's two multi-voice packages about them (06:44, 18 April 1997 and 06:43, 23 April 1997). There was one appearance each for the UK Independence, Natural Law, Pro-Life Alliance, Rainbow, Socialist Labour, BNP, Liberal, and Loony parties, that would have been heard only by some of the smallest audiences to the programme because they were scheduled before 07:00. In addition to the concentration on the three 'main parties' – and most surprisingly – there was a very large imbalance *between* the three 'main parties', which did not at all reflect their representation in the previous poll. The Conservatives were accorded more than twice the number of Labour's appearances, and the biggest

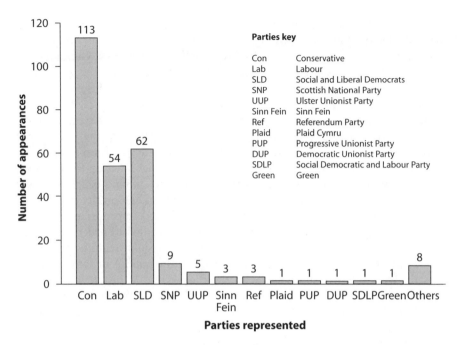

Figure 7.1 Appearances on *Today* of party representatives during the 1997 campaign

opposition party was even beaten to *Today*'s microphones by the Social and Liberal Democrats, whose representation at Westminster had been tiny even in comparison to Labour's.

To Labour's total could be added a very small number of appearances by trade unionists (18), at least some of whom were probably also Labour Party members. However, to do so would itself be a misrepresentation because they appeared not as party representatives but in their capacity as trade unionists, threatening, for example, industrial action over planned cuts to the fire service in Essex. This was not at all a message Labour party strategists would have welcomed, as an unhelpful reminder of past industrial strife under the previous 1974–9 Labour government of first Harold Wilson (1916–95) and then James Callaghan (1912–2005). Similarly, appearances by members of the CBI or the Institute of Directors, or appointees of quangos were not attributed to the Conservative total, even though they were statistically more likely to be members of that party than of Labour. For whatever reason, it seemed *prima facie* that in 1997 a clear advantage was given to the ruling party. *Today* also discriminated between the minor parties, often unfairly. Somehow the Scottish Nationalists must have merited nine times the invitations given to Plaid Cymru, even though the Labour policy of devolution – one of the campaign issues – applied to both Scotland and Wales. The one party had certainly not enjoyed nine times the number of seats of the other in the previous parliament.

This simple count of appearances, however, is too reductive an analysis to be considered alone. For instance, the Conservatives' greater number of appearances could have been doubly gruelling interviews compared to Labour's. Alternatively, many of the Conservatives' appearances could have served as unwelcome reminders of the 'sleaze' issue, and could therefore have been perceived by Labour as beneficial to their own prospects. Figure 7.2 shows the allocation between the parties of the so-called 'set piece' interviews, prime-time slots at the 'top' of the hour, following the main news bulletin, which catches large numbers of listeners tuning in for a news briefing. The most prestigious interviewees were very often lined up for this slot, rather than positioned elsewhere in the programme running order, amongst the sport, *Thought for the Day*, business bulletins and so on. Its timing also allows for the item to be extended when considered appropriate, whereas items that precede the news are often abruptly curtailed in order to accommodate the weather and programme trails that are regular features before the immovable Greenwich Time Signal at the top of the hour. An example of this was the exclusive live interview with the then Prime Minister, John Major, conducted on location in 10 Downing Street (2 April 1997), which ran from 08:10 to 08:28. It would have been inconceivable for such an event to be placed between the 'God slot' and the weather forecast preceding the news and thus, due to the time constraints imposed by the programme's regular format, have to be greatly reduced in duration to five minutes.

Where these slots were occupied by 'set piece' interviews with main parties, their distribution was as follows: 52.4 per cent Conservatives, 28.6 per cent Labour, and 9.5 per cent Liberal Democrats. Here, *Today* favoured the Conservatives over both the other two 'main parties' as well as the minority parties, most of which were not featured at all. Unlike the regional parties, the Green, Referendum and UK Independence Parties were national parties with candidates in most or all of the constituencies in England, yet they were deprived of this important opportunity to make themselves heard. Both Labour's post-7 am appearances were 'double headers' in which they were interviewed with representatives of other parties. By contrast, Conservatives were interviewed alone or with other Conservatives in seven post-7 am slots. It is also worth noting the placing of these items. In the final three weeks of the campaign (arguably the most important as they more immediately preceded the poll itself), the ratio of Conservative interviewees to others in these slots shifted even farther in their favour. It would be easy to construe from this that there was a desire to over-represent the Conservative Party, and that that desire grew as the poll approached.

Outside the 'set-piece' opportunities to 'have the floor', some political parties benefited elsewhere from the relatively unconstrained access to the programme's microphones that was afforded by being interviewed, as opposed to being recorded and used as a clip in a multi-voice package or as a stimulus preceding an interview with someone else. Scheduling these interviews outside the prime slots may have reduced exposure to the

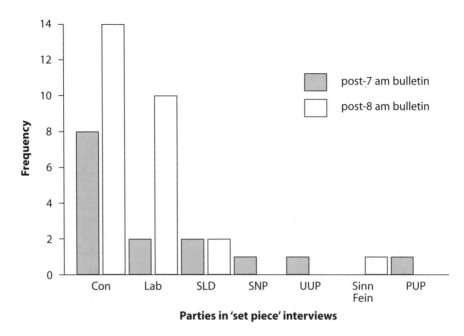

Figure 7.2 Distribution of post-news 'set piece' interviews on *Today* during the 1997 campaign

audience – and thus potential impact – but their lesser importance does not obviate the need to consider their effect on any overall 'balance' within the programmes. This analysis counted what have here been called 'apparently complete' interviews – in that each one began and ended with some form of welcome and expression of gratitude respectively, whether in the studio or involving some live link – although in the case of undeclared recordings, any editing would probably not have been discernible. Again, these were what can be termed party representatives, in that almost all were then or had been spokespeople for their party, and might readily have been put up for interview by their leadership. Each of them appeared to be broadly supportive of their own parties' campaigns and critical at times of their opponents.

The results in Figure 7.3 demonstrate a significant imbalance, with the Conservatives receiving a disproportionate advantage in frequency over Labour. The imbalance created in the prime slots appeared to be compounded across the rest of the programmes, albeit to a lesser extent. Curiously, the Social and Liberal Democrats, although very poorly represented in the prime 'set-piece' slots, were otherwise interviewed more often than Labour. Effectively therefore, SLD representatives were much more likely to be interviewed outside prime slots than in them, while only four of the regional parties were featured in 'apparently complete' interviews at all.

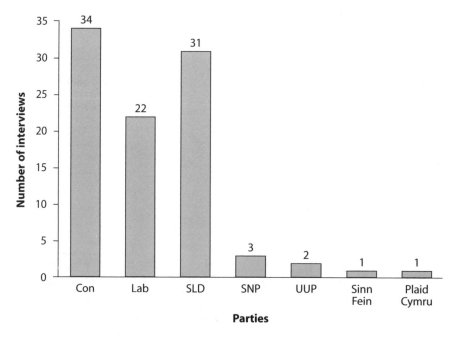

Figure 7.3 Distribution of other 'apparently complete' interviews on *Today* during the 1997 campaign

Of course, not all 'apparently complete' interviews on the programmes were with party representatives. There were other voices on the programme and who they were and what they said may also be significant. However, the difficulties inherent in such an analysis of the texts are considerable. Identifying which speakers are sympathetic to which party without on-air explanation would require a large amount of detective work: certainly beyond the resources of most listeners. Usually, the relationship between interviewee and any party was left unexplained, and so individuals within the audience who considered the issue had to draw their own conclusions from any prior knowledge they might have had. That, too, is problematic: for example, the Essex firefighters – would their appearances have been widely read as supportive of Labour, or as likely to be harmful to that party? Paradoxically, Labour had for years been actively courting business leaders and the party had secured the support of some of them. It would not have been as safe in 1997 as it had been even five years earlier, to assume that business and the CBI were automatically sympathetic to the Conservatives. Without an on-air declaration, then, listeners were left to make disparate – and inevitably often incorrect – assumptions. In the following analysis, then, the assumptions of any party allegiance are left to the reader. In accordance with grounded theory of data analysis (Glaser and Strauss, 1967; Strauss and Corbin, 1990) Table 7.1 allocates interviewees to categories, even the definition of which is inevitably problematic because the act of categorization itself creates an additional hermeneutic layer. When, for instance, does a businessman become a business leader? For this reason, the categories are as broad as seems usefully possible. Items with no obvious relevance to the British general election (such as violence in Israel, mass suicides in America and the Dalai Lama's visit to Taiwan) were excluded.

Table 7.1 Interviewees *not* billed as party representatives in other 'apparently complete' interviews on *Today* during the 1997 campaign

trade unionists	18	SLD voters	3
businessmen or women	12	Conservative voters	1
university academics	8	'likely' Labour voters	3
newspaper editors (pro-Labour)	8	don't knows	4
newspaper editors (pro-Conservative)	0	bishops	5
newspaper journalists/columnists	8	barristers	1
magazine editors	5	charities	1
market analysts	2	QUANGOs	10
government economic adviser	1	privatized utilities	3
economists	2	pressure groups	5
Institute of Fiscal Studies	1	advertising industry	1
Centre for Policy Studies	1	spokesman for Mohammed Al Fayed	1
OECD (Organisation for Economic Co-operation and Development)	1	grant maintained schools association	1
judge 'supports SLD'	1	headteachers	3
policemen	2	gay foster parent	1
architect (pro-Labour)	1	pupils	2
playwright ('wrote cynical play about Labour')	1	parent governor	1
US drugs czar	1	student union president	1
novelist	1	Fawcett Society	1
writer	1	British Veterinary Association	1
fisherman	1	Safeway	1
archaeologist	1	hereditary peer	1
council officer	1	lobbyist (Ian Greer)	1
health visitor	1	environmentalist	1
abattoir manager	1	children's author	1
benefit claimant	1	loyalist	1
foreign nationals	4	comedian	1

However little Labour may have welcomed airtime being given to trade unionists, for example, most of the interviewees in that category could be assumed to be Labour supporting as that is the party to which most of their unions were politically affiliated. Similarly, whatever their personal views, it was possible for the relatively media literate to make assumptions about the on-air contributions of editors of Labour-supporting newspapers. As there were no appearances in this context from the editors of either the *Daily Mail* or the *Daily Telegraph*, the fifth category has, exceptionally, a zero value. Again, reasonable assumptions may be made about those voters described as 'Conservative', 'SLD' or 'likely Labour', if those on-air descriptions were correct. With no further indicators, the majority of the remaining descriptors offer few clues as to party allegiance (if any) or ideological positioning. (A small number of exceptions included the 'right-wing' Centre for Policy Studies.) Certainly, from the parties' perspective there is a distinction between having the opportunity to speak for oneself, and being characterized by someone else, however sympathetic.

Overall, the allocation of actual interview time to the three main parties was more representative of their standing in the previous parliament. A tendency to interview Labour for longer helped redress in part the lower *frequency* of their inclusion. For example, the mean running time of each party's 'set-piece' interviews, in minutes, was as follows: Conservative 3.4, Labour 4.73, and SLD 3.21 (including questioning but not the cues). This, and other longer interviews meant that the total share of all 'apparently complete' interview time was divided as shown in Figure 7.4 below.

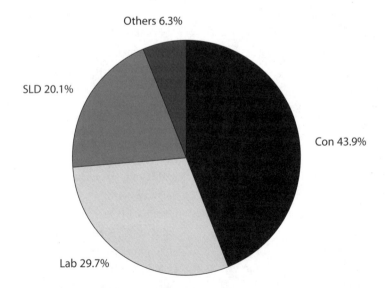

Figure 7.4 Share of all 'apparently complete' interview time with party representatives during the 1997 campaign (post-news and at all other times)

Today also favoured the Conservatives and disadvantaged Labour during *Yesterday in Parliament*: in the audio clips used the Conservatives spoke longer and therefore had longer to make their views known. The Conservative, Labour and SLD parties were each accorded 793, 527 and 320 seconds respectively over 33, 22 and 10 separate appearances. The only other party to be featured, Plaid Cymru, appeared once for 20 seconds. The Labour disadvantage was once again disproportionate to its parliamentary representation in the previous 1992 result when compared to the Conservatives and the SLD, who against such a criterion were both vastly over-represented on air. Clearly, as far as *Yesterday in Parliament*'s coverage was concerned, MPs from the Scottish Nationalist and the Northern Ireland parties might have more profitably gone campaigning in their constituencies, because their presence in the two chambers was not noted in any way.

Most of the 1997 programmes concluded with an 'election panel'. While the most frequent panelist was the BBC's political researcher, Bill Bush, the next and the only two other very significant contributors in terms of their frequency of appearance, were Ian Hargreaves and Charles Moore, then editors of the *New Statesman* and the *Daily Telegraph* respectively. Bush's role was frequently stated to be as a 'neutral' observer – a representative of the BBC – while one might suppose the predominance of Hargreaves and Moore was because they were intended, as if binary opposites, to represent left and right-wing political opinion respectively. No other contributor appeared in these debates more than three times; no one else assumed the same importance in the constitution of the panel as these three. Certainly, an approximate balance was achieved between the two editors in terms of frequency of appearance (but not necessarily in terms of duration 'on air' or freedom of expression). The only panellists with obvious party affiliations were Des Wilson, formerly of the original Liberal Party and Simon Brook, described as ex-Head of Broadcasting, Conservative Central Office. In a post-election irony, Bill Bush left the BBC and joined the staff at 10 Downing Street in 1999.

As well as frequency and duration overall, this study closely considered the series of interviews with the three 'main' party leaders. Although Paddy Ashdown (SLD) benefited from an additional interview on the first programme of the campaign on 18 March, 'apparently complete' appearances by these three party leaders were otherwise relatively infrequent, being broadcast in two cycles, as shown in Table 7.2.

Disparities of duration and scheduling are immediately apparent: in the first cycle, all three were broadcast in the prime post 08:00 news slot, whereas, in the second cycle Ashdown was relegated to second item, being preceded by a recorded interview with Labour's Gavin Strang. John Major, as the Conservative leader, had two obvious benefits: having much longer durations than the others and in being scheduled on both occasions to his advantage. In the first cycle, Major came first, while Ashdown had to wait until last, but in the second cycle, when proximity to the actual poll was a far

Table 7.2 Dates, times and durations of interviews with three 'main' party leaders

Weds 2 April 1997	08:10	John Major (Con) *17'37"*	by John Humphrys
Thurs 3 April 1997	08:10	Tony Blair (Lab) *15'40"*	by James Naughtie
Fri 4 April 1997	08:10	Paddy Ashdown (SLD) *13'37"* – following 'wavering SLD voter' *41"*	by John Humphrys
Fri 25 April 1997	08.17	Paddy Ashdown (SLD) *12'50"*	by James Naughtie
Mon 28 April 1997	08:10	Tony Blair (Lab) *18'17"*	by John Humphrys
Tues 29 April 1997	08:10	John Major (Con) *19'49"*	by James Naughtie

greater issue, Major had the 'final word' of the three. Meanwhile, in the second cycle the intervening weekend pushed Ashdown back to the previous Friday, as many as six days before polling took place. There is no legal, as opposed to logistical, reason why this second cycle could not have begun on the Monday, allowing even Ashdown the ability to speak at length to *Today* listeners in the final week.

The privileges of incumbency were also extended to Major on a linguistic level: both his interviews were clearly billed on air as being conducted 'in 10 Downing Street'. Given that trust and fitness for office were key issues in the campaign (both Blair and Ashdown lacking Major's experience of government), for the programme to place such an emphasis on location could reasonably be read as according the Conservatives a further advantage. Even if the programme had to travel to Downing Street to interview Major, it did not *need* to reveal the logistics of its operation, but it *chose* to do so for effect. The semiotic richness of John Humphrys' introduction 'I am in Downing Street with the Prime Minister' (2 April 1997) could not have been lost on party managers. For a televised interview they would undoubtedly have preferred as a backdrop the stately setting of this historic seat of government to a television studio. This contrasts with James Naughtie's description the following day of Tony Blair as being interviewed 'at his campaign headquarters' – a binary opposition of which an extreme reading might place the king in his castle and the guerrilla leader in his lair.

Today also chose to positively identify Major as 'the Prime Minister' rather than the equally correct, but politically more neutral 'leader of the Conservative Party'. This policy ran throughout the 1997 campaign, and continued in 2001 and 2005, as the status of certain other interviewees was consistently reinforced as 'the home secretary', 'the foreign secretary' and so on, where more neutral descriptors were readily available. An early example was James Naughtie's cue to a pre-recorded interview with the then Secretary of State for Defence, Michael Portillo: 'I spoke to him *not* about the election, but about his Russian visit' (07:51, 18 March 1997). (Neither that day's *Telegraph* nor *Guardian* newspapers had covered the visit in detail.) By consciously choosing to do this, the programme was reminding the audience of the nature of the status quo: naturalizing the Conservatives in power. Others may of course argue that this worked against the Conservatives in those listeners who were inclined towards change, although it should be remembered that Labour's poll lead fell, rather than rose, over the seven weeks of the campaign. With less value-laden possibilities at their disposal, for 'impartial' broadcasters to systematically choose language which is more likely to favour one party, can be read as negligent or malign, depending on one's perspective. Certainly, such a policy cannot easily be interpreted as even-handed.

Only Paddy Ashdown was deliberately placed after a 'wavering voter' who was having doubts about supporting his party. Neither Major nor Blair was subject to such a challenging juxtapositioning of recorded stimulus and live response. This is another example of an opportunity for equal treatment of alike elements being passed over in favour of disadvantaging one participant or advantaging another. Again, it was not to the detriment of the Conservatives. The choice of interviewer was interesting in each case, too. Whether by accident or by design, each leader was interviewed once by James Naughtie, and once by John Humphrys, but in each cycle Tony Blair was treated differently from the other two. It would be a brave, even foolhardy commentator who would impute any overt party political leanings to either of these two experienced journalists, but inevitably, as they are different *people*, the experience of being interviewed by one is likely to differ in at least some respects from being interviewed by the other. Supposing Humphrys were the 'easier' interviewer, Blair might have been given an easier ride in the crucial second cycle, or if the reverse were true, he would have been subjected to a more searching scrutiny just before the poll. In fact, Table 7.3 shows that Major was allowed to speak without interruption for significantly longer than the other two interviewees, and Blair was the most constricted. Although Naughtie was more inclined to interrupt Major than Ashdown, Blair was the most interrupted of the three by a wide margin. This last point may, of course, be a result of the answering style of the three politicians, but Blair's shorter average answering times do suggest that John Humphrys was significantly less inclined to allow the Labour leader to finish his answers than Naughtie had been with the others.

Table 7.3 Temporal latitude afforded to 'main' party leaders in the final cycle of interviews on *Today* during the 1997 campaign

	Average length of uninterrupted interviewee speech	*Total number of interruptions by interviewer*	*Total number of questions and non-questions*
Ashdown by Naughtie	14.57 seconds	13	35
Blair by Humphrys	13.97 seconds	43	47
Major by Naughtie	17.47 seconds	19	44

In the 2001 and 2005 campaigns, *Today* treated the three 'main parties' quite differently. In 2001 neither of the two biggest parties had the kind of advantage over the other given to the Conservatives in 1997, but in 2005 Labour also benefited from incumbency, being favoured over the Conservatives and the Liberal Democrats, according to a number of the criteria explored above. In 2001 the programme 'balanced' almost equal numbers of 'set piece' interviews with Labour (18) and the Conservatives (16), while the Liberal Democrats had only four: all at 07:09. The UK Independence Party, the British National Party and the Green Party each featured once, again in the earlier slot. Paradoxically, in 2005 'set piece' interviews were overwhelmingly of Labour representatives, numbering at 07:09 and 08:10 respectively three and 13, to the Conservatives' three and nine and the Lib Dems' six and six, while only one other appeared: Dave Nellist described as a Socialist Alternative candidate and 'formerly of Labour'. That the Conservatives and Liberal Democrats should have had equal access to these two prime timeslots is surprising, given the Lib Dems' continued third party status. Figures 7.5 and 7.6 reveal how the number of appearances of party representatives and the apportionment of total airtime to them overall were decidedly more 'balanced' in 2001, but skewed dramatically to Labour's advantage in 2005.

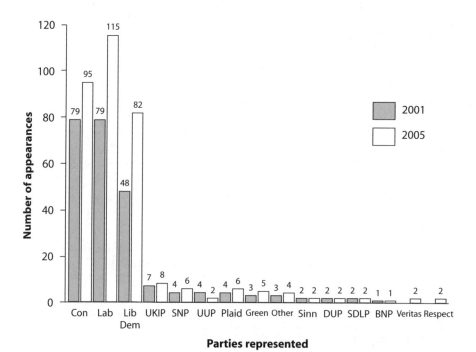

Figure 7.5 Appearances on *Today* of party representatives during the 2001 and 2005 campaigns

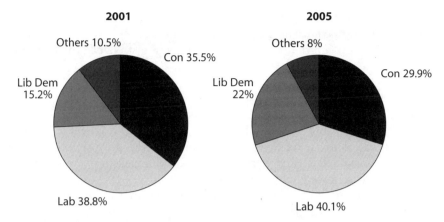

Figure 7.6 Share of all airtime given to party representatives on *Today* during the 2001 and 2005 campaigns

In addition, on each occasion there was potential for harm in the programme's use of repeated patterns of discourse, which are reductive and potentially damaging in the extreme (see Chapter 5), although *Today* was not alone in using them. Examples include the 'two-horse race' script, reinforcing the unlikelihood of the third party to prevail in a British general election, the 'spin script', naturalizing readings of Labour as overly reliant on spin doctors, and the 'sleaze script', assimilating into the programme's discourse that of others who in 1997 wished the Conservatives to be perceived as corrupt.

In summary, in 1997 *Today* chose to disadvantage Labour in favour of the Conservatives according to several important criteria, and gave the Social and Liberal Democrats advantages that were disproportionate to each party's share of votes cast in the 1992 ballot. There is little evidence that such Conservative advantages then were 'balanced' by other aspects of the programming, or even that the news agenda being followed highlighted Conservative negatives in sufficient measure to reduce their positive advantage. However, in 2005 many of the advantages of incumbency in government became Labour's, and the other parties suffered as a result. Whether that bias was intentional or accidental, the audience's apparent ignorance of it (see Chapter 4) may be the reason *Today* managed to conduct itself thus with such impunity.

This is not, however, 'balance' over a 'reasonable period of time'. Misleading representations of elections serve democracy poorly, and may corrupt it. It seems unlikely that *Today* alone won the 2005 election for Labour or lost it for the Conservatives or the smaller parties. However, the phenomena uncovered here may have had some effect on the outcomes of those political processes in some constituencies, and, if repeated more widely by others in the media, that effect may have been magnified. Although there is no data available from audiences to 'prove' it, in 1997 *Today* may have contributed to the shortening of Labour's opinion poll lead over the long, seven-week campaign that was the Conservatives' last chance to cling onto power.

The three case studies above use a number of measurable parameters to examine programmes made by broadcasters on whom there are statutory and moral responsibilities to be 'balanced'. They are not, however, exhaustive accounts of the texts they describe, because the polysemic nature of most media artefacts means there may be yet more measurable phenomena to consider. Discourse analysis of individual words, phrases and questions, detailed examination of paralinguistic elements within them and the retracing through remaining paperwork of original production decisions are but three further strategies that could each unearth more data to combine with that already generated. However, hoping to prove or disprove production bias through reliance on ever more profound criteria may be seen as unnecessarily desperate, when those who would be perceived as unbiased can make relatively simple production decisions over representation that apportion and schedule airtime, select and reject evidence, deploy language and challenge politicians and others in ways that are appropriate to the most likely consensual notions of balance.

Hell hath no fury ... reality and representation in press coverage of the Millennium Dome

Finally, what of representation in the press, where we have already noted far greater editorial freedom? The almost complete absence of regulatory pressure we discussed in Chapter 3 allows the press far greater latitude in its treatment of controversial issues than many broadcasters enjoy. We saw that partisan editorializing, often along party political lines, is almost *de rigeur*, in that newspapers are frequently aligned with particular collectives because they share similar objectives within the democratic process. In press treatment of matters of public controversy, neither overt nor covert bias would surprise the more media literate reader any more than readers of tabloid newspapers would be surprised by the destructive, yet essentially lucrative practice of promoting personalities from the fashion, sport, music or entertainment *milieux* up to the point at which their celebrity value becomes just as compelling a reason for attempting to destroy them again, once some imperfection, ill-advised dalliance or character flaw is exposed. In neither case is the presentation of only partial evidence uncommon, and the result is that much reporting in the press amounts to deliberate misrepresentation of 'realities' of which journalists are more aware, but which as proxies they choose to distort when communicating them to their audiences.

Partisanship sometimes requires alignment with perspectives that are unpalatable, but on occasions even a government's most fervent supporters in the press cannot bring themselves to support a particular measure. An interesting example of the breakdown of press partisanship in the UK lays in the press coverage of the Millennium Dome, erected in Greenwich, London, in the years preceding the beginning of the twenty-first century. A controversial project since it was first proposed by the Conservative government of John Major in 1994, the Dome was the venue for the country's largest midnight celebration of the arrival of the new millennium, as well as a planned year-long visitor attraction styled partly in the mould of the Great Exhibition of 1951. Unusually, and because of the projected £750 million cost of the construction deals being done by the Conservatives in order to clear and make safe this derelict peninsular, which was bordered on three sides by a meander in the River Thames, as well as to begin construction in a timely manner, Labour in opposition gave guarantees that they would continue with the project should they come to power in the forthcoming general election. So, one of Labour's first acts in government was to embrace the project and secure its financial position in its first budget, despite the compromise this represented of its own policy agenda – and that of its traditional supporters in the press – to prioritize public spending in essential public services, foremost among them, health and education.

The press coverage of the construction phase varied from the broadly supportive to the dismissive, which tended to concentrate on the likelihood of its readiness for the televised party and its grand opening to paying visitors the following morning. Among the various incidental 'attractions' inside it were life-sized caricatures of builders, shown still working to complete the project, in a wry dig at what did in fact turn out to be inaccurate press speculation. The front-bench pre-election consensus around the project had come under strain as decisions were taken to commission a longer-lasting structure, which would prolong the site's usefulness well beyond the life of the original exhibition, and to devise content which would be overwhelmingly educational, rather than purely for pleasure. To be found among the walkthrough body, the performing jugglers, the Faith Zone and a number of other big exhibits including a fake beach, were a giant seagull made from recycled kitchen utensils, a six-foot-tall hamster and a Test Your Strength machine with five hammers. However, Conservative scepticism was initially constrained by the party being the initiators of the project and so endorsing the main principles behind it.

Furthermore, the spectacular millennium night party was a resounding televisual success: certainly on a par with any such event arranged elsewhere in the world, and more lavish than most, as well as being far more ambitious a staged event than any New Year celebration mounted by a television channel either before or after. An estimated 19 million viewers were tuned in to the BBC's extended coverage of the celebrations. The event itself was positively reviewed by many in the press (McCrumb, 2000). The *Sun*'s leader had a single word for it: 'WOW!' (1 January 2000), while with the headline 'A Dome-ful of fun, thanks to the Sun' the newspaper congratulated itself for taking 'winning families' who had won a competition to the 'spectacular bash' and who agreed 'there was no place like Dome' (3 January 2000). By contrast, the *Observer* noted that a party of 250 000 'revellers' gathered in the regenerated Liverpool docks was 'the closest the North-West has come to mimicking the magnificence of the Millennium Dome' (Paton Walsh, 2000).

Once the Dome was open, some early press coverage enthused along the lines of the *Observer*'s headline 'There ain't nothing like a Dome, say enthusiastic public' (2 January 2000), which described 'the public's verdict' as 'favourable', and led with such quotes as 'The Dome is breathtaking. I feel like Alice in Wonderland' and 'This has been good value for money and I think it's wonderful' (Thorpe, 2000). One feature article in *The Times* listed dozens of things 'You can't get through 2000 without ...' including 'the Dome: it'll be cool. Honestly' (1 January 2000), while another headlined 'Wake up to our trips for travel' enthusiastically described the reviewer's son Leo's press trip round the Dome on Christmas Eve (1 January 2000). Far from being negative, the news item on page seven, 'Body zone hard to stomach', was a glowing description of the 'most striking attraction' in the Dome. The *Guardian*'s leader reported the next day that the Dome was 'up, running and magnificent', 'a stunning architectural statement, matched by an equally impressive feat of engineering' (3 January 2000). Attendance in the first few days was very promising, with 10,000 people paying to pass through the turnstiles on the first. By the end of the year, the Millennium Dome had measurably become the second most visited paying attraction in Europe, second only to the Euro Disney resort (now renamed Disneyland Resort Paris) east of Paris which, although open almost continuously since 1992, has still failed to make a profit for its US and European backers.

Unfortunately, it would be an understatement to describe the Millennium Dome project as less than successful. Despite displaying considerable project management skills in opening it on time, the organizers' greatest mistake was arguably the public relations disaster that had already unfolded on Millennium eve. Many of the 10,000 would-be partygoers became stuck for several hours, effectively corralled on their feet, at Stratford station, while officials struggled to implement the security checks that had been deemed necessary for all those arriving by Underground at an event attended by several members of the Cabinet and the Royal Family. Many of them were raffle winners, employees of sponsoring organizations, nominees of registered charities and others lucky enough to have been invited to the event, and apparently all of them sufficiently motivated to attend to have refused any other invitations they may have received. Among them were what were described as 'VIPs', and the most significant of them for the success or failure of the project were a large number of newspaper editors, columnists and journalists. To a select group of people quite accustomed to privileged access to all manner of prestigious events, the inconvenience and indignity of being squashed and physically restrained at Stratford without even a drink may have been too much to endure.

Certainly, when the editors had had time to recover from the weekend's excesses and the press coverage of the Dome began to quickly turn sour, the minister responsible perceived a desire among them to exact revenge on the Dome organizers for what must have been one of the least satisfactory 'freebies' of their careers (Watson-Smyth, 2000). Even before the honeymoon was over, and just as with celebrities past their sell-by dates, representations of the Dome quickly turned from positive to negative. The partial nature of their attacks on the Dome is revealed by their duplicity. At first, they concentrated not on the content, but on the organizational infrastructure. The large numbers of visitors paying to enter in the first few days were soon presented not as an indicator of success, but of incompetence and because of queues of 'up to an hour' to pass through the most popular exhibit, the body, they were enough of a problem to make the sponsors reconsider their commitment to the project (Gibbons, 2000). The word in the tabloid and broadsheet press was that going to the Dome meant the distress and disappointment of prolonged queuing, even though *aficionados* of theme parks – such as Euro Disney – are likely to have experienced even longer waits for the most popular attractions in peak periods. The *Daily Mail* headlined 'An hour's wait: Welcome to the Queueing Zone' (3 January 2000).

Perhaps because the adverse press coverage in those first few days killed it, perhaps because an initial rush of enthusiasts was just an inevitable but unrepresentative passing phenomenon, or simply because the school holidays ended – we can never know – visitor numbers went into serious decline, to the extent that turnstile income fell well below the levels needed to sustain the project within its initial budgets. Rather than suggesting these were better times to visit the Dome without queuing, coverage now variously focused on the 'unattractiveness' of the exhibits, their 'over-didactic' nature, the 'inevitability' of New Labour directing the project managers down politically-correct routes in the selection of necessarily unappealing material and so on. By the summer, the lower than predicted visitor numbers had provoked a financial crisis, and the spiralling bad publicity of high-profile resignations and political recriminations may well have depressed them further. On 6 September 2000 the *Sun* called a new injection of public funds to sustain the project 'scandalous', the *Independent* labelled the whole site 'a disaster zone', and 'Close it today' demanded the *Daily Express*. Few chose to remark on the irony of the then Conservative leader, William Hague calling it 'an empty pointless tent in the middle of nowhere' (CNN, 2000). Perhaps, indeed, hell hath no fury like an editor scorned.

There is an obvious dichotomy in media proxies being able to represent the same 'reality' to readers either positively or negatively according to the predilection of newspaper editors, and in effect influence events for better or for worse. It is one of the most remarkable, and at the same time disturbing, aspects of the considerable power that control of the mass media places in the hands of very few people. Whatever perspective one brings to such political controversies as that over the Dome, the wielding of that power in ways which can directly affect individuals – losing their jobs, for instance, because the economic prospects of an enterprise are damaged, or on a larger scale, influencing the outcomes of democratic processes – reinforces the importance of understanding balance and bias in all their forms.

Conclusion

Defining 'balance' around consensual *fulcra* on matters of controversy is as problematic in principle as achieving a 'balanced' discourse is in practice. In most cases democratic principles are best served by those making journalistic representations at least *striving* towards a balance around which a consensus might gather. However, this renders inevitable the existence of bias in almost every media representation of the realities that audiences cannot perceive first hand. In some instances – and especially where the safety of individuals and even the democratic nation state are at risk – such bias may even be desirable, if not essential. In others it is only regulation (and perhaps only through public service broadcasting) that may be relied upon to provide limited safeguards against bias.

We have considered the chronic instability of realism in all its forms, an inadequacy of representation by proxy that has been only marginally mitigated since ancient philosophers and orators articulated persuasive yet partial accounts of the realities they observed. Such historic discourse as has been preserved for us to consume as audiences provides valuable insight into the experiences of eyewitnesses, but its incompleteness leaves gaping holes in our knowledge of those times. The recent relatively rapid development of communication technology still falls short of offering today's audiences the full experience of witnessing events at first hand, however much media constructs characterize themselves as 'reality TV', 'fly on the wall', documentary or drama-documentary. Future historians will be almost as inadequately equipped to draw complete conclusions about our realities as we are about our past. More pertinently, the epistemological instability surrounding the controversies of our own time may endanger now the democracies on whose proper functioning we depend.

What, then, of the proxies themselves: the journalists, broadcasters and others whose job it is to represent the realities they perceive? At best, notions of professionalism that are underpinned by peer expectation, institutional values and formative experience may combine with regulation, statutory obligation and the risk of litigation to produce such 'fairness' as may be possible. At worst, journalistic representation is deliberately biased, often in order to pursue political agendas that aim to distort democratic processes, and it might, if audiences are affected by what they perceive insofar as they will change their opinion or their vote. We have argued that there is a strong case for content regulation of the press, in order to curb its representational excesses, because complete freedom of expression is only illusory. Such freedom is already qualified in several respects, and only in the most auto-cratic of states is broadcasting so tightly regulated that this form of control is widely perceived to be harmful.

We have usefully categorized bias according to where it occurs: *produc-tion* bias in the various acts of encoding, and *reception* bias in the different ways in which individuals within audiences decode media representations. Due to a range of epistemological concerns about the collection of data from audiences, some valid, yet contradictory accounts of audience perceptions were deliberately *not* used to draw conclusions about production bias in the texts on which they reported. However, they suggested that individuals' perceptions of balance and bias may be unreliable indicators of the presence or absence of both. So in drawing some conclusions about a number of media texts in contexts where 'balance' is a statutory requirement, we concentrated on measurable elements in production, while recognizing the inadequacy of such an approach in embracing the immeasurable.

Throughout the book, pragmatic approaches to its subject matter have attempted to recognize – and where possible accommodate – the essential pragmatism required of others, in order to engage with their own subject matter within the various resource constraints imposed upon them by their own circumstances. We are all of us fallible in our ability to represent faith-fully what we perceive, and not just because of the physical inadequacies of the media contexts and technology upon which we rely. Rather than feigning infallibility, we as journalists need to recognize that fallibility and in turn encourage in our audiences a corresponding awareness of it, so that through media literacy, rather than ignorance or passive acceptance, their own read-ings of our representations may be as epistemologically robust as possible. In the struggle to come between competing globalizing and resistive forces democracy will surely depend on it.

Notes

Preface

1. Although the Italian Guglielmo Marconi (1874–1937) first used wireless telegraphy to send Morse code over long distances, it was the Canadian Reginald Fessenden (1866–1932) who first broadcast a sound radio programme consisting of voice and music, on 24 December 1906. He called it 'wireless radiotelephony'.

Chapter 1

1. Examples of Romantic art include Paul Gustav Doré's (1832–3) illustrations of Don Quixote, an obviously fictional character from Spanish literature.
2. Notably among them, Gustave Courbet (1819–77) depicted working class people around a grave in 'A burial at Ornans' (1850).
3. For example, Honoré de Balzac's (1799–1850) long series of novels and stories *La Comédie Humaine* and Gustave Flaubert's (1821–80) seminal work, *Madame Bovary* (1857).
4. Such as Émile Zola's (1840–1902) 20 stories named after the dynastic family, les Rougon-Macquarts.
5. Among the surrealists were the artists Pablo Picasso (1881–1973), René Magritte (1898–1967) and Salvador Dalí (1904–89), and the filmmaker Luís Buñuel (1900–83). For example, Magritte's picture of a pipe was entitled 'Ceci n'est pas une pipe' ('This is not a pipe', 1929), and Dalí painted the deliberately unlikely 'Women with flower heads finding the skin of a grand piano on the beach' (1936).
6 http://www.aim.org/
   http://www.fair.org/
   http://www.medialit.org/
   http://www.freedomforum.org/
7. http://www.bbc.co.uk/radio4/today/listenagain/ram/today2_arafat_20041111.ram (accessed 12 November 2004)

Chapter 7

1. Interview with the author, 2 April 1996.

Bibliography and Further Reading

ABC (2005) *History of ABC Radio*, Sydney: Australian Broadcasting Corporation, http://www.abc.net.au/radio/celebrate100/history.htm (accessed 17 February 2005).

Ahmed, K. (2003) 'Bully ministers will wreck us – BBC chairman', *Observer*, 27 July, http://www.observer.co.uk/politics/story/0,6903, 1006939,00.html (accessed 17 February 2005).

Al-Jazeera (2004) *Aljazeera Code of Ethics*, Qatar: Al-Jazeera, http://english.aljazeera.net/NR/exeres/07256105-B2FC-439A-B255-D830BB238EA1.htm (accessed 12 July 2005).

Allan, S. (2004) *News Culture*, Maidenhead: Open University Press.

Allan, S. (2005) 'Hidden in plain sight: journalism's critical issues', in *Journalism: Critical Issues*, Maidenhead: Open University Press.

Alia, V. (2004) *Media Ethics and Social Change*, Edinburgh, Edinburgh University Press.

Amber, A. (2000) 'Making the debates happen: a television producer's perspective', in Coleman, S., *Televised Election Debates: International perspectives*, Basingstoke: Macmillan.

Anania, F. (1995) 'Italian public television in the 1970s: a predictable confusion', *Historical Journal of Film, Radio and Television*, August, Abingdon: Carfax Publishing.

Antoine, F. (2003) 'Méthodologie de la mesure de l'audience en radio: diversité des methodes et divergences des resultats, le cas de la Belgique' in Cheval, J.-J. (ed.), *Audiences, Publics et Pratiques Radiophoniques*, Pessac: Maison des Sciences de l'Homme d'Aquitaine.

Aristotle (2004 edition) *Rhetoric*, tr. W. Rhys Roberts, Montana: Kessinger.

Atton, C. (2004) *An Alternative Internet: Dissent, transgression and creativity in a digital age*, Edinburgh: Edinburgh University Press.

Ba, A. (2003) 'Les radios de proximité en Afrique de l'Ouest', in Cheval, J.-J. (ed.), *Audiences, Publics et Pratiques Radiophoniques*, Pessac: Maison des Sciences de l'Homme d'Aquitaine.

Bagdikian, B. (1997) 'The US media: supermarket or assembly line?' in Iyengar, S. and Reeves, R. (eds), *Do the Media Govern? Politicians, voters and reporters in America*, London: Sage.

Baldwin, T (2003) 'Life is stricter already in Downing Street and at BBC', *The Times*, 27 September.

BARB (2005) *Weekly Viewing Summary*, http://www.barb.co.uk/viewing summary/weekreports.cfm?report=total (accessed 28 June 2005).

Bartle, J., Atkinson, S. and Mortimore, R. (2002) *Political Communications: The general election campaign of 2001*, London: Frank Cass.

Batty, D. (2004) 'Timeline: MMR row', *Guardian*, 24 February, http://society.guardian.co.uk/publichealth/story/0,,1154945,00.html (accessed 12 November 2004).

BBC (1996) *Radio Times*, London: British Broadcasting Corporation, 27 April–3 May.

BBC (1998) *BBC Radio Collection: Today*, London: British Broadcasting Corporation.

BBC (2003) *Board of Governors: Minutes of a private meeting held in private session, Sunday 6 July 2003 6.30pm to 8.50pm in Room 2364 Broadcasting House*, London: British Broadcasting Corporation.

BBC (2004a) *Producers' Guidelines*, London: British Broadcasting Corporation, http://www.bbc.co.uk/info/policies/producer_guides/pdf/section3.pdf (accessed 9 October 2004).

BBC (2004b) *BBC World Service Remains World's Leading International Radio Broadcaster*, London: British Broadcasting Corporation, 21 June, http://www.bbc.co.uk/pressoffice/pressreleases/stories/2004/06_june/21/ws_figures.shtml (accessed 15 June 2005).

BBC (2005a) *Editorial Guidelines*, London: British Broadcasting Corporation, http://www.bbc.co.uk/guidelines/editorialguidelines/assets/guidelinedocs/Producersguidelines.pdf (accessed 22 February 2006).

BBC (2005b) *About Breakfast with Frost*, London: British Broadcasting Corporation, 29 May, http://news.bbc.co.uk/1/hi/programmes/breakfast_with_frost/2405429.stm (accessed 23 August 2005).

Becker, G. (ed.) (1963) *Documents of Modern Literary Realism*, Princeton: Princeton University Press.

Bell, P. and van Leeuwen, T. (1994) *The Media Interview: Confession, contest, conversation*, Sydney: University of New South Wales Press.

Belsey, A. and Chadwick, R. (1992) *Ethical Issues in Journalism and the Media*, London: Routledge.

BFI (2001) *Northern Ireland: The Troubles*, London British Film Institute, http://www.bfi.org.uk/collections/catalogues/troubles/troubles.pdf (accessed 18 February 2005).

Bhaskar, R. (1989) *The Possibility of Naturalism*, Brighton: Harvester.

Bignell, J. (2005) *Big Brother: Reality TV in the twenty-first century*, Basingstoke: Palgrave.

Blumer, H. (1969) *Symbolic Interactionism: Perspective and method*, London: Prentice-Hall.

Born, G. (2004) *Uncertain Vision: Birt, Dyke and the reinvention of the BBC*, London: Secker and Warburg.

Boseley, S. (2002) 'Chief medical officer urges TV campaign to counter MMR fears', *Guardian*, 11 February.

Bourdieu, P. (1986) *Distinction: A social critique of the judgement of taste*, London: Routledge.

Boyd, A. (2001) *Broadcast Journalism*, Oxford: Focal.

Boykoff, M. T. and Boykoff J. M. (2004) 'Balance as bias: global warming and the US prestige press', *Global Environmental Change* 14, 125–36, Orlando: Elsevier, http://www.colorado.edu/geography/courses/geog_2412_f04/balance%20as%20bias.pdf (accessed 12 November 2004).

Bradlee, B. (1997) 'Lying', in Iyengar, S. and Reeves, R. (eds), *Do the Media Govern?*, London: Sage.

Brants, K. and van Kempen, H. (2002) 'The ambivalent watchdog: the changing culture of political journalism and its effects', in Kuhn, R. and Neveu, E. (eds), *Political Journalism: New challenges, new practices*, London: Routledge.

Briggs, A. (1961) *The History of Broadcasting in the United Kingdom, Vol. 1: The Birth of Broadcasting*, London: OUP.

Brown, P., Fitzwalter, R., Harvey, S., Jones, H. and Wailes Fairbairn, F. (2003) 'Representation in the nations and regions' in Ralph, S., Manchester, H. and Lees, C. (eds), *Diversity or Anarchy? Papers from the 31st Manchester Broadcasting Symposium*, Luton: University of Luton Press.

Bull, P. (1994) 'On identifying questions, replies and non-replies in political interviews', *Journal of Language in Social Psychology* 13(2), 115–31.

Bumpus, B. and Skelt, B. (1986) *Seventy Years of International Broadcasting*, Paris: UNESCO.

Bunker, D. (1996) 'The Radio Four audience', in *Invitation to Tender: Programme commissions for April 1997 to March 1998*, London: British Broadcasting Corporation.

Burgess, M. (2004) *Coroner's Statement*, 6 January, http://www.surreycoroner.info/inquests.html (accessed 8 December 2004).

Burns, T. (1977) *The BBC, Public Institution and Private World*, London: Macmillan.

Butler, D. and Kavanagh, D. (1997) *The British General Election of 1997*, Basingstoke: Macmillan.

Butler, D. and Kavanagh, D. (2001) *The British General Election of 2001*, Basingstoke: Macmillan.

Caine, G., Bartlett, R. and Crossley, D. (2004) *Corporate Governance in the Australian Broadcasting Corporation: Follow-up audit*, Canberra: Australian National Audit Office.

Calcutt, D. (1990) *Report of the Committee on Privacy and Related Matters*, London: HMSO.

Calcutt, D. (1993) *Review of Press Self-Regulation*, London: HMSO.

Capella, J. and Jamieson, K. (1997) *Spiral of Cynicism: The press and the public good*, New York: Oxford University Press.

Carey, J. W. (1988) *Communication as Culture*, Boston: Unwin Hyman.

Carpenter, H. (2000) *That Was Satire, That Was: Beyond the fringe, the establishment club, 'Private Eye' and 'That Was the Week That Was'*, London: Weidenfeld and Nicolson.

Carter, H. (2005) 'Labourer gets life for Murrell murder', *Guardian*, 7 May, http://www.guardian.co.uk/crime/article/0,2763,1478524,00.html (accessed 31 July 2005).

Carter, T. (2003) 'Castro regime jamming US broadcasts into Iran', *Washington Times*, 15 July.

Chantler, P. and Harris, S. (1992) *Local Radio Journalism*, Oxford: Focal.

Chaparro Escudero, M. (2002) *Sorprendiendo al Futuro, Comunicación para el Desarrollo e Información Audiovisual*, Barcelona: Los Libros de la Frontera.

Charasse, D. (1981) *Lorraine Coeur D'acier*, Paris: Petite Collection Maspero.

Cheval, J.-J. (1997) *Les Radios en France: Histoire, état et enjeu*, Rennes: Editions Apogée.

Chippendale, P. and Horrie, C. (1992) *Stick It Up Your Punter: The rise and fall of the Sun*, London: Mandarin.

Chomsky, N. (1989) *Necessary Illusions*, London: Pluto.

Chong, D. (2001) *The Girl in the Picture: The remarkable story of Vietnam's most famous casualty*, London: Penguin.

Clark, H. (2000) 'The worm that turned: New Zealand's 1996 general election and the televised 'worm' debates', in Coleman, S. (ed.), *Televised Election Debates: International perspectives*, Basingstoke: Macmillan.

CNN (2000) 'London Dome's new chief wonders why it was ever built', CNN.com, 6 September, http://archives.cnn.com/2000/TRAVEL/NEWS/09/06/britain.dome.reut/index.html (accessed 17 February 2006).

Cockerell, M. (1988) *Live from Number 10: The inside story of prime ministers and television*, London: Faber and Faber.

Coleman, S. (2000) 'Meaningful political debate in the age of the sound-bite', in Coleman, S. (ed.), *Televised Election Debates: International perspectives*, Basingstoke: Macmillan.

Collett, P. and Lamb, R. (1986) *Watching People Watching Television: Final report to the IBA*, Oxford: University of Oxford, Department of Experimental Psychology.

Cone, S. (1998) 'Presuming a right to deceive: Radio Free Europe, Radio Liberty, the CIA and the news media', *Journalism History* 24(4), 148–56, Ohio: Ohio University.

Council of Europe (1989) *Television without Frontiers* Directive (89/552/EEC) Brussels: Council of Europe.

Cozens, C. (2005) 'BBC news ratings double', *Guardian*, 8 July, http://media.guardian.co.uk/overnights/story/0,7965,1524235,00.html (accessed 14 July 2005).

Crawford, Earl of (1926) *Report of the Broadcasting Committee, 1925*, London: HMSO.

Crawford, N. (1924) *The Ethics of Journalism* (1969 edition, New York: Greenwood).

Crisell, A. (1994) *Understanding Radio*, London: Routledge.

Critchlow, J. (1999) 'Western Cold War broadcasting', *Journal of Cold War Studies* 1(3), 168–75, Massachusetts: MIT Press.

Crook, T. (1998) *International Radio Journalism*, London: Routledge.

CSA (2000) *Nouvelles Modalités Adoptées par le CSA pour L'évaluation du Respect du Pluralisme Politique dans les medias*, Paris: Conseil Supérieur de l'Audiovisuel, http://www.csa.fr/infos/textes/textes_detail.php?id=8546 (accessed 17 February 2005).

Curran, J. and Seaton, J. (1997) *Power Without Responsibility*, London: Routledge.

DCA (2003) *The Hutton Inquiry: Hearing transcripts*, 18 September, London: Department for Constitutional Affairs, http://www.the-hutton-inquiry.org.uk/content/transcripts/hearing-trans38.htm (accessed 19 November 2004).

DCMS (2005) *Review of the BBC's Royal Charter: A strong BBC, independent of government*, London: Department of Culture, Media and Sport, http://www.bbccharterreview.org.uk/have_your_say/green_paper/bbc_cr_greenpaper.pdf (accessed 5 March 2005).

Deacon, D., Pickering, M., Golding, P. and Murdock, G. (1999) *Researching Communications*, London: Arnold.

Denver, D., Fisher, J., Cowley, P. and Pattie, C. (1998) *British General Elections and Parties Review, Vol. 8: The 1997 general election*, London: Frank Cass.

Dimbleby, J (2004) 'The coming war', *Observer*, 30 October, http://observer.guardian.co.uk/waronterrorism/story/0,1373,1340175,00.html (accessed 17 December 2004).

Domenget, J.-C. (2003) 'Au quotidien et au fil de l'âge, pratiques radiophoniques des retraités' in Cheval, J.-J. (ed.), *Audiences, Publics et Pratiques Radiophoniques*, Pessac: Maison des Sciences de l'Homme d'Aquitaine.

Donovan, P. (1997) *All Our Todays: Forty years of the Today programme*, London: Jonathan Cape.

Duelfer, C. (2004) *Comprehensive Report of the Special Advisor to the DCI on Iraq's WMD*, Washington, DC: Central Intelligence Agency, http://www.cia.gov/cia/reports/iraq_wmd_2004/ (accessed 19 November 2004).

Dyke, G. (2004) *Inside Story*, London: HarperCollins.

EDR (2005) *Global 2005: International air travellers survey*, London: European Data and Research.

El-Nawawy, M. and Iskandar Farag, A. (2002) *Al-Jazeera: How the Free Arab News Network scooped the world and changed the Middle East*, Boulder: Westview Press.

EthicNet (2002) *Databank for European Codes of Journalism Ethics*, Tampere, Finland: University of Tampere, http://www.uta.fi/laitokset/tiedotus/ethicnet/index.html.

Fairclough, N. (1989) *Language and Power*, Harlow: Longman.

Fairclough, N. (1995) *Media Discourse*, London: Arnold.

Fallows, J. (1997) *Breaking the News: How the media undermine American democracy*, New York: Vintage.

Ferguson, R. (2000) *Representing Race*, London: Arnold.

Fink, C. (1988) *Media Ethics*, New York: McGraw-Hill.

Fowler, R. (1991) *Language in the News: Discourse and ideology in the press*, London: Routledge.

Frankel, L. (1969) 'The role of accuracy and precision of response in sample surveys', in Johnson, W. and Smith Jnr, H. (eds), *New Developments in Survey Sampling*, London: Wiley.

Franklin, B. (1994) *Packaging Politics*, London: Arnold.

Franklin, B. (1997) *Newszac and News Media*, London: Routledge.

Frost, C. (2000) *Media Ethics and Self-Regulation*, Harlow: Pearson Education.

Galtung, J. and Ruge, M. (1965) 'The structure of foreign news: the presentation of the Congo, Cuba and Cyprus crises in four foreign newspapers', *Journal of International Peace Research* 1, 64–91.

Garton, G., Montgomery, M. and Tolson, A. (1991) 'Ideology, scripts and metaphors in the public sphere of a general election', in Scannell, P. (ed.), *Broadcast Talk*, London: Sage.

Gerbner, G., Gross, L., Morgan, M. and Signorielli, N. (2002) 'Growing up with television: cultivation processes', in Bryant, J. and Zillman, D. (eds), *Media Effects*, Mahwah: Erlbaum.

Gibbons, F. (2000) 'Boots stamps out Dome queues', *Guardian*, 7 January, http://www.guardian.co.uk/2000/article/0,,196626,00.html (accessed 17 February 2006).

Gibson, O. (2005) 'BBC licence fee safe – at least until 2016', *Guardian*, 3 March, http://media.guardian.co.uk/site/story/0,14173,1429200,00. html (accessed 3 May 2005).

Giddens, A. (1984) *The Constitution of Society: Outline of the theory of structuration*, Cambridge: Polity Press.

Glaser, B. and Strauss, A. (1967) *The Discovery of Grounded Theory: Strategies for qualitative research*, London: Weidenfeld and Nicolson.

Glasgow University Media Group (1976) *Bad News*, London: Routledge.

Gledhill, R. and Sherwin, A. (2003) 'BBC is hostile and biased, says Archbishop' *The Times*, 30 September.

Golding, P. and Elliott, P. (1976) *Making the News*, Leicester: Centre for Mass Communications Research.

Goodwin, G. and Smith, R. (1994) *Groping for Ethics in Journalism*, Ames: Iowa State University Press.

Goody, E. N. (ed.) (1978) *Questions and Politeness*, Cambridge: Cambridge University Press.

Gopsill, T. (1999) 'Lord Wakeham's new clothes', *Free Press* 112, London: Campaign for Press and Broadcasting Freedom.

Grant, D. (1970) *Realism*, London: Methuen.

Greenslade, N. (2005) 'A lonely Tribune out in left field', *Observer*, 6

February, http://observer.guardian.co.uk/business/story/0,6903,1406736, 00.html (accessed 18 March 2005).

Guardian, (1997) 'Election results', 3 May.

Gunter, B. (1987) *Poor Reception: Misunderstanding and forgetting broadcast news*, Hillsdale: Lawrence Earlbaum Associates.

Gunter, B. (1997) *Measuring Bias on Television*, Luton: University of Luton Press.

Hall, S. (1974) 'Media power: the double bind', *Journal of Communication* 24(4), 19–26.

Hall, S. (1981) 'The determinations of news photographs', in Cohen, S. and Young, J. (eds), *The Manufacture of News*, London: Sage Constable.

Harris, S. (1991) 'Evasive action: how politicians respond to questions in political interviews', in Scannell, P. (ed.), *Broadcast Talk*, London: Sage.

Harrison, J. (2006) *News*, London: Routledge.

Hassan, R. (2004) *Media, Politics and the Network Society*, Maidenhead: Open University Press.

Hay, J. (ed.) (1996) *Serving the Citizen: Broadcasting and the general election* (transcript), Gravesend: Voice of the Listener and Viewer.

Heil, A. (2003) *The Voice of America: A history*, New York: Columbia University Press.

Hendy, D. (2000) *Radio in the Global Age*, Cambridge: Polity.

Henley, J. (2003) 'Gigantic sleaze scandal winds up as former Elf oil chiefs are jailed', *Guardian*, 13 November, http://www.guardian.co.uk/france/story/0,11882,1083784,00.html (accessed 14 March 2005).

Hernan, E. and Chomsky, N. (1994) *Manufacturing Consent: The political economy of mass media*, New York: Pantheon.

HM Government (1990) *The Broadcasting Act 1990*, London: HMSO.

Hobbs, A. (1996) Entries on Plato, Aristotle, Greek Political Theory and the Sophists in *Concise Oxford Dictionary of Politics*, Oxford: Oxford University Press.

Hochheimer, J. (1993) 'Organizing democratic radio, issues in praxis', *Media, Culture and Society* 15(3), 473–86.

Hodgson, J. (2001) 'Dyke: why I apologised', *Guardian*, 18 September, http://www.guardian.co.uk/september11/story/0,11209,601375,00.html (accessed 23 August 2005).

Homer (2004 edition) *The Odyssey*, tr. T. E Lawrence, Illinois: Barnes and Noble.

Hood, S. (1980) *On Television*, London: Pluto.

Hutchby, I. (2005) *Media Talk: Conversation analysis and the study of broadcasting*, Maidenhead: Open University Press.

Hutchby, I. (2006) *Confrontation Talk: Arguments, asymmetries, and power on talk radio*, New Jersey: Lawrence Erlbaum Associates.

Hutton, Lord (2004) *Report of the Inquiry into the Circumstances Surrounding the Death of Dr David Kelly C.M.G.*, London: House of Commons.

ISC (2003) *Iraqi Weapons of Mass Destruction: Intelligence and assessments*, London: Intelligence and Security Committee, 11 September.

Iyengar, S. (1997) 'Use of the media in the policy process: overview', in Iyengar, S. and Reeves, R. (eds), *Do the Media Govern? Politicians, voters and reporters in America*, London: Sage.

Jackson, K. (2003) *Media Ownership Regulation in Australia*, Canberra: Parliament of Australia, http://www.aph.gov.au/library/intguide/sp/media_ regulations.htm (accessed 10 March 2005).

Katz, E., Blumler, J. and Gurevitch, M. (1974) 'Utilization of mass communication by the individual', in Blumler, J. and Katz, E. (eds), *The Uses of Mass Communication*, London: Sage.

Kaye, M. and Popperwell, A. (1995) *Making Radio: A guide to basic radio techniques*, London: Broadside Books.

Knight, P. (ed.) (2003) *Conspiracy Theories in American History: An encyclopaedia*, Santa Barbara: ABC-CLIO.

Knights, M. (2004) *Representation and Misrepresentation in Later Stuart Britain: Partisanship and political culture*, Oxford: Oxford University Press.

Koch, T. (1990) *The News as Myth: Fact and context in journalism*, New York: Greenwood Press.

Kuhn, R. (1995) *The Media in France*, London: Routledge.

Kuhn, R. (2002) 'The first Blair government and political journalism', in Kuhn, R. and Neveu, E. (eds), *Political Journalism: New challenges, new practices*, London: Routledge.

Lamont, D. (2003) 'Speaking ill of the dead', *Guardian*, 11 August, http://media.guardian.co.uk/mediaguardian/story/0,,1015945,00.html (accessed 15 March 2005).

Lasswell, H. (1927) *Propaganda Techniques in the First World War*, New York: Knopf.

Leavis, F. R. and Thompson, D. (1933) *Culture and Environment: The training of critical awareness*, London: Chatto and Windus.

Lewis, J., Inthorn, S. and Wahl-Jorgensen, K. (2005) *Citizens or Consumers? What the media tell us about political participation*, Maidenhead: Open University Press.

Lewisohn, M. (2003) *The bbc.co.uk Guide to Comedy: Spitting Image*, London: British Broadcasting Corporation, http://www.bbc.co.uk/comedy/ guide/articles/s/spittingimage_7775945.shtml (accessed 19 May 2005).

Littleton, S. (1992) *The Wapping Dispute: An examination of the conflict and its impact on the national newspaper industry*, Aldershot: Avebury.

Livingstone, S. (1990) *Making Sense of Television: The psychology of audience interpretation*, Oxford: Pergamon.

Lloyd, J. (2003) 'Constructing our reality: 24/7', *Index on Censorship* 4, 28 September.

MacGregor, B. (1997) *Live, Direct and Biased? Making television news in the satellite age*, London: Arnold.

MacLeod, M. and Foster, K. (2005) 'Wark's Labour links: now Tory leaders demand action by BBC', *Scotland on Sunday*, 9 January, http://news.scotsman.com/topics.cfm?tid=1232&id=25492005&20050218111053 (accessed 18 February 2005).

Maslow, A. (1954) *Motivation and Personality*, London: Harper and Row.

Masterman, L. (1985) *Teaching the Media*, London: Comedia.

McAllister, I., Jones, R., Papadakis, E. and Gow, D. (1990) *Australian Election Survey, 1990*, Canberra: Australian National University.

McArthur, B. (1988) *Eddy Shah: Today and the newspaper revolution*, Newton Abbot: David and Charles.

McChesney, R. (2000) *Rich Media, Poor Democracy: Communication politics in dubious times*, New York: New Press.

McCombs, M. and Shaw, D. (1972) 'The agenda-setting function of the mass media', *Public Opinion Quarterly* 36.

McCrumb, R. (2000) 'Putting on the Blitz', *Observer*, 2 January, http://www.guardian.co.uk/2000/article/0,,196644,00.html (accessed 17 February 2006).

McLeish, R. (1994) *Radio Production*, Oxford: Focal.

McLuhan, M. (2001) *Understanding Media* (Routledge Classics), London: Routledge (first published 1964).

McManus, J. (1994) *Market-Driven Journalism: Let the citizen beware*, California: Sage.

McNair, B. (1994) *News and Journalism in the UK: A textbook*, London: Routledge.

McNair, B. (1998) *The Sociology of Journalism*, London: Arnold.

McNair, B. (2000) *Journalism and Democracy: An evaluation of the political public sphere*, London: Routledge.

McNair, B. (2002) 'Journalism and democracy in contemporary Britain', in Kuhn, R. and Neveu, E. (eds), *Political Journalism: New challenges, new practices*, London: Routledge.

McQuail, D. (1992) *Media Performance: Mass communication and the public interest*, London: Sage.

McQuail, D. (2005) *McQuail's Mass Communication Theory*, London: Sage.

McQuail, D., Blumler, J. and Brown, J. (1972) 'The television audience: a revised perspective', in McQuail, D. (ed.), *Sociology of the Mass Media*, London: Penguin.

McWhinnie, D. (1959) *The Art of Radio*, London: Faber and Faber.

Menduni, E. (2002) *Televisione e Società Italiana*, Milan: Studi Bompiani.

Mickelson, S. (1983) *America's Other Voice: The story of Radio Free Europe and Radio Liberty*, Westport: Praeger.

Miles, H. (2005) *Al-Jazeera: How Arab TV News challenged the world*, London: Abacus.

Miller, D. (1992) *Jamming the Switchboards: The government attack on BBC coverage of the NHS*, Stirling: University of Stirling, www.staff.stir.ac.uk/david.miller/publications/Jamming.html.

Miquel, P. (1984) *Histoire de la Radio et de la Télévision*, Paris: Perrin.

Mitterrand, F. (1981) *Ici et Maintenant*, Paris: Livre de Poche.

Moloney, E. (1991) 'Closing down the airwaves: the story of the broadcasting ban', in Rolston, B. (ed.), *The Media and Northern Ireland*, Basingstoke: Palgrave.

Monteleone, F. (2003) *Storia della Radio e della Televisione in Italia*, Venice: Marsilio.

Montgomery, M. (1991) 'Our tune: a study of a discourse genre' in Scannell, P. (ed.), *Broadcast Talk*, London: Sage.

MORI (2004) *British 'Favour ID Cards'*, London: MORI, 23 April 2005, http://www.mori.com/polls/2004/detica-top.shtml (accessed 23 August 2005).

MORI (2005) *Attitudes to the Hunting Ban*, London: MORI, 16 February 2005, http://www.mori.com/contacts.shtml (accessed 18 February 2005).

Murialdi, P. (1996) *Storia del Giornalismo Italiano*, Bologna: il Mulino.

Murschetz, P. (1998) 'State support for the daily press in Europe: a critical appraisal: Austria, France, Norway and Sweden compared', *European Journal of Communication* 13(3).

Neil, R. (2004) *The BBC's Journalism after Hutton: the report of the Neil review team*, London: BBC, http://www.bbc.co.uk/info/policies/pdf/neil_report.pdf (accessed 19 November 2004).

Nelson, M. (1997) *War of the Black Heavens: The battles of western broadcasting in the cold war*, Syracuse, NY: Syracuse University Press.

North, A. (2004) *'Heavy Poll Bias' towards Karzai*, London: BBCi, 4 October, http://news.bbc.co.uk/1/hi/world/south_asia/3712460.stm (accessed 3 May 2005).

NUJ (2004) *Code of Conduct*, London: National Union of Journalists, http://www.nuj.org.uk/inner.php?docid=59 (accessed 18 February 2005).

Ofcom (2005) *The Ofcom Broadcasting Code*, London: Office of Communications.

Olson, K. W. (2003) *Watergate: The presidential scandal that shook America*, Lawrence: University Press of Kansas.

O'Neill, O. (2002) *A Question of Trust: The BBC Reith Lectures 2002*, Cambridge: Cambridge University Press.

Orans, M. (1996) *Not Even Wrong: Margaret Mead, Derek Freeman and the Samoans*, San Francisco: Chandler and Sharp.

Paton-Walsh, N. (2000) 'Club Mersey parties the long night away', *Observer*, 2 January, http://www.guardian.co.uk/2000/article/0,196642,00.html (accessed 17 February 2006).

Patterson, T. (1996) 'Bad News, Bad Governance', *Annals of the American Academy of Political and Social Science*, 546, July.

Pew Research Centre (2004) *News Audiences Increasingly Polarised*, Washington DC: Pew Research Centre for the People and the Press, http://people-press.org/reports/display.php3?ReportID=215 (accessed 8 April 2005).

Pierce, A. (2002) 'Palace fury at BBC's missing black tie', *The Times*, 2

April, http://www.timesonline.co.uk/article/0,,2-254788,00.html (accessed 2 December 2004).

Pilger, J. (1998) *Hidden Agendas*, London: Vintage.

Plato (2004 edition) *Gorgias*, tr. W. Hamilton, London: Penguin.

Plett, B. (2004) *Yassir Arafat's Unrelenting Journey*, London: BBC News, http://news.bbc.co.uk/1/hi/programmes/from_our_own_correspondent/ 3966139.stm (accessed 12 November 2004).

Puddington, A. (2000) *Broadcasting Freedom: The cold war triumph of Radio Free Europe and Radio Liberty*, Lexington: University of Kentucky Press.

Pujas, V. (2002) 'A comparative analysis of the exposure of corruption in Italian, French and Spanish Media', in Kuhn, R. and Neveu, E. (eds), *Political Journalism: New challenges, new practices*, London: Routledge.

RAJAR (2005) *Quarterly Summary, 2nd quarter*, London: Radio Joint Audience Research Ltd, http://www.rajar.co.uk/QuarterlySummary/ (accessed 21 June 2005).

Robbe-Grillet, A. (1963) *Pour un Nouveau Roman*, Paris: Les Éditions de Minuit.

Roberts, B. (2003) *Drinking in the Last Chance Saloon: Individual privacy, media intrusion and the Press Complaints Commission*, Manchester: University of Manchester.

Roncarolo, F. (2002) 'A crisis in the mirror: old and new elements in Italian political communication', in Kuhn, R. and Neveu, E. (eds), *Political Journalism: New challenges, new practices*, London: Routledge.

Ross, K. (2004) 'Political talk radio and democratic participation: caller perspectives on Election Call', *Media, Culture and Society* 26(6), 1 November.

Rowan, F. (1984) *Broadcast Fairness: Doctrine, practice, prospects: a reappraisal of the fairness doctrine and equal time rule*, New York: Longman.

Sabbagh, D. (2005) 'CNN lightens up in a quest for more viewers', *The Times*, 1 July.

Sabo, W. (2002) 'The portable people meter is your friend', *Radio and Records*, 18 October.

Sandall, R. (2003) 'MMR RIP?', *Sunday Times Magazine*, 14 December, found at http://www.vaccinationnews.com/DailyNews/2003/December/ ENewsMMRRIP16.htm (accessed 12 November 2004).

Sanders, K. (2003) *Ethics and Journalism*, London: Sage.

Scannell, P. (ed.) (1991) *Broadcast Talk*, London: Sage.

Scannell, P. and Cardiff, D. (1991) *A Social History of British Broadcasting*, Vol. 1, Oxford: Blackwell.

Schiller, H. (1989) *Culture Inc: The corporate takeover of public expression*, Oxford: Oxford University Press.

Schlesinger, P. (1987) *Putting 'Reality' Together*, London: Methuen.

Scott, D. and Usher, R. (1993) *Education and Meaning: Philosophy in practice*, London: Routledge.

Scott, R. (1996) *Scott Report: Return to an Address of the Honourable the House of Commons Dated 18 July 1996 for the Appendices to the Report of the Inquiry into the Export of Defence Equipment and Dual-Use Goods to Iraq and Related Prosecutions*, London: HMSO.

Seaton, J. (2003) 'Rows and consequences', *British Journalism Review* 14(4).

Seymour-Ure, C. (1974) *The Political Impact of Mass Media*, London: Constable.

Shanahan, M. and Neill, K. (2005) *The Great New Zealand Radio Experiment*, Wellington: Dunmore Press.

Sheridan Burns, L. (2002) *Understanding Journalism*, London: Sage.

Shingler, M. and Wieringer, C. (1998) *On Air: Methods and meanings of radio*, London: Arnold.

Snow, J. (2004) *Shooting History: A personal journey*, London: HarperCollins.

Som, R. K. (1973) *A Manual of Sampling Techniques*, London: Heinemann.

Sosin, G. (1999) *Sparks of Liberty: An insider's memoir of Radio Liberty*, Pennsylvania: Pennsylvania University Press.

Speers, T. and Lewis, J. (2003) 'MMR and the Media: misleading reporting?', *Nature Reviews Immunology* 3(11): 913–18.

Speers, T. and Lewis, J. (2004) 'Jabbing the scientists: media coverage of the MMR vaccine in 2002', *Communication and Medicine* 1(2): 171–82.

Starkey, G. (2001) *Balance and Bias in Radio Four's Today Programme, during the 1997 general election campaign*, PhD thesis, University of London Institute of Education.

Starkey, G. (2003) 'Radio audience research: challenging the "gold standard"', *Cultural Trends* 45.

Starkey, G. (2004a) *Radio in Context*, Basingstoke: Palgrave.

Starkey, G. (2004b) 'Radio Five Live: Extending choice through 'radio bloke'?', in Crisell, A. (ed.), *More than a Music Box: Radio cultures and communities in a multi-media world*, Oxford: Berghahn.

Starkey, G. (2004c) 'Estimating audiences: sampling in television and radio audience research', *Cultural Trends* 13(1), March.

Stopher, P. and Meyburg, A. (1979) *Survey Sampling and Multivariate Analysis for Social Scientists and Engineers*, Massachusetts: Lexington.

Strauss, A. and Corbin, J. (1990) *Basics of Qualitative Research: Grounded theory procedures and techniques*, London: Sage.

Street, J. (2001) *Mass Media, Politics and Democracy*, Basingstoke: Palgrave.

Street, S. (2002) *A Concise History of British Radio*, Tiverton: Kelly.

Summerskill, B. (2003) 'Crime down but we refuse to believe it', *Observer*, 27 April, http://observer.guardian.co.uk/crimedebate/story/ 0,12079, 944386,00.html (accessed 8 March 2005).

Sutter, D. (2001) 'Can the media be so liberal? The economics of media bias', *Cato Journal* 20(3), Washington DC http://www.cato.org/pubs/journal/ cj20n3/cj20n3-7.pdf (accessed 8 March 2005).

Thompson, H. (1966) *Hell's Angels: A strange and terrible saga*, New York: Ballantine.

Thompson, J. B. (1990) *Ideology and Modern Culture*, Cambridge: Polity.

Thompson, J. B. (1995) *The Media and Modernity*, Cambridge: Polity.

Thorpe, V. (2000) 'There ain't nothing like a Dome, say enthusiastic public', *Observer*, 2 January, http://www.guardian.co.uk/2000/article/ 0,,196639, 00.html (accessed 17 February 2006).

Tiffen, R. (2002) 'Media escalation and political anti-climax in Australia's 'Cash for Comment' scandal', in Kuhn, R. and Neveu, E. (eds), *Political Journalism: New challenges, new practices*, London: Routledge.

Times Mirror Centre (1995) *Ordinary Americans More Cynical than Journalists: News media differs with public and leaders on watchdog issues*, Washington: Times Mirror Center on the People and the Press.

Timms, D. (2004) 'US election spend breaks £100 million', *Guardian*, 20 July, http://media.guardian.co.uk/advertising/story/0,,1264673,00.html (accessed 18 February 2005).

Tolson, A. (2005) *Media Talk: Spoken discourse on television and radio*, Edinburgh: Edinburgh University Press.

Tomlinson, H. (ed.) (2002) *Privacy and the Media: The developing law*, London: Matrix Chambers.

Travis, A. (2004) 'Iraq given a low priority by voters', *Guardian*, 18 August, http://politics.guardian.co.uk/polls/story/0,11030,1285307,00.html (accessed 16 September 2004).

Trinity Mirror (2005) *2004 Preliminary Results*, London: Trinity Mirror plc, http://www.trinitymirror.com/ir/results/2004prelims/tm_objectid= 15241259%26method=full%26siteid=111046%26headline=nationals %2ddivision-name_page.html (accessed 3 May 2005).

Tweedy, N. and Barrow, B. (2002) 'Scoop that could have changed the course of history', *Daily Telegraph*, 30 September, http://www.telegraph.co.uk/ news/main.jhtml?xml=/news/2002/09/30/nmajor330.xml (accessed 21 May 2005).

Underwood, D. (1993) *When MBAs Rule the Newsroom: How markets and managers are shaping today's media*, New York: Columbia.

United Kingdom Parliament (2004) *Register of Members' Interests*, London: United Kingdom Parliament, http://www.publications.parliament.uk/pa/ cm/cmregmem/050128/memi13.htm (accessed 10 March 2005).

Van Leeuwen, T. (1999) *Speech, Music, Sound*, Basingstoke: Macmillan.

Verhulst, S. (1998) 'Regulating the changing media in the United Kingdom', in Goldberg, D., Prosser, T. and Verhulst, S. (eds), *Regulating the Changing Media: A comparative study*, Oxford: Clarendon Press.

Wall, T. (2005) 'National regulation in an age of global radio', paper at 'Un solo mundo, voces múltiples', V Congreso de Radios y Televisiones Locales, Públicas y Alternativas, Sevilla, 24 February 2005.

Ward, I. and Walsh, M. (2000) 'Leaders' debates and presidential politics in

Australia', in Coleman, S. (ed.), *Televised Election Debates: International perspectives*, Basingstoke: Macmillan.

Watson-Smyth, K. (2000) 'Mandelson accuses editors of Dome "vendetta"', *Independent*, 10 January, http://news.independent.co.uk/uk/this britain/ article293221.ece (accessed 17 February 2006).

Wells, M. (2002) 'Campbell foe set for top job at Today: Leading candidate accused of anti-Labour bias', *Guardian*, 14 November.

Wells, M. (2003a) 'BBC's public stance hid doubts on Gilligan', *Guardian*, 13 August.

Wells, M. (2003b) 'Today host rapped by Chairman', *Guardian*, 30 August.

Welsh, T. and Greenwood, W. (2003) *McNae's Essential Law for Journalists*, London: LexisNexis UK.

Wilby, P. and Conroy, A. (1994) *The Radio Handbook*, London: Routledge.

Williams, R. (1976) *Communications*, London: Penguin.

Wilson, J. (1996) *Understanding Journalism*, London: Routledge.

Winston, B. (1995) *Claiming the Real: The documentary film revisited*, London: British Film Institute.

Index